TOURISM EMPLOYMENT

TOURISM EMPLOYMENT

Atul Shrivastava

CENTRUM PRESS
NEW DELHI-110002 (INDIA)

CENTRUM PRESS

H.O.: 4360/4, Ansari Road, Daryaganj,
New Delhi-110002 (India)
Tel: 23278000, 23261597, 23255577, 23286875

B.O.: No. 1015, Ist Main Road, BSK IIIrd Stage,
IIIrd Phase, IIIrd Block, Bangalore-560085 (INDIA)
Tel: 080-41723429

Email: centrumpress@gmail.com
Visit us at: www.centrumpress.com

Tourism Employment

First Edition, 2010

ISBN 978-93-80540-06-1

PRINTED IN INDIA

Printed at Mehra Offset Press, Delhi

Contents

Preface

Tourism with its wide range of constituent sub sectors is now world's largest industry. The dramatic growth of tourism over the last twenty five years is one of the most remarkable economic and social phenomena of the period.

Tourism activity has long lasting socio-economic impacts on the host economy and community. The employment impact of tourism goes beyond employment in sectors in which tourists directly spend their money, such as hotels, restaurants and airlines. The establishments which receive tourists also buy goods and services from other sectors that generate employment in those sectors through multiplier effect.

In India, there has been 220.1 million domestic tourist visits in the year 2000 that increased to 234.8 million in the year 2001 and 273.3 million in 2002. In the year 2003, 2.75 million tourists visited the country. Conservative estimates of tourism related employment (base year 2002) by our professionals reveal that tourism generates about 7.5 million full time job equivalents in India. It translates to about 11 million actual jobs.

Our professionals discussed with various stakeholders in the local tourism markets. Such discussions brought out various constraints faced by tourism industry at various tourist destinations in the country. Major constraints are poor quality of infrastructure, malpractices by operators, manpower not being qualified resulting in poor quality of service, absence of a diversified value bundle as a product offer to the tourists, proper marketing and promotion, air connectivity and concerns related with carrying capacity and environment.

The emerged picture of tourism potential and related employment coupled with the identification of gaps in planning, provision, positioning and marketing of tourism point towards the requisite interventions at macro as well as micro level. Macro interventions are related with macro economic policy framework in which tourism industry operates in the country. On the other hand, micro interventions are related with spatial planning, efficient provision and marketing of tourist destinations.

Above observations coupled with timely and efficient implementation of programs and plans outlined in the tourism policies of respective States can catalyze the growth of tourism industry in the country resulting in creation of more tourism related jobs. Besides above, some additional measures are required to improve the air and surface connectivity of all these destinations. Further, the issues related with environment and fragility of eco-systems needs special attention.

Special attention is also required for increasing the employment of women in the tourism industry. Employers should set up programs and schemes encouraging women to move into non-traditional occupations, invest in women's training, appoint them in managerial positions, and re-appoint them after years of diminished involvement due to family responsibilities. To sum up, Indian tourism has vast potential for generating employment and earning large sums of foreign exchange besides giving a fillip to the country's overall economic and social development. Much has been achieved by way of increasing air seat capacity, increasing trains and railway connectivity to important tourist destinations, four-laning of roads connecting important tourist centres and increasing availability of accommodation by adding heritage hotels to the hotel industry and encouraging paying guest accommodations. But much more remains to be done. Since tourism is a multi-dimensional activity, and basically a service industry, it would be necessary that all wings of the Central and State governments, private sector and voluntary organizations become active partners in the endeavour to attain sustainable growth in tourism if India is to become a world player in the tourist industry.

India has been a tourist destination from ancient times. Fahien and Hiuen Tsiang from China, Mark Twain and few Christian apostles from the west came to India many years ago. But still many beautiful treasures of our country are little known or unknown to our own people. With this objective in mind the author has planned this Encyclopaedia by covering independently each state with detailed analysis of its cultural, geographical, natural and as well as social resources. The earning from tourism have made it one of the world's largest industries. It is the fasted growing sector of global trade. Hence the great importance of tourism planning and Human Resource Development. Aim of this book is to provide to our readers different aspects of tourism planning and Human Resource Developments. Selection of the material has been made in accordance with the course contents of various studies being organised by universities and training institutions of travel and tourism."

—Atul Shrivastava

1

Kind of Tourism

Accessible Tourism

Accessible tourism is the ongoing endeavour to ensure tourist destinations, products and services are accessible to all people, regardless of their physical limitations, disabilities or age. It encompasses publicly and privately owned tourist locations. The improvements not only benefit those with permanent physical disabilities, but also parents pushing buggies, elderly travellers, people with temporary injuries, such as a broken leg, as well as their relatives, friends and other companions.

Overview

Modern society is increasingly aware of concepts such as ageing and integration of people with disabilities. Issues such accessibility and Design for All are featured in international symposia and bodies such as the European Commission have taken steps to promote guidelines and good practices and now dedicate major resources in these fields.

As of 2008, there were more than 50 million persons with disabilities in Europe, and more than 600 million around the world. When expanded to include all beneficiaries of accessible tourism, as defined above, the number grows to some 130 million people in Europe alone. In addition to the social benefits, the market represents an opportunity with new investment opportunities and new service requirements, rarely provided by the regular travel agencies, transport providers and other key players in the tourism sector.

According to ENAT, the European Network for Accessible Tourism, accessible tourism includes:

- Barrier-free destinations: infrastructure and facilities.

- Transport: by air, land and sea, suitable for all users.
- High quality services: delivered by trained staff.
- Activities, exhibits, attractions: allowing participation in tourism for everyone.
- Marketing, booking systems, Web sites & services: accessible for all.

Specific Needs and Requirements

Specific problems found by travellers or tourists with disabilities include:

- Inaccessible, or only partly accessible, web sites.
- Lack of accessible airport transfer.
- Lack of wheelchair accessible vehicles.
- Lack of well-adapted hotel rooms.
- Lack of professional staff capable of informing and advising about accessibility issues.
- Lack of reliable information about a specific attraction's level of accessibility.
- Lack of accessible restaurants, bars, etc.
- Lack of adapted toilets in restaurants and public places.
- Inaccessible streets.
- Lack of technical aids and disability equipment (wheelchairs, bath chairs, toilet raisers, electric scooters).

Brief History

Europe and United States of America share the majority of the existing companies in this niche. However, around the world many companies are starting to appear as the result of a growing need, largely driven by "senior tourism" due to increasing life expectancy in developed countries. Portugal, Spain, the United Kingdom, Germany, France and other northern European countries are increasingly prepared to receive tourists in wheelchairs, and to provide disability equipment and wheelchair accessible transport.

Adventure Travel

Access to inexpensive consumer technology, with respect to Global Positioning Systems, flash packing, social networking and photography, have increased the worldwide interest in adventure travel. The interest in independent adventure travel has also increased as more specialist travel websites emerge offering previously niche locations and sports.

Tour Operators, Travel Agencies & Retailers

Many organizations and companies worldwide cater to adventure clientele. Some geographic regions are promoted by both private and public agencies as adventure travel destinations, such as the Arenal Volcano in Costa Rica, one of the worldwide leaders.

ElderTreks specializes in adventure travels for those who are now over the hill. From the safaris of Africa to the explorations of Peru the trips provide adventurous, cultural, and nature focused experiences.

For the eco-friendly traveller, Adventure Life provides custom trips to South and Central America and Antarctica, raising ecological and cultural awareness.

Intrepid offers over 500 trips to around 100 destinations including North America, Europe, The Middle East, Africa, Australasia and The Pacific.

Some other tour operators specializing in adventure travel are: Wilderness Journeys, for travels to Africa, South America, and Asia; Trek America, for adventures in Canada, continental United States, Alaska, and Mexico; and Contiki Tours, covering among its areas Australia and North America.

Along with information on adventure travels from tour companies, travellers can find useful trip facts, tour availability, and travel tips by directly visiting online the destination of choice. Prom Peru promotes, through its tourist channel, legendary Peru. It offers itinerary ideas that cater to the history aficionado, with its visit to historic sites such as Machu Picchu, as well as to the daring explorer, with its variety of adventure travels such as paragliding, mountaineering, trekking, mountain biking, and rafting.

Motorbiking opportunities in Patagonia are listed on the region's website along with a myriad of other adventure travels. Visit their glaciers, trek alongside the Andes with tours offered by Patagonia-Argentina.

Without venturing outside of the United States, but still keeping adventure in mind, Colorado offers a multitude of activities that cater to the different types of travellers. The official website promotes skiing, climbing, and hiking, as well as train trips through a mine and trekking through Picketwire Canyon.

Disabled

With the trend of increasing accessible tourism, available to disabled persons around the world, some tourism areas are developing adventure tourism specifically for the disabled. Whistler, British Columbia and Vancouver, British Columbia, Canada have been taking the lead with the 2010 Winter Paralympics. Adventure travel for the disabled has become a $13 billion USD a year industry in North America. Notable disabled adventurers include: Erik Weihenmayer, the first blind person to climb Mount Everest; Casey Pieretti, an amputee skater; and Caroline Walsh, founder of the Access to Marine Conservation for All International.

Some adventure travel destinations offer diverse programs and job opportunities developed specifically for the disabled. Esprit Rafting, located in Pontiac Regional County Municipality, in Quebec, Canada, designs rafting trips for people with spinal cord damage, and is a rollerskate/RollerBlade free zone.

Types of Adventure Travel

Disaster Tourism

Disaster tourism is the act of travelling to a disaster area as a matter of curiosity. The behaviour can be a nuisance if it hinders rescue, relief, and recovery operations.

If not done because of pure curiosity, it can be catalogued as disaster learning.

Ghetto Tourism

Ghetto tourism refers to the growing popularity of tourism in ghettos.

Jungle Tourism

Jungle tourism is a rising subcategory of adventure travel defined by active multifaceted physical means of travel in the jungle regions of the earth. Although similar in many respects to adventure travel, jungle tourism pertains specifically to the context of region, culture and activity. According to the Glossary of Tourism Terms, jungle tours have become a major component of green tourism in tropical destinations and are a relatively recent phenomenon of Western international tourism.

Overland Travel

Overland travel or overlanding refers to an "overland journey"- perhaps originating with Marco Polo's first overland expedition in the 13th century from Venice to the Chinese court of Kublai Khan. Today overlanding is a form of extended adventure holiday, embarking on a long journey, often in a group.

Overland companies provide a converted truck or a bus plus a tour leader, and the group travels together overland for a period of weeks or months. Since the 1960s overlanding has been a popular means of travel between destinations across Africa, Europe, Asia (particularly India), the Americas and Australia. The "Hippie trail" of the 60s and 70s saw thousands of young westerners travelling through the Middle East to India and Nepal.

Urban Exploration

Urban exploration (often shortened as urbex or UE) is the examination of the normally unseen or off-limits parts of urban areas or industrial facilities. Urban exploration is also commonly referred to as infiltration, although some people consider infiltration to be more closely associated with the exploration of active or inhabited sites. It may also be referred to as "draining" (when exploring drains) "urban spelunking", "urban caving", or "building hacking".

The nature of this activity presents various risks, including both physical danger and the possibility of arrest and punishment. Many, but not all, of the activities associated with urban exploration could be considered trespassing or other violations of local or regional laws.

Ethno Tourism

Ethno tourism refers to visiting a foreign location for the sake of observing the indigenous members of its society for the sake of non-scientific gain. Some extreme forms of this include attempting to make first contact with tribes that are protected from outside visitors.

Two controversial issues associated with ethno tourism include bringing natives into contact with diseases they do not have immunities for, and the possible degradation or destruction of a unique culture and/or language.

Agritourism

Agritourism is a style vacation that normally takes place on a farm or ranch. This may include the chance to help with farming and ranching tasks during the visit. Agritourism is considered to be a niche or uniquely adapted form of tourism and is often practiced in wine growing regions such as Australia, Italy, Portugal, Spain, and North America. Tourists engage in farm activities ranging from picking fruit or feeding animals, or planting crops.

Agritourism in the United States

In America, agritourism is widespread and includes any farm open to the public at least part of the year. Tourists can pick fruits and vegetables, ride horses, taste honey, learn about wine, shop in farm gift shops and farm stands for local and regional produce or hand-crafted gifts. Such "U-pick" farms were at their most popular in the 1970s. Other terms associated with agritourism are "farm direct marketing", "sustainable agriculture" and "agritainment".

According the USDA, Cooperative State, Education and Extension Service, "Tourism is becoming increasingly important to the U.S. economy. A conservative estimate from the Federal Reserve Board in Kansas, based on 2000 data, shows that basic travel and tourism industries accounted for 3.6 percent of all U.S. employment. Even more telling, data from the Travel Industry Association of America indicate that 1 out of every 18 people in the U.S. has a job directly resulting from travel expenditures."

Through the Small Farm Centre at the University of California, "Agricultural tourism or agritourism, is one alternative for improving the incomes and potential economic viability of small farms and rural communities. Some forms of agritourism enterprises are well developed in California, including fairs and festivals. Other possibilities still offer potential for development."

They have developed a California Agritourism Database that "provides visitors and potential entrepreneurs with information about existing agritourism locations throughout the state." In the, *Agricultural Tourism: Helpful Agricultural Tourism (Agritourism) Definitions* fact sheet by the Small Farm Centre, definitions are provided for terminology associated in agritourism including the actual phrase, "Agricultural Tourism" which is defined as referring to the "act of visiting a working farm or any agricultural, horticultural or agribusiness operation for the purpose of enjoyment, education, or active involvement in the activities of the farm or operation."

In Western North Carolina they are using agritourism to develop their local economy, craft trades, and educate their visitors to current agriculture practices. On the web site, *Home Made in America*, they look at agritourism this way, "...this niche market not only assists communities with solutions to help diversify their economic base, but it also helps our regional urban centres and increasingly suburban populations to understand the important role that farming and rural life plays in our history, by highlighting the need for it in our contemporary society. Agritourism projects reinforce the need to support local growers and sources and allow the visitor to experience what it is to be part of the land."

In the publication, *Promoting Tourism in Rural America*, it explains the need for planning and marketing your rural community and to weigh the pros and cons of tourism impacts. Local citizen participation is helpful and should be included in starting any kind of a tourism program. Being prepared by planning tourism can assist in a successful program that enhances the community.

Reasons for popularity

People are more interested in how their food is produced and want to meet the producers and talk with them about what goes into food production. Children who visit the farms often have not seen a live duck, or pig, and have not picked an apple right off the tree. This form of expanded agritourism has given birth to what are often called "entertainment farms." These farms cater to the pick-your-own crowd, offering not only regular farm products, but also food, mazes, open-pen animals, train rides, picnic facilities and pick-your-own produce.

Agritourism was featured in the satirical NBC television comedy *The Office* in the episode entitled "Money" from season. The character Dwight Schrute lives on and maintains a beet farm, which is well known to everybody in the office. In the episode Dwight explains that Trip Advisor is the lifeblood of the agritourism industry. The characters Jim and Pam then proceed to visit the farm, where they choose the "irrigation" themed room and proceed to plow the fields, make wine from beets, and watch a table making demonstration.

Dude Ranches

Dude (or guest) ranches offer tourists the chance to work on cattle ranches and sometimes include cattle drives. The fact sheet, *Promoting the Farm and Ranch Recreation Business*, gives farmers and ranchers an insight on how to market their facilities and how to develop a strategy to help gain tourism dollars. They are more common in the United States and Australian Outback.

Archaeological Tourism

Archaeotourism or Archaeological tourism is an alternative form of cultural tourism, which aims to promote the passion for historical-archaeology and the conservation of historical sites.

Establishment

Like Ecological tourism (or Ecotourism), Archaeological tourism is promoted to encourage the development of cultural associations, and companies and cooperatives can be found that dedicate themselves to offer this type of service.

The best definition of archaeotourism can be found in the words of its founders:

The passion by the past is something inherent to the human being. As it says well: «Town that does not know from where town comes that does not know to where it goes».

The Archaeotourism or archaeological tourism is ideal for which they look for a higher knowledge and sublimates, tie to the meditation and the relaxation, in perfect syntony with the surroundings or ecosystem that is, integration with the Mother Nature, but always in old places, next to the ruins of the "enigmatic missing civilizations".

Sites and places magician-monks or asylums. From the most remote prehistoric times. From the era of the dinosaurs to the Medieval Age. In order to develop his activities it has a nourished group of authentic experts in each one of the matters.

Therefore, archaeologists, palaeontologists, anthropologists, historians and specialists in trips will unite their knowledge under a same objective: to offer to the traveller a wonderful and unforgettable experience, an intensive course and of introduction to each one of these manifestations of the human knowledge. This way the visitor will not be a simple traveller, will be in addition an apprentice in sciences to the past.

Some times will feel a paleontologist discovering tracks of dinosaurs and others will feel like Indiana Jones in the Damn Temple, mainly when penetrating in the mysterious caverns and artificial caves that long ago served from temples our ancestors. Enigmatic places loaded of an atmosphere of magic and mystery that, sometimes, surpass to all fiction created by the cinema.

Other Definitions

Archaeological tourism can include all products associated with public archaeological promotion, including visits to archaeological sites, museums, interpretation centres, reinactment of historical occurrences, the rediscovery of native products, festivals, or theatre.

Although archaeological tourism is quite recent, many international institutions and governments have already begun to contemplate viable alternative activity for the sustainable economic-social development. Several countries have for years had programs resembling the main points of Archaeological tourism for economic income, including Egypt, Mexico and Peru.

Birth Tourism

In the United States

The Fourteenth Amendment to the United States Constitution guarantees citizenship to those born in the U.S. It has been reported that some women, wishing their children to be born in the United States, engage in "birth tourism" so that their children become U.S. citizens.

This practice is believed to be popular among women in Korea, Hong Kong and Taiwan. According to Edward Chang, a scholar of Asian American Studies at the University of California, Riverside, the practice is popular among the elite of South Korea, since sons of these women can avoid compulsory military service. Temporary homes for these mothers are often located in residential neighbourhoods, which neighbours allege decrease the quality of life in the neighbourhood, primarily due to increases in traffic and other business-like effects.

Being US citizens, these children do not have to meet the stricter international student rules to enter U.S. universities and colleges. In addition, when they turn 21, they become eligible to petition for a grant of permanent residency for their parents through family reunification. Some prospective mothers misrepresent their intentions of coming to the United States, a violation of U.S. immigration law. However, it is not illegal for a woman to come to the U.S. to give birth.

In Canada

Canada's citizenship law has, since 1947, generally conferred Canadian citizenship at birth to anyone born in Canada, regardless of the citizenship or immigration status of the parents. The only exception is for children born in Canada to representatives of foreign governments or international organizations. In the mid-1990s, the Canadian government considered a proposal to limit jus soli citizenship in cases where neither parent was a citizen or permanent resident of Canada, but the idea was eventually dropped and never became part of Canadian law.

In Mexico

The Mexican Constitution of 1917 states that children born on Mexican soil are citizens of the country.

In Ireland

The Twenty-seventh Amendment of the Constitution of Ireland abolished birthright citizenship in Ireland. It is suggested that fears of birth tourism played a role in the amendment.

Bookstore Tourism

Bookstore tourism is a type of cultural tourism that promotes independent bookstores as a group travel destination. It started as a grassroots effort to support locally owned and operated bookshops, many of which have struggled to compete with large bookstore chains and online retailers.

The project was initiated in 2003 by Larry Portzline, a writer and college instructor in Harrisburg, Pennsylvania who led "bookstore road trips" to other cities and recognized its potential as a group travel niche and marketing tool. He promoted the concept with a how-to book and a web site, and groups around the U.S. soon began offering similar excursions, usually via a chartered bus, and often incorporating book signings, author home tours, and historical sites. In 2005-06, two regional booksellers associations — the Southern California Booksellers Association and the Northern California Independent Booksellers Association — embraced Bookstore Tourism, offering trips to independent bookstores in Los Angeles, San Diego and San Francisco.

The Bookstore Tourism movement encourages schools, libraries, reading groups, and organizations of all sizes to create day-trips and literary outings to cities and towns with a concentration of independent bookstores. It also encourages local booksellers to attract bibliophiles to their communities by employing bookstore tourism as an economic development tool. Others benefiting include local retailers, restaurants, bus companies, and travel professionals.

The effort also provides organizations with an outreach opportunity to support reading and literacy.

Portzline has travelled across the country to promote the concept. In 2006 he created a promotional video featuring group "bookstore road trips" in New York City's Greenwich Village and in Los Angeles area "beach towns" and posted it on the Bookstore Tourism website.

Portzline took a year off in 2008, and in early 2009 began to promote the effort again, partly in response to the effects of the U.S. financial crisis on independent booksellers.

Christian Tourism

Christian tourism is a subcategory of religious tourism. As one of the largest branches of religious tourism, it is estimated that seven percent of the world's Christians — about 150 million people — are "on the move as pilgrims" each year.

Definition

Christian tourism refers to the entire industry of Christian travel, tourism, and hospitality. In recent years it has grown to include not only Christians embarking individually or in groups on pilgrimages and missionary travel, but also on religion-based cruises, leisure (fellowship) vacations, crusades, rallies, retreats, monastery visits/guest-stays and Christian camps, as well as visiting Christian tourist attractions.

Statistics

Although no definitive study has been completed on Christian tourism, some segments of the industry have been measured:

- According to the Religious Conference Management Association, in 2006 more than 14.7 million people attended religious meetings (RCMA members), an increase of more than 10 million from 1994 with 4.4 million attendees.
- The United Methodist Church experienced an increase of 455% in Volunteers in Mission between 1992 with almost 20,000 volunteers and 2006 with 110,000 volunteers.
- The Christian Camp and Conference Association states that more than eight million people are involved in CCCA member camps and conferences, including more than 120,000 churches.
- Short-term missions draw 1.6 million participants annually.
- Christian attractions including Sight & Sound Theatre attracts 800,000 visitors a year while the Holy Land Experience and Focus on the Family welcome centre each receives about 250,000 guests annually. Recently launched Christian attractions include the Creation Museum and Billy Graham Library, both of which are expected to receive about 250,000 visitors each year as well.

Culinary Tourism

Judging by the surge since 2001 in the number of times "culinary tourism" has appeared as a subject matter or in a session title in tourism industry conferences and programs, we can see that Culinary Tourism is valued by tourism industry professionals as one of the most popular niches in the world's tourism industry. This makes sense, given recent consumer focus on healthy and organic eating, culinary/food pedigrees, and the simple fact that all travellers must eat. Not every visitor goes shopping or visits museums, but all travellers eat. For anyone who doubts, look at the increase in cooking shows featured on The Travel Channel or travel shows featured on The Food Network, as examples.

Culinary Tourism is defined as the pursuit of unique and memorable eating and drinking experiences, according to the International Culinary Tourism Association. Culinary Tourism differs from agritourism in that culinary tourism is considered a subset of cultural tourism (cuisine is a manifestation of culture) whereas agritourism is considered a subset of rural tourism, according to Culinary Tourism: The Hidden Harvest. That said, culinary tourism and agritourism are inextricably linked, as the seeds of cuisine can be found in agriculture.

Culinary Tourism is not just experiences of the highest calibre-that would be gourmet tourism. This is perhaps best illustrated by the notion that Culinary Tourism is about what is "unique and memorable, not what is necessarily pretentious and exclusive". Similarly, wine tourism, beer tourism and spa tourism are also regarded as subsets of culinary tourism.

Cultural Tourism

'Cultural tourism' (or culture tourism) is the subset of tourism concerned with a country or region's culture, specifically the lifestyle of the people in those geographical areas, the history of those peoples, their art, architecture, religion(s), and other elements that helped shape their way of life.

Cultural tourism includes tourism in urban areas, particularly historic or large cities and their cultural facilities such as museums and theatres. It can also include tourism in rural areas showcasing the traditions of indigenous cultural communities (i.e. festivals, rituals), and their values and lifestyle.

It is generally agreed that cultural tourists spend substantially more than standard tourists do. This form of tourism is also becoming generally more popular throughout the world, and a recent OECD report has highlighted the role that cultural tourism can play in regional development in different world regions.

Cultural tourism has been defined as 'the movement of persons to cultural attractions away from their normal place of residence, with the intention to gather new information and experiences to satisfy their cultural needs'.

Destinations

One type of cultural tourism destination is living cultural areas. For an indigenous culture that has stayed largely separated from the surrounding majority, tourism can present both advantages and problems. On the positive side are the unique cultural practices and arts that attract the curiosity of tourists and provide opportunities for tourism and economic development.

On the negative side is the issue of how to control tourism so that those same cultural amenities are not destroyed and the people do not feel violated. Other destinations include historical sites, modern urban districts, theme parks and country clubs, coastal or island ecosystems, and inland natural areas.

Key Principles

Destination Planning

As the issue of globalization takes place to this modern time, the challenge of preserving the few remaining cultural community around the world is becoming hard. In a tribal based community, reaching economic advancement with minimal negative impacts is an essential objective to any destination planner. Since they are using the culture of the region as the main attraction, sustainable destination development of the area is vital for them to prevent the negative impacts due to tourism.

Management Issues

Certainly, the principle of "one size fits all" doesn't apply to destination planning. The needs, expectations, and anticipated benefits from tourism vary greatly from one destination to another. This is clearly exemplified as local communities living in regions with tourism potential (destinations) develop a vision for what kind of tourism they want to facilitate, depending on issues and concerns they want to be settled or satisfied.

Destination Planning Resources

Planning Guides

Culture: the heart of development policy;

It is important that the destination planner takes into account the diverse definition of culture as the term is subjective. Satisfying tourists' interests such as landscapes, seascapes, art, nature, traditions, ways of life and other products associated to them-which may be categorized cultural in the broadest sense of the word, is a prime consideration as it marks the initial phase of the development of a cultural destination.

The quality of service and destination, which doesn't solely depend on the cultural heritage but more importantly to the cultural environment, can further be developed by setting controls and policies which shall govern the community and its stakeholders. It is therefore safe to say that the planner should be on the ball with the varying meaning of culture itself as this fuels the formulation of development policies that shall entail efficient planning and monitored growth.

Local community, tourists, the destination and sustainable tourism

While satisfying tourists' interests and demands may be a top priority, it is also imperative to ruminate the subsystems of the destination's *(residents)*. Development pressures should be anticipated and set to their minimum level so as to conserve the area's resources and prevent a saturation of the destination as to not abuse the product and the residents correspondingly. The plan should incorporate the locals to its gain by training and employing them and in the process encourage them to participate to the travel business. Keep in mind that the plan should make travellers not only aware about the destination but also concern on how to help it sustain its character while broadening their travelling experience.

Planning Tools

Sources of Data: The core of a planner's job is to design an appropriate planning process and facilitate community decision. Ample information which is a crucial requirement is contributed through various technical researches and analyses. Here are some of the helpful tools commonly used by planners to aid them:

1. Key Informant Interviews.
2. Libraries, Internet, and Survey Research.
3. Census and Statistical Analysis.
4. Spatial Analysis with Geographical Information System (GIS) and Global Positioning System (GPS) technologies.

Key Institutions

Participating structures are primarily led by the government's local authorities and the official tourism board or council, with the involvement of various NGOs, community and indigenous representatives, development organizations, and the academe.

Case Studies: Mountainous Regions of Central Asia and in the Himalayas

Tourism is coming to the previously isolated but spectacular mountainous regions of Central Asia, the Hindu Kush and the Himalayas. Closed for so many years to visitors from abroad, it now attracts a growing number of foreign tourists by its unique culture and splendid natural beauty. However, while this influx of tourists is bringing economic opportunities and employment to local populations, helping to promote these little-known regions of the world, it has also brought challenges along with it: to ensure that it is well-managed and that its benefits are shared by all.

As a response to this concern, the Norwegian Government, as well as the UNESCO, organized an interdisciplinary project called the Development of Cultural and Ecotourism in the Mountainous Regions of Central Asia and the Himalayas project.

It aims to establish links and promote cooperation between local communities, national and international NGOs, and tour agencies in order to heighten the role of the local community and involve them fully in the employment opportunities and income-generating activities that tourism can bring. Project activities include training local tour guides, producing high-quality craft items and promoting home-stays and bed-and-breakfast type accommodation.

As of now, the project is drawing on the expertise of international NGOs and tourism professionals in the seven participating countries, making a practical and positive contribution to alleviating poverty by helping local communities to draw the maximum benefit from their region's tourism potential, while protecting the environmental and cultural heritage of the region concerned.

The University of Travel host, Dallas, Texas has an extensive travel library continually gathering travel related research and tourism economic impact studies nationwide.

Dark Tourism

Dark tourism (also black tourism or grief tourism) is tourism involving travel to sites associated with death and suffering. Thanatourism, derived from the Ancient Greek word *thanatos* for the personification of death, is associated with dark tourism but refers more specifically to violent death; it is used in fewer contexts than the terms dark tourism and grief tourism. This includes castles and battlefields such as Culloden near Inverness, Scotland, Chernobyl in ex USSR, or Bran Castle, Poienari Castle in Romania; sites of disaster, either natural or man made such as Ground Zero in New York; prisons now open to the public such as Beaumaris Prison in Anglesey, Wales; and purpose built centres such as the London Dungeon.

Disaster Tourism

Disaster tourism is the act of travelling to a disaster area as a matter of curiosity. The behaviour can be a nuisance if it hinders rescue, relief, and recovery operations.

If not done because of pure curiosity, it can be catalogued as disaster learning.

Hurricane Katrina

Disaster tourism took hold in the Greater New Orleans Area in the aftermath of Hurricane Katrina. There are now guided bus tours to neighbourhoods that were severely damaged by storm-related flooding. Some local residents have criticized these tours as unethical, because the tour companies are profiting from the misery of their communities and families.

The Army Corps of Engineers has noted that traffic from tour buses and other tourist vehicles have interfered with the movement of trucks and other cleanup equipment on single-lane residential roads. Furthermore, during the first six months after the storm, most of these neighbourhoods lacked electricity, phone access, street signs, or access to emergency medical or police assistance. Simply travelling to these neighbourhoods was hazardous. For these reasons, organized disaster tours are now banned from two of the most severely damaged areas in the city, the Lower 9th and St. Bernard Parish near the Industrial Canal.

On the other hand, such communities as Gentilly and Lakeview, along the 17th Street Canal, have welcomed organized tour groups as a means to publicize the scale of the destruction and attract more aid to the city. Much of the recovery effort in the New Orleans relies on out-of-state volunteers and donations. Numerous non-profit organization, including Habitat for Humanity International and Catholic Charities, have converged on the city to gut and rebuild homes. There is also a movement by local residents to bring congressmen and other national leaders to the city and view the damage in person, since recovery efforts have been hampered by the failure of many homeowners and businesses to receive claims from their insurance providers.

Drug Tourism

Drug tourism is travel for the purpose of obtaining or using drugs for personal use that are unavailable or illegal in one's home jurisdiction. Drug tourism can be also defined as the phenomenon by which one's travel experience involves the consumption and usage of drugs that are considered to be illegal or illegitimate in either the visited destination or the tourist's country of origin. This would include crossing a national border to obtain drugs over the counter that are not sold in one's own country, or travelling to another country in order to obtain or use narcotics that are illegal in one's own country, or even travelling from one U.S. state to another in order to buy alcohol or tobacco more easily. Drug tourism to other countries is also popular among college students in the United States younger than 21 who are not yet of the legal drinking age for alcohol purchasing and consumption. Empirical studies show that drug tourism is heterogeneous and might involve either the pursuit of mere pleasure and escapism or a quest for profound and meaningful experiences through the consumption of drugs.

Drug tourism has many legal implications, and persons engaging in it sometimes risk prosecution for drug smuggling or other drug-related charges in their home jurisdictions or in the jurisdictions they are visiting, especially if they bring their purchases home rather than using them abroad. The act of travelling for the purpose of buying or using drugs is itself a criminal offence in some jurisdictions.

In Europe, Amsterdam is a popular destination for drug tourists, due to the Dutch government's liberal attitude toward marijuana use and possession. Another Dutch city which is visited frequently by drug tourists is Maastricht because of its position close to the borders of Germany and Belgium. Drug tourism thrives because legislation controlling the sale, possession, and use of drugs varies dramatically from one jurisdiction to another.

In Australia, the Australian Capital Territory and South Australia have a more liberal approach to marijuana use, promoting interstate drug tourism, particularly from Victoria and New South Wales. In addition, some areas of northern New South Wales have a liberal recreational drug culture, particularly areas around Nimbin where the annual Mardi Grass festival is held. Other popular destinations include Melana, India where famous Indian hashish is produced, and the Rif

Mountains in Morocco where hashish is produced. In South America, some tourists are attracted to Amazonian villages to try a local liquid called ayahuasca which is a mixture of psychedelic plants that is used in traditional ceremonies. Similarly, tourists in Peru try hallucinogenic cactus called San Pedro which originally has been used by local tribes.

Ecotourism

Eotourism (also known as ecological tourism) is travel to fragile, pristine, and usually protected areas that strives to be low impact and (often) small scale. It helps educate the traveller; provides funds for conservation; directly benefits the economic development and political empowerment of local communities; and fosters respect for different cultures and for human rights. Eco tourism is very important so that future generations can experience the wonderful environment we have today. As defined by the co-founder of the Centre for Responsible Travel, Martha Honey, Ph.D., in her book *Ecotourism and Sustainable Development, Second Edition: Who Owns Paradise?*. Most serious studies of ecotourism including several university programs now use this as the working definition. Ecotourism appeals to ecologically and socially conscious individuals. Generally speaking, it focuses on volunteering, personal growth and learning new ways to live on the planet. It typically involves travel to destinations where flora, fauna, and cultural heritage are the primary attractions. Ecotourism is a conceptual experience, enriching those who delve into researching and understanding the environment around them. It gives us insight into our impacts as human beings and also a greater appreciation of our own natural habitats.

Responsible ecotourism includes programs that minimize the negative aspects of conventional tourism on the environment and enhance the cultural integrity of local people. Therefore, in addition to evaluating environmental and cultural factors, an integral part of ecotourism is the promotion of recycling, energy efficiency, water conservation and creation of economic opportunities for the local communities.

Criteria

Ecotourism is a form of tourism that involves travelling to tranquil and unpolluted natural areas. According to the definition and principles of ecotourism established by The International Ecotourism Society (TIES) in 1990, ecotourism is "Responsible travel to natural areas that conserves the environment and improves the wellbeing of local people." (TIES, 1990). Martha Honey, expands on the TIES definition by describing the seven characteristics of ecotourism, which are:

* Involves travel to natural destinations.
* Minimizes impact.
* Builds environmental awareness.
* Provides direct financial benefits for conservation.
* Provides financial benefits and empowerment for local people.
* Respects local culture.
* Supports human rights and demographic movements.

Ideally, ecotourism should satisfy several criteria, such as:

* conservation of biological diversity and cultural diversity through ecosystem protection
* promotion of sustainable use of biodiversity, by providing jobs to local populations
* sharing of socioeconomic benefits with local communities and indigenous peoples by having their informed consent and participation in the management of ecotourism enterprises
* tourism to unspoiled natural resources, with minimal impact on the environment being a primary concern.
* minimization of tourism's own environmental impact.
* affordability and lack of waste in the form of luxury.
* local culture, flora and fauna being the main attractions.

For many countries, ecotourism is not simply a marginal activity to finance protection of the environment, but is a major industry of the national economy. For example, in Costa Rica, Ecuador, Nepal, Kenya, Madagascar and Antarctica, ecotourism represents a significant portion of the gross domestic product and economic activity.

The concept of ecotourism is widely misunderstood and in practice is often used as a marketing tool to promote tourism, which is related to nature. This is an especially frequent malpractice in the realm of Jungle tourism. Critics claim that these green washing practices, carried out in the name of ecotourism, often consist of placing a hotel in a splendid landscape, to the detriment of the ecosystem. According to them, ecotourism must above all sensitize people to the beauty and the fragility of nature. They condemn some operators as green washing their operations: using the labels of "green" and "eco-friendly", while behaving in environmentally irresponsible ways.

Although academics disagree about who can be classified as an ecotourist and there is precious little statistical data, some estimate that more than five million ecotourists-the majority of the ecotourist population-come from the United States, with others from Western Europe, Canada and Australia.

Currently, there are various moves to create national and international ecotourism accreditation programs, although the process is also controversial. National ecotourism certification programs have been put in place in countries such as Costa Rica, Australia, Kenya and Sweden.

History

Ecotourism, responsible tourism, jungle tourism and sustainable development have become prevalent concepts since the late 1980s, and ecotourism has experienced arguably the fastest growth of all sub-sectors in the tourism industry. The popularity represents a change in tourist perceptions, increased environmental awareness, and a desire to explore natural environments. Such changes have become as much a statement affirming one's social identity, educational sophistication, and disposable income as it has about preserving the Amazon rainforest or the Caribbean reef for posterity.

Criticisms

Definitional problems and green washing: To approach an understanding of the problem, a clear definition must delineate what is, and is not, ecotourism. Ideally, ecotourism satisfies several general criteria, including the conservation of biological diversity and cultural diversity through ecosystem protection, promotion of sustainable use of biodiversity, share of socioeconomic benefits with local communities through informed consent and participation, increase in environmental and cultural knowledge, affordability and reduced waste, and minimization of its own environmental impact. In such ways, it contributes to the long term benefits to both the environment and local communities.

However, in the continuum of tourism activities that stretch from conventional tourism to ecotourism proper, there has been a lot of contention to the limit at which biodiversity preservation, local socioeconomic benefits, and environmental impact can be considered "ecotourism". For this reason, environmentalists, special interest groups, and governments define ecotourism differently. Environmental organizations have generally insisted that ecotourism is nature-based, sustainably managed, conservation supporting, and environmentally educated.

The tourist industry and governments, however, focus more on the product aspect, treating ecotourism as equivalent to any sort of tourism based in nature. As a further complication, many terms are used under the rubric of ecotourism. Nature tourism, low impact tourism, green tourism, bio-tourism, ecologically responsible tourism, and others have been used in literature and marketing, although they are not necessary synonymous with ecotourism.

The problems associated with defining ecotourism have led to confusion among tourists and academics alike. Definitional problems are also subject of considerable public controversy and concern because of green washing, a trend towards the commercialization of tourism schemes disguised as sustainable, nature based, and environmentally friendly ecotourism.

According to McLaren, these schemes are environmentally destructive, economically exploitative, and culturally insensitive at its worst. They are also morally disconcerting because they mislead tourists and manipulate their concerns for the environment. Despite objections, green washing continues to grow unabated. The Nature's Sacred Paradise, a theme park in Quintana Roo, Mexico, is responsible for displacing local Mayan communities and illegally keeping endangered species in captivity to attract visitors. The development and success of such large scale, energy intensive, and ecologically unsustainable schemes are a testament to the tremendous profits associated with being labelled as ecotourism.

Negative Impact of Tourism

Ecotourism has become one of the fastest-growing sectors of the tourism industry, growing annually by 10-15% worldwide. One definition of ecotourism is "the practice of low-impact, educational, ecologically and culturally sensitive travel that benefits local communities and host countries". Many of the ecotourism projects are not meeting these standards. Even if some of the guidelines are being executed, the local communities are still facing other negative impacts. South Africa is one of the countries that are reaping significant economic benefits from ecotourisms, but negative effects-including physical displacement of persons, gross violation of fundamental rights, and environmental hazards-far outweigh the medium-term economic benefits. A tremendous amount of money is being spent and human resources continue to be used for ecotourism despite the lack of success, and even more money is put into public relation campaigns to dilute the effects of criticism. Ecotourism channels resources away from other projects that could contribute more sustainable and realistic solutions to pressing social and environmental problems.

"The money tourism can generate often ties parks and managements to ecotourism". But there is a tension in this relationship because ecotourism often causes conflict and changes in land-use rights, fails to deliver promises of community-level benefits, damages environments, and has plenty of other social impacts. Indeed many argue repeatedly that ecotourism is neither ecologically nor socially beneficial, yet it persists as a strategy for conservation and development. While several studies are being done on ways to improve the ecotourism structure, these examples provide rationale for stopping it altogether.

The ecotourism system exercises tremendous financial and political influence. The evidence above shows that at the very least a strong case exists for restraining such activities. Funding could be used for field studies aimed at finding alternative solutions to tourism and the diverse problems Africa faces in result of urbanization, industrialization, and over exploitation of agriculture. At the local level ecotourism has become a source of conflict over control of land, resources, and tourism profits.

There are many problems with the idea of ecotourism. Environmental, the effects on the local people, and conflicts over profit distribution are only a few of the negative effects of ecotourism. In a perfect world more efforts would be made towards educating tourists of the environmental and social effects of their travels. Very few regulations or laws stand in place as boundaries for the investors in ecotourism. These should be implemented to prohibit the promotion of unsustainable ecotourism projects and materials which project false images of destinations, demeaning local and indigenous cultures.

Direct Environmental Impacts

Ecotourism operations occasionally fail to live up to conservation ideals. It is sometimes overlooked that ecotourism is a highly consumer-centred activity, and that environmental conservation is a means to further economic growth.

Although ecotourism is intended for small groups, even a modest increase in population, however temporary, puts extra pressure on the local environment and necessitates the development of additional infrastructure and amenities. The construction of water treatment plants, sanitation facilities, and lodges come with the exploitation of non-renewable energy sources and the utilization of already limited local resources. The conversion of natural land to such tourist infrastructure is implicated in deforestation and habitat deterioration of butterflies in Mexico and squirrel monkeys in Costa Rica. In other cases, the environment suffers because local communities are unable to meet the infrastructure demands of ecotourism. The lack of adequate sanitation facilities in many East African parks results in the disposal of campsite sewage in rivers, contaminating the wildlife, livestock, and people who draw drinking water from it.

Aside from environmental degradation with tourist infrastructure, population pressures from ecotourism also leaves behind garbage and pollution associated with the Western lifestyle. Although ecotourists claim to be educationally sophisticated and environmentally concerned, they rarely understand the ecological consequences of their visits and how their day-to-day activities append physical impacts on the environment. As one scientist observes, they "rarely acknowledge how the meals they eat, the toilets they flush, the water they drink, and so on, are all part of broader regional economic and ecological systems they are helping to reconfigure with their very activities." Nor do ecotourists recognize the great consumption of non-renewable energy required to arrive at their destination, which is typically more remote than conventional tourism destinations. For instance, an exotic journey to a place 10,000 kilometres away consumes about 700 litres of fuel per person.

Ecotourism activities are, in of itself, issues in environmental impact because they disturb fauna and flora. Ecotourists believe that because they are only taking pictures and leaving footprints, they keep ecotourism sites pristine, but even harmless sounding activities such as a nature hike can be ecologically destructive. In the Annapurna Circuit in Nepal, ecotourists have worn down the marked trails and created alternate routes, contributing to soil impaction, erosion, and plant damage. Where the ecotourism activity involves wildlife viewing, it can scare away animals, disrupt their feeding and nesting sites, or acclimate them to the presence of people. In Kenya, wildlife-observer disruption drives cheetahs off their reserves, increasing the risk of inbreeding and further endangering the species.

Environmental Hazards

Unfortunately, industrialization, urbanization, and unsustainable agriculture practices have all had serious effects on the environment. Ecotourism is now also playing a role in this depletion. While the term ecotourism may sound relatively benign, one of its most serious impacts is its consumption of virgin territories. These invasions often include deforestation, disruption of ecological life systems and various forms of pollution, all of which contribute to environmental degradation. The number of motor vehicles crossing the park increases as tour drivers search for rare species.

The number of roads has disrupted the grass cover which has serious effects on plant and animal species. These areas also have a higher rate of disturbances and invasive species because of all the traffic moving off the beaten path into new undiscovered areas. Ecotourism also has an effect on species through the value placed on them. "Certain species have gone from being little known or valued by local people to being highly valued commodities. The commodification of plants may erase their social value and lead to overproduction within protected areas. Local people and their images can also be turned into commodities". Kamuaro brings up a relatively obvious contradiction, any commercial venture into unspoiled, pristine land with or without the "eco" prefix as a contradiction in terms. To generate revenue you have to have a high number of traffic, tourists, which inevitably means a higher pressure on the environment.

Local People

Most forms of ecotourism are owned by foreign investors and corporations that provide few benefits to local communities. An overwhelming majority of profits are put into the pockets of investors instead of reinvestment into the local economy or environmental protection. The limited numbers of local people who are employed in the economy enter at its lowest level, and are unable to live in tourist areas because of meager wages and a two market system.

In some cases, the resentment by local people results in environmental degradation. As a highly publicized case, the Masai nomads in Kenya killed wildlife in national parks to show aversion to unfair compensation terms and displacement from traditional lands. The lack of economic opportunities for local people also constrains them to degrade the environment as a means of sustenance. The presence of affluent ecotourists encourage the development of destructive markets in wildlife souvenirs, such as the sale of coral trinkets on tropical islands and animal products in Asia, contributing to illegal harvesting and poaching from the environment. In Suriname, sea turtle reserves use a large portion of their budget to guard against these destructive activities.

Displacement of People

One of the most powerful examples of communities being moved in order to create a park is the story of the Masai. About 70% of national parks and game reserves in East Africa are on Masai land. The first undesirable impact of tourism was that of the extent of land lost from the Masai culture. Local and national governments took advantage of the Masai's ignorance on the situation and robbed them of huge chunks of grazing land, putting to risk their only socioeconomic livelihood. In Kenya the Masai also have not gained any economic benefits. Despite the loss of their land, employment favours better educated workers. Furthermore the investors in this area are not local and have not put profits back into local economy. In some cases game reserves can be created without informing or consulting local people, who come to find out about the situation when an eviction notice is delivered. Another source of resentment is the manipulation of the local people by their government. "Ecotourism works to create simplistic images of local people and their uses and understandings of their surroundings. Through the lens of these simplified images, officials direct policies and projects towards the local people and the local people are blamed if the projects fail". Clearly tourism as a trade is not empowering the local people who make it rich and satisfying. Instead ecotourism exploits and depletes, particularly in African Masai tribes. It has to be reoriented if it is to be useful to local communities and to become sustainable.

Threats to Indigenous Cultures

Ecotourism often claims that it preserves and "enhances" local cultures. However, evidence shows that with the establishment of protected areas local people have illegally lost their homes, and most often with no compensation. Pushing people onto marginal lands with harsh climates, poor soils, lack of water, and infested with livestock and disease does little to enhance livelihoods even when a proportion of ecotourism profits are directed back into the community. The establishment of parks can create harsh survival realities and deprive the people of their traditional use of land and natural resources. Ethnic groups are increasingly being seen as a "backdrop" to the scenery and wildlife.

The local people struggle for cultural survival and freedom of cultural expression while being "observed" by tourists. Local indigenous people also have strong resentment towards the change, "Tourism has been allowed to develop with virtually no controls. Too many lodges have been built, too much firewood is being used and no limits are being placed on tourism vehicles. They regularly drive off-track and harass the wildlife. Their vehicle tracks crisscross the entire Masai Mara. Inevitably the bush is becoming eroded and degraded".

Mismanagement

While governments are typically entrusted with the administration and enforcement of environmental protection, they often lack the commitment or capability to manage ecotourism sites effectively. The regulations for environmental protection may be vaguely defined, costly to implement, hard to enforce, and uncertain in effectiveness. Government regulatory agencies, as political bodies, are susceptible to making decisions that spend budget on politically beneficial but environmentally unproductive projects. Because of prestige and conspicuousness, the construction of an attractive visitor's centre at an ecotourism site may take precedence over more pressing environmental concerns like acquiring habitat, protecting endemic species, and removing invasive ones. Finally, influential groups can pressure and sway the interests of the government to their favour. The government and its regulators can become vested in the benefits of the ecotourism industry which they are supposed to regulate, causing restrictive environmental regulations and enforcement to become more lenient.

Management of ecotourism sites by private ecotourism companies offers an alternative to the cost of regulation and deficiency of government agencies. It is believed that these companies have a self interest in limited environmental degradation, because tourists will pay more for pristine environments, which translates to higher profit. However, theory indicates that this practice is not economically feasible and will fail to manage the environment.

The model of monopolistic competition states that distinctiveness will entail profits, but profits will promote imitation. A company that protects its ecotourism sites is able to charge a premium for the novel experience and pristine environment. But when other companies view the success of this approach, they also enter the market with similar practices, increasing competition and reducing demand. Eventually, the demand will be reduced until the economic profit is zero. A cost-benefit analysis shows that the company bears the cost of environmental protection without receiving the gains. Without economic incentive, the whole premise of self interest through environmental protection is quashed; instead, ecotourism companies will minimize environment related expenses and maximize tourism demand.

The tragedy of the commons offers another model for economic unsustainability from environmental protection, in ecotourism sites utilized by many companies. Although there is a communal incentive to protect the environment, maximizing the benefits in the long run, a company will conclude that it is in their best interest to utilize the ecotourism site beyond its sustainable level. By increasing the number of ecotourists, for instance, a company gains all the economic benefit while paying only a part of the environmental cost. In the same way, a company recognizes that there is no incentive to actively protect the environment; they bear all the costs, while the benefits are shared by all other companies. The result, again, is mismanagement.

Taken together, the mobility of foreign investment and lack of economic incentive for environmental protection means that ecotourism companies are disposed to establishing themselves in new sites once their existing one is sufficiently degraded.

Improving Sustainability

Regulation and accreditation: Because the regulation of ecotourism is poorly implemented or nonexistent, ecologically destructive greenwashed operations like underwater hotels, helicopter tours, and wildlife theme parks are categorized as ecotourism along with canoeing, camping, photography, and wildlife observation. The failure to acknowledge responsible, low impact ecotourism puts these companies at a competitive disadvantage.

Many environmentalists have argued for a global standard of accreditation, differentiating ecotourism companies based on their level of environmental commitment. A national or international regulatory board would enforce accreditation procedures, with representation from various groups including governments, hotels, tour operators, travel agents, guides, airlines, local authorities, conservation organizations, and non-governmental organizations. The decisions of the board would be sanctioned by governments, so that non-compliant companies would be legally required to disassociate themselves from the use of the ecotourism brand.

Crinion suggests a Green Stars System, based on criteria including a management plan, benefit for the local community, small group interaction, education value and staff training. Ecotourists who consider their choices would be confident of a genuine ecotourism experience when they see the higher star rating.

In addition, environmental impact assessments could be used as a form of accreditation. Feasibility is evaluated from a scientific basis, and recommendations could be made to optimally plan infrastructure, set tourist capacity, and manage the ecology. This form of accreditation is more sensitive to site specific conditions.

Guidelines and Education

An environmental protection strategy must address the issue of ecotourists removed from the cause-and-effect of their actions on the environment. More initiatives should be carried out to improve their awareness, sensitize them to environmental issues, and care about the places they visit.

Tour guides are an obvious and direct medium to communicate awareness. With the confidence of ecotourists and intimate knowledge of the environment, they can actively discuss conservation issues. A tour guide training program in Costa Rica's Tortuguero National Park has helped mitigate negative environmental impacts by providing information and regulating tourists on the parks' beaches used by nesting endangered sea turtles.

Small Scale, Slow Growth and Local Control

The underdevelopment theory of tourism describes a new form of imperialism by multinational corporations that control ecotourism resources. These corporations finance and profit from the development of large scale ecotourism that causes excessive environmental degradation, loss of traditional culture and way of life, and exploitation of local labour. In Zimbabwe and Nepal's Annapurna region, where underdevelopment is taking place, more than 90 percent of ecotourism revenues are expatriated to the parent countries, and less than 5 percent go into local communities.

The lack of sustainability highlights the need for small scale, slow growth, and locally based ecotourism. Local peoples have a vested interest in the well being of their community, and are therefore more accountable to environmental protection than multinational corporations. The lack of control, westernization, adverse impacts to the environment, loss of culture and traditions outweigh the benefits of establishing large scale ecotourism.

The increased contributions of communities to locally managed ecotourism create viable economic opportunities, including high level management positions, and reduce environmental issues associated with poverty and unemployment. Because the ecotourism experience is marketed to a different lifestyle from large scale ecotourism, the development of facilities and infrastructure does not need to conform to corporate Western tourism standards, and can be much simpler and less expensive. There is a greater multiplier effect on the economy, because local products, materials, and labour are used. Profits accrue locally and import leakages are reduced.

However, even this form of tourism may require foreign investment for promotion or start up. When such investments are required, it is crucial for communities for find a company or non-governmental organization that reflects the philosophy of ecotourism; sensitive to their concerns and willing to cooperate at the expense of profit. The basic assumption of the multiplier effect is that the economy starts off with unused resources, for example, that many workers are cyclically unemployed and much of industrial capacity is sitting idle or incompletely utilized. By increasing demand in the economy it is then possible to boost production. If the economy was already at full employment, with only structural, frictional, or other supply-side types of unemployment, any attempt to boost demand would only lead to inflation. For various laissez-faire schools of economics which embrace Say's Law and deny the possibility of Keynesian inefficiency and underemployment of resources, therefore, the multiplier concept is irrelevant or wrong-headed.

As an example, consider the government increasing its expenditure on roads by $one million, without a corresponding increase in taxation. This sum would go to the road builders, who would hire more workers and distribute the money as wages and profits. The households receiving these incomes will save part of the money and spend the rest on consumer goods. These expenditures in turn will generate more jobs, wages, and profits, and so on with the income and spending circulating around the economy.

The multiplier effect arises because of the induced increases in consumer spending which occur due to the increased incomes — and because of the feedback into increasing business revenues, jobs, and income again. This process does not lead to an economic explosion not only because of the supply-side barriers at potential output (full employment) but because at each "round", the increase in consumer spending is less than the increase in consumer incomes. That is, the marginal propensity to consume (mpc) is less than one, so that each round some extra income goes into saving, leaking out of the cumulative process. Each increase in spending is thus smaller than that of the previous round, preventing an explosion. Ecotourism has to be implemented with care.

Natural Resource Management

Natural resource management can be utilized as a specialized tool for the development of ecotourism. There are several places throughout the world where the amount of natural resources are abundant. But, with human encroachment and habitats these resources are depleting. Without knowing the proper utilization of certain resources they are destroyed and floral and faunal species are becoming extinct. Ecotourism programmes can be introduced for the conservation of these resources. Several plans and proper management programmes can be introduced so that these resources remain untouched. Several organizations, NGO's, scientists are working on this field.

Natural resources of hill areas like Kurseong in West Bengal are plenty in number with various flora and fauna, but tourism for business purpose poised the situation. Researcher from Jadavpur University presently working in this area for the development of ecotourism which can be utilized as a tool for natural resource management.

Tour Operators, Travel Agencies & Retailers

Some companies specialise in ecotourism, designing their trips to be environmentally, culturally and socially friendly. Companies such as Intrepid Travel, Adventure Life, Frontier, and Marine Conservation Society, Family Nature Summit, Peregrine Adventures, World Expeditions, Explore Worldwide and Exodus offer trips catering for the thoughtful traveller. Some tour operators are keenly aware of the impacts that they may have on specific areas and rotate clients around to different sites for snorkelling, bird watching, and other activities. Others are just beginning to see the advantage of "green" travel destinations.

Extreme Tourism

Extreme tourism or shock tourism is a type of niche tourism involving travel to dangerous places or participation in dangerous events. Extreme tourism overlaps with extreme sport. The two share the main attraction, "adrenaline rush" caused by an element of risk, and differing mostly in the degree of engagement and professionalism.

Extreme tourism is a growing business in the countries of the former Soviet Union and in South American countries like Peru, Chile and Argentina. The mountainous and rugged terrain of Northern Pakistan has also developed into a popular extreme tourism location.

While traditional tourism requires significant investments in hotels, roads, etc., extreme tourism requires much less to jump-start a business. In addition to traditional travel-based tourism destinations, various exotic attractions are suggested, such as flyovers in MiGs at Mach 2.5, ice diving in the White Sea, or travelling across the Chernobyl zone.

Ghetto Tourism

Ghetto tourism refers to the growing popularity of tourism in ghettos.

Studies

Michael Stephens first examined the subject in the cultural-criticism journal, Pop Matters, in 2005. Ghetto tourism includes all forms of entertainment — "gangsta rap," video games, movies, TV, and other forms that allow consumers to traffic in the inner city without leaving home.

As Stevens says, "digital media achieves more detailed simulations of reality. The quest for thrills mutates into a desire, not just to see bigger and better explosions, but to cross class and racial boundaries and experience other lifestyles." International tourists to New York City in the 1980s led to a successful tourism boom in Harlem. By 2002, Philadelphia began offering tours of blighted inner-city neighbourhood. After Hurricane Katrina, tours were offered in flood-ravaged Lower Ninth Ward, a notoriously violent and poor section of New Orleans.

Musical Influence

With respect to the vast historic references to landmarks, neighbourhood and streetscapes within music, ghetto or "urban tourism" often encompasses travel to destinations made famous by direct or indirect mention by popular artists. Travel to certain parts of Detroit that include 8 Mile Road, known for the role the travel route played in the similarly titled 8 Mile film starring Eminem, or to Crenshaw Boulevard in South Central Los Angeles, a metropolitan area that inspired an entire generation of pioneering musical influence, could potentially be included as urban tourism. The Jane-Finch area of Toronto, Canada is gaining notoriety as another area in transition.

Graffiti Travel

Artists have been featured in The Source magazine and some individuals travel to different urban settings to adapt and learn new graffiti styles.

Jungle Tourism

Jungle tourism is a rising subcategory of adventure travel defined by active multifaceted physical means of travel in the jungle regions of the earth. Although similar in many respects to adventure travel, jungle tourism pertains specifically to the context of region, culture and activity. According to the *Glossary of Tourism Terms*, jungle tours have become a major component of green tourism in tropical destinations and are a relatively recent phenomenon of Western international tourism.

Of the regions that take part in tourism-driven sustainable development practices and eco tourism, Mexican, Central and South American practices are the most pervasive in the industry; notably Mayan jungle excursions. Other regions include jungle territories in Africa, Australia, and the South Pacific.

Jungle Tourism in Central and South America

The majority of jungle tour operators are concentrated in what is known as the Mayan World or "Ruta Maya". The Mayan World encompasses five different countries that hosted the entirety of the Mayan Civilization: Mexico, Guatemala, Belize, Honduras and El Salvador. Most tours consist of visits to popular Mayan archaeological sites such as Tikal, Guatemala, Chichen Itza, and Copan. These day visits will usually consist of a guided tour of a heavily tourist-concentrated Mayan and archaeological site. Tikal and Chichen Itza are prime examples of popular day-visit sites. Such sites involve a tour guide, designated either by the state government or by a private company, for the tourists. These tour guides are predominantly trained professionals, certified to take large parties of fifty through heavily populated archaeological sites.

Although most of the visits to these more prominent sites involve day trips, there are also many jungle tour operators that showcase less-known, remote Mayan jungle ruins such as Nakum, Yaxha, and El Mirador. These tours involve much more preparation, time and funding to explore as they are usually in very remote and generally inaccessible regions of the Mayan jungles. These ruins and sites are reached by alternative and physically taxing means of travel such as bicycle, canoe, horseback or hiking. This is what essentially differentiates jungle tourism from any other sort of adventure travel tours. There are several tour operators that will even employ the use of machetes during tours.

Another significant and noteworthy difference is the fact that the majority of tour operators that travel deep into the Central and South American Jungle will cap the number of persons travelling in the group at ten to fifteen. This is done to minimize the impact on the jungle flora and fauna. Federal laws in some countries prohibit any given group large than fifteen people travelling through the Mayan jungle, a generally protected region, but very limited resources have kept such practices from occurring under the radar.

Mountain Biking

Mountain biking is an ever evolving sport that has recently seen a huge flux of popularity but has firm roots in experimentation with non "mountain" style bicycles. The sport consists of riding bicycles off-road, often over rough terrain, with specially equipped mountain bikes or hybrid/cross road bikes. Most mountain bikes share similar characteristics with other bicycles but they underscore durability and performance in rough terrain: knobby tires, large frame tubing, front fork suspension or dual suspension shock absorbers, 26 inch and also 29 inch tires. The durability factor results a far heavier bicycle weight to rider ratio than their road touring bicycles. Levered shifters for gear rations and lever brake systems are common. Recent trends find riders using fixed gear systems, single speed systems and internal gear systems.

Mounatin Biker's tend to be environmentally conscious individuals who practice Karma based policies on and off the trail. Cooperating with land-owners and Governments for land access and legal trails, pro-active trail building concepts and maintenance International Mountain Bicycling Association (IMBA), helping other bikers in need and positive advocacy for the sport. Mountain biking is growing but can generally be broken down into multiple categories for example: XC cross country, DH downhill, FR freeride AM All Mountain Urban trials/street riding, DJ Dirt Jumping. Each has differing levels of safety-consciousness and varrying types of mountain bikes and riding gear. A combination sport named mountain bike orienteering adds the skill of map navigation to mountain biking.

This individual sport requires endurance, core strength and balance, bike handling skills (time in the saddle) and self-reliance. Advanced riders exhibit extreme risk taking performing aerial manoevers and steep technical decents. It can be performed almost anywhere from a back yard to a gravel road, but the majority of mountain bikers ride off-road trails, whether country back roads, fire roads, or *singletrack* (narrow trails that wind through forests, mountains, deserts, or fields). There are aspects of mountain biking that are more similar to trail running than regular bicycling. Because riders are often far from civilization, there is a strong ethic of self-reliance in the sport. Riders learn to repair their broken bikes or flat tires to avoid being stranded miles from help. This reliance on survival skills accounts for the group dynamics of the sport. Club rides and other forms of group rides are common, especially on longer treks.

History

The history of the mountain bike includes contributions from cyclo-cross in Europe, the Roughstuff Fellowship in the UK, and modified heavy cruiser bicycles used for freewheeling down mountain trails in Marin County, California. However, it was not until the late 1970s and early 1980s that road bicycle companies started to manufacture mountain bicycles using high-tech lightweight materials. Throughout the 1990s and 2000s, mountain biking moved from a little-known sport to a mainstream.

Equipment

Mountain bikes differ from road bicycles in several ways. They have a smaller, reinforced frame, knobby, wide and high profile tyres which are mounted on a rim stronger than those used on most non-mountain bicycles, a larger range of gears to facilitate climbing up steep hills and over obstacles, a wider flat or upwardly-rising handlebar that allows a more upright riding position, and often some form of suspension system for either the front wheel or both wheels. Mountain bikes sometimes come with disc brakes similar to those used in automobiles, rather than rim brakes used on road bikes.

Bicycle pedals vary from simple *platform* pedals, where the rider simply places the shoes on top of the pedals, to *clipless*, where the rider uses a specially equipped shoe with a sole that engages mechanically into the pedal. Pedals with toe cages (*clips*) are rarely used anymore as they take longer to get out of than clipless or platform if one takes a fall on the rough terrain.

Helmets provide important head protection, as falls can occur over rough, rocky, sandy, or mountainous terrain. Helmets include full-faced helmets or regular. Gloves differ from road touring gloves, are made of heavier construction, and often have covered thumbs or all fingers covered for hand protection. They are sometimes made with padding for the knuckles.

Glasses with little or no difference from those used in other cycling sports, help protect against debris while on the trail. Filtered lenses, whether yellow for cloudy days or shaded for sunny days, protect the eyes from strain. Shoes generally have gripping soles similar to those of hiking boots for scrambling over un-ridable obstacles, unlike the smooth-bottomed shoes used in road cycling. The shank of mountain bike shoes is generally more flexible than road cycling shoes.

Clothing is chosen for comfort during physical exertion in the backcountry, and its ability to withstand falls. Road touring clothes are often inappropriate due to their delicate fabrics and construction. Hydration systems are important for mountain bikers in the backcountry, ranging from simple water bottles to water bags with drinking tubes in lightweight backpacks.

GPS System is sometimes added to the handlebars and is used to display and monitor progress on trails downloaded from the internet or pre-made mapping systems, record trails on the fly, and keep track of trip times and other data. The GPS system is often a hand-held GPS device with colour screen and rugged, waterproof (IPX7) design. Pump to inflate flat tires.

Bike tools and extra bike tubes are important, as mountain bikers frequently find themselves miles from help, with flat tires or other mechanical problems that must be handled by the rider.

Body armour Similar to the armour worn on motorcross bikes. These can consist of knee pads, elbow pads, padded shorts or armoured under jackets. These are made by companies like Dainese, sixsixone, Alpinestars and others. It is especially popular with downhill cycling.

Injuries and Protective Gear

Prevention

The risk of injury is inherent in the sport of mountain biking, especially in the more extreme disciplines such as downhill biking. Injuries range from relatively minor wounds, such as cuts and abrasions from falls on gravel to serious injuries such as striking the head or spine on a boulder or tree. Protective equipment can protect against minor injuries, and reduce the extent or seriousness of major impacts, but it cannot protect a rider against the most serious impacts or accidents. To truly reduce the risk of injury, a rider needs to take steps to make injuries less likely, such as picking trails that they can handle given their experience level, ensuring that they are fit enough to deal with the trail they have chosen, and keeping their bike in top mechanical shape. If a mountain biker wishes to explore more dangerous trails or disciplines (types of mountain biking) such as downhill riding, they will need to learn new skills, such as jumping and avoiding obstacles. Fitness is another issue; if a rider is not in good enough shape to ride a certain class of trail, they will become fatigued, which puts them at a higher risk of having an accident. Lastly, maintenance of one's bike needs to be done more frequently for mountain biking than for casual commuter biking in the city. Mountain biking places much higher demands on every part of the bike. Jumps and impacts can crack the frame or damage the derailleurs or the tire rims, and steep, fast descents can quickly wear out brake pads. Thus, whereas a casual in-the-city rider may only check over and maintain their bike every few months, a mountain biker should check and lube the bike before every ride.

Protective Gear

The style and level of protection worn by individual riders varies greatly and is affected by many factors including terrain, environment, weather, potential obstacles on the trail, experience, technical skill, fitness, perceived risk, desired style and others too numerous to mention. As a general rule, if everyone else at the bike park is wearing a lot of protective gear it is a fair guess that a degree of protection is desirable. However, it does not follow that if someone is wearing no protection at all it is a good idea to copy them. They may be a very good rider, completely foolhardy or have no idea whatsoever what he/she is doing or how dangerous what they are about to ride is. A cross-country helmet and simple long fingered gloves are a good minimum for the majority of riding.

Limb protection becomes important when speeds rise, surfaces become loose and sketchy, terrain technical and crashes more common and more severe. Full-face helmets and armoured suits or jackets are more suited to "gravity" and "air"-orientated disciplines which use jumps and drops, where their extra bulk and weight is outweighed by the bigger and more frequent crashes with worse consequences. Still, within XC community, the typical road-racing attire is what most riders use. Whatever protection is used it should fit well, be comfortable (or it won't be worn) on the bike as well as in the shop and suited for the particular type of riding. Gloves can offer increased comfort while riding, by alleviating compression and friction, and protection in the event of strikes to the back or palm of the hand or when putting the hand out in a fall. Gloves also protect the hand, fingers, and knuckles from abrasion on rough surfaces such as concrete. Many different styles of gloves exist, with various fits, sizes, finger lengths, palm padding and armour options available. Armoring knuckles and the backs of hands with plastic panels is common in more extreme types of mountainbiking.

Helmets

The use of helmets, in one form or another, is almost universal amongst all mountain bikers. Those who choose not to wear helmets are often ridiculed for their lack of safety and image concerns. The main three types are cross-country, rounded skateboarder style (nicknamed "half shells" or "skate style") and full face. Cross-country helmets tend to be light and well ventilated, and more comfortable to wear for long periods, especially while perspiring in hot weather. In XC competitions, most bikers use the usual road racing style helmets, for their lightweight and aerodynamic qualities. Skateboard helmets are simpler and cheaper than other helmet types; provide greater coverage of the head and resist minor scrapes and knocks. Unlike road biking helmets, skateboard helmets typically have a thicker, hard plastic shell which can take multiple impact before it needs to be replaced. The trade-off for this is that they tend to be much heavier and less ventilated (sweatier), therefore not suitable for endurance-based riding.

Full-face helmets (BMX-style) provide the highest level of protection, being stronger again than skateboard style and including a jaw guard to protect the face. The weight is the main issue with this type but nowadays they are often relatively well ventilated and made of high-tech materials, such as carbon fibre. As all helmets should meet minimum standards, SNELL B.95 (American Standard) BS EN 1078:1997 (European Standard), DOT or "motorized ratings" are making their way into the market.

The choice of helmet often comes down to rider preference, likelihood of crashing and on what features or properties of a helmet they place emphasis. Helmets are mandatory at competitive events and almost without exception at bike parks, most organisations also stipulate when and where full-face helmets must be used.

Body Armour and Pads

Many companies also produce other items of protective gear, often nicknamed "armour" to protect limbs and trunk in the event of a crash. While initially made for and marketed at downhillers, freeriders and jump/street riders, body armour has trickled into other areas mountain biking as trails have become faster and more technical.

Armour ranges from simple neoprene sleeves for knees and elbows to complex, articulated combinations of hard plastic shells and padding that cover a whole limb or the entire body.

Some companies market body armour jackets and even full body suits designed to provide greater protection through greater coverage of the body and more secure pad retention. Most upper body protectors also include a spine protector that comprises plastic or metal reinforced plastic plates, over foam padding, which are joined together so that they arcticulate and move with the back. Some mountain bikers also use BMX-style body armour, such as chest plates, abdomen protectors, and spine plates. New technology has seen an influx of integrated neck protectors that fit securely with full face helmets.

There is a general correlation between increased protection and increased weight/decreased mobility, although different styles balance these factors differently. Different levels of protection are deemed necessary/desirable by different riders in different circumstances. Backpack hydration systems such as Camelbaks where a water filled bladder is held close to the spine used by some riders for their perceived protective value. However, there is only anecdotal evidence of protection and with the exception of one specific product by the company Deuter, they are never sold as spine protection.

First Sid

In addition to preventing injuries with protective gear, mountain bike riders need to know how to deal with injuries that occur. Mountain biking groups typically travel with first aid kits, so that they are able to clean and dress cuts and abrasions or splint broken limbs. Experienced mountain bike guides may also have training in dealing with suspected spinal injuries. In the event of serious injuries, such as suspected spinal injury, bikers may have to be removed by a 4X4 truck, or if there are no vehicle-accessible roads, airlifted from the trail with a helicopter.

Types

Mountain biking is dominated by these major categories:

Downhill (DH) is, in the most general sense, riding mountain bikes downhill. The rider usually travels to the point of descent by other means than cycling, such as a ski lift or automobile, as the weight of the downhill mountain bike often precludes any serious climbing. While cross country riding inevitably has a downhill component, Downhill (or DH for short) usually refers to racing-oriented downhill riding. Downhill-specific bikes are universally equipped with front and rear suspension, large disc brakes, and use heavier frame tubing than other mountain bikes. Because of their extremely steep terrain (often located in summer at ski resorts), downhill courses are one of the most extreme and dangerous venues for mountain biking. They include large jumps (up to and including 12 meters (40 feet)), drops of 3+ meters (10+ feet), and are generally rough and steep top to bottom. To negotiate these obstacles at race speed, racers must possess a unique combination of total body strength, aerobic and anaerobic fitness, and mental control. Minimum body protection in a true downhill setting is knee pads and a full face helmet with goggles, although riders and racers commonly sport full body suits to protect themselves. Downhill bikes now weigh around 16-20 kilos (35-45 lbs), while professional downhill mountain bikes can weigh as little as 15 kilos (33 lbs), fully equipped with custom carbon fibre parts, air suspension, tubeless tires and more. Downhill frames get anywhere from 170-250 millimetres (7 to 10 inches) of travel and are usually mounted with an 200 millimetre (8 inch) travel dual-crown fork.

All-mountain (AM) bike category typically provides 125-180 millimetres (5-7 inches) of rear and front suspension travel and stronger components then XC models, while still providing overall weight suitable for climbing and descending on a variety of terrain.

Four Cross/Dual Slalom (4X) is sport in which riders compete either on separate tracks, as in Dual Slalom; or on a short slalom track, as in 4X. Most bikes used are light hard-tails, although the last World Cup was actually won on a full suspension bike. The tracks on which the racers race on have dirt jumps, berms, and gaps. Professionals in gravity mountain biking tend to concentrate either on downhill mountain biking or 4X/dual slalom as each is very different. However, some riders, such as Cedric Gracia, still do 4X and DH, although that is becoming rarer as 4X takes on its own identity.

Freeride/Big Hit/Hucking. Freeride, as the name suggests is a 'do anything' discipline that encompasses everything from downhill racing without the clock to jumping, riding 'North Shore' style (elevated trails made of interconnecting bridges and logs), and generally riding trails and/or stunts that require more skill and aggressive techniques than XC. Freeride bikes are generally heavier and more amply suspended than their XC counterparts, but usually retain much of their climbing ability. It is up to the rider to build his or her bike to lean more toward a preferred level of aggressiveness. "Slopestyle" type riding is an increasingly popular genre that combines big-air, stunt-ridden freeride with BMX style tricks. Slopestyle courses are usually constructed at already established mountain bike parks and include jumps, large drops, quarter-pipes, and other wooden obstacles. There are always multiple lines through a course and riders compete for judges' points by choosing lines that highlight their particular skills. A "typical" freeride bike is hard to define, but 13-18 kilos (30-40) lbs with 150-250 millimetres (6-10 inches) of suspension front and rear.

Dirt Jumping (DJ) is one of the names given to the practice of riding bikes over shaped mounds of dirt or soil and becoming airborne. The idea is that after riding over the 'take off' the rider will become momentarily airborne, and aim to land on the 'landing'. Dirt jumping can be done on almost anything but the bikes are generally smaller and more manoeuvrable hardtails so that tricks e.g. backflips, are easier to complete. The bikes simpler so that when a crash occurs there are less components that are liable to dysfunction and cause the rider injury.

Trials riding consists of hopping and jumping bikes over obstacles, without touching a foot onto the ground. It can be performed either off-road or in an urban environment. It requires an excellent sense of balance. As with Dirt Jumping and BMX-style riding, emphasis is placed on style, originality and technique. Trials bikes look almost nothing like mountain bikes. They use either 20", 24" or 26" wheels and have very small, low frames, some types without a saddle.

Urban/Street is essentially the same as urban BMX (or Freestyle BMX), in which riders perform tricks by riding on/over man made objects. The bikes are the same as those used for Dirt Jumping, having

24" or 26" wheels. Also, they are very light, many in the range of 25-30 lbs, and having 0-100 millimetres or front suspension. As with Dirt Jumping and Trials, style and execution are emphasized.

Cross-Country (XC) is the most popular form of mountain biking, and the standard for most riders. It generally means riding point-to-point or in a loop including climbs and descents on a variety of terrain. A typical XC bike weighs around 9-13 kilos (20-30 lbs), and has 0-125 millimetres (0-5 inches) of suspension travel front and sometimes rear.

Short Cross or Speed Cross (SC) is the newest form of mountain biking. The idea is to ride short, narrow forest paths with rocks, roots and dints, but not necessarily any ramps on them. The optimal length of the paths are from a few tens to hundreds of meters. The shortness is to provide extreme speed and thrilling to get through the hindrances as fast as possible without crashing. The altitude of the paths does not have to vary much. The ultimate direction of the paths from vertical aspect can be the both ways, either up or down. The transitions between these essential parts are to be taken lightly and stopping at the beginning of every path is to provide maximum amount of thrilling action gained through the speed. This form of mountain biking is similar to what might be experienced in a XC or downhill race. The bikes for this purpose can vary from XC to FR.

Advocacy

Mountain bikers have faced land access issues from the beginnings of the sport. Areas where the first mountain bikers have ridden have faced serious restrictions or elimination of riding.

Many trails were originally fireroads, animal paths, hiking trails, or multi-use paths that were simply used for these new trail users. Single-track mountain biking creates more conflict with hikers, particularly in forested areas. There is also some concern single-track biking leads to erosion. Because of these conflicts, the interpretation of the Wilderness Act was revised in 1984 by the National Park Service to be able to exclude bicycles in certain areas.

Opposition to the sport has led to the development of local, regional, and international mountain bike groups. The different groups that formed generally work to create new trails, maintain existing trails, and help existing trails that may have issues. Groups work with private and public entities from the individual landowner to city parks departments, on up through the state level at the DNR, and into the federal level. Different groups will work individually or together to achieve results. Advocacy organizations work through a variety of means including education, trail work days, and trail patrols. Examples of the education an advocacy group can provide include: Educate local bicycle riders, property managers, and other user groups on the proper development of trails, and on the International Mountain Bicycling Association's rules of the Trail. Examples of trail work days can include: Flagging, cutting, and signing a new trail, or removing downed trees after a storm. A trail patrol is a bike rider who has had some training to help assist other (including non cyclists) trail users.

The International Mountain Bicycling Association (IMBA), is a non-profit advocacy group whose mission is to create, enhance and preserve trail opportunities for mountain bikers worldwide. IMBA serves as an umbrella organization for mountain biking advocacy worldwide, and represents more than 700 affiliated mountain biking groups. In 1988, five California mountain bike clubs linked to form IMBA. The founding clubs were: Concerned Off Road Bicyclists Association, Bicycle Trails Council East Bay, Bicycle Trails Council Marin, Sacramento Rough Riders, and Responsible Organized Mountain Pedalers. IMBA developed "Rules of the Trail" to promote responsible and courteous conduct on shared-use trails.

IMBA Rules of the Trail

1. Ride On Open Trails Only.
2. Leave No Trace.
3. Control Your Bicycle.
4. Yield to Others.
5. Never Scare Animals.
6. Plan Ahead.

Environmental Impact

Studies reported in the IMBA (International Mountain Bike Association) Trail Solutions manual found that a mountain bike's impact is comparable to that of a hiker and substantially less than that of an equestrian. Studies that find mountain biking has little environmental impact have been criticized as underestimating the real impact of mountain biking on the environment. In 2003, Jason Lathrop wrote a critical literature review on the ecological impacts of mountain biking, raising some questions found nowhere else. He quotes the BLM: "An estimated 13.5 million mountain bicyclists visit public lands each year to enjoy the variety of trails. What was once a low use activity that was easy to manage has become more complex". He also notes that few studies take mountain biking into account.

The environmental impacts of mountain biking can be greatly reduced by not riding on muddy or sensitive trails, not skidding, and by staying on the trail.

Naked Hiking

Naked walking, also known as naked hiking or freehiking, is a sub-category of the modern form of social nudity.

Naturism has traditionally been an activity engaged in within a private space, landed club environment or designated beach. Modern naturism is moving towards a public space, as well including a more active component.

Although naturists have always been interested in health and fitness—indeed this was a prerequisite to many early gatherings—and most clubs have volleyball nets and table tennis tables, there has always been a slight reluctance to walk, run or cycle naked. One reason for this has been the secluded nature of the early clubs, private from prying eyes and textiles, and the limited area in which the early pioneers had to work with. Modern naturism in nude-tolerant societies is moving out of the private enclosure and towards the arena of public nudity, where it is deemed OK to be not only naked in public, but also to be active in the nude. The point about being active is that many people appear to find static nudity acceptable, for example in the media (porn magazines or page 3 girls in newspapers), and theatre (non-moving Greek statue-like nudity), but moving nudity, in contrast, seems to generate heated feeling.

Attention and Opinion

Nude hikers go out of their way to be discreet, and are to be seen walking in remote mountain areas, through quiet forests and woods, across distant fields and scrubland, and not in densely populated areas, often not meeting anyone else at all, e.g. in remote areas in Alaska. In the United Kingdom, Steve Gough, known as The Naked Rambler, received much media coverage for walking naked from Land's End to John o' Groats in 2003–2004 and again in 2005–2006. He was arrested and released several times during both his walks while in England, but has been imprisoned in Scotland.

This does not happen to everybody who hikes naked. Indeed, in both 2005 and 2006 the European Alps were crossed naked during a one week hiking (tour), and there was little media coverage. No one was arrested or troubled, and there was no police involvement whatsoever. Most naked hikers report friendly reactions from people they meet, however the risk of being booked on a charge such as public indecency (and this varies between countries and individual police forces) may be present when hiking in the nude, and one should try to keep away from population centres where practical. Some jurisdictions have regulations formally prohibiting this activity, and can impose fines or other punishments. A local bylaw to this effect was adopted, for example, by the 2009 General Meeting (*Landsgemeinde*) of the residents of the Swiss canton Appenzell Innerrhoden. Even so, it's not clear that the ban is legally enforceable under the Swiss Federal Constitution.

Special Considerations

Although extremists might insist that naked hiking should be all-naked, and nothing but naked, as in all things one should remain practical and sensible about such activities. Sensible footwear might mean bare feet on the beach, but wearing mountain boots in the mountains.

Sunstroke or sunburn is a danger by any activity, naked or not, but naked hiking in the high mountains exposes the body to an increased level of sunshine not found at sea level, so sunscreen and a sun hat are essential items. Bugs, such as mosquitoes and midges, can be particularly troublesome, especially in sensitive areas, so anti-bug formulas are often needed by participants in this activity. Walking through a bunch of stinging nettles, poison oak, or a field full of high thistles, can be an interesting experience (even with shorts on). Naturally, extra care must be taken

River Trekking

River trekking or river tracing is a form of hiking or outdoor adventure activity, particularly popular in Hong Kong and Taiwan, and, in some ways, similar to canyoning or canyoneering. River trekking is a combination of trekking and climbing and sometimes swimming along the river. It involves particular techniques like rock climbing, on wet surfaces, understanding the geographical features of river and valleys, knotting, dealing with sudden bad weather and find out possible exits from the river.

Taiwan

This sport is popular throughout Taiwan, where it is generally called river tracing.

Philippines

In the Philippines, River Trekking is just gaining its popularity especially with the introduction of Mapawa Nature Park in Cagayan de Oro in Mindanao on one of their must-do activities. There are 5 challenges in the river which includes swimming, rapelling, jumping and sliding among others. The particular nature park was featured on GMA 7's now defunct reality show Extra Challenge.

South Africa

The South African version of river trekking is called kloofing and has gained a similar following from both an informal recreational and commercial point of view.

Rating of Difficulties

As river trekking has a certain level of risk, experienced river trekkers or hiking groups have developed rating systems about difficulties on different rivers. The ratings usually are various from 1 to 5 stars, even though a few rivers can be more than 5 stars because of their extreme difficulties. Such ratings are largely subjective, depends largely on river trekker's own experience. Therefore, different people or hiking groups would give different number of stars on the same river. According to Hong Kong Adventurer, an English Website about hiking and river trekking in Hong Kong, difficult scale of different rivers as:

Number of Stars	*Description*
1	can be handled by normal healthy persons.
2	not too easy.
3	fairly difficult.
4	difficult, absolutely not for beginners.
5	very difficult, very demanding in term of strength and skill.

Risk and danger

River trekking has certain level of risk. There are occasional accidents in river trekking, including falls from steep cliffs or waterfalls, drownings, exhaustion, or getting lost. Risks that should be prepared for include the following:

First, sudden changes in weather, like rainstorms, can cause rapid rises in water levels and speed in the river. Also, the number of viable paths and climbing areas inside the river valley would be reduced suddenly in a very short period. Besides this, bad or misty weather would also cause low visibility. Low visibility may come in to quickly for trekkers to adapt to. Therefore, a torch (flashlight), preferably a head-mounted one, is a must for river trekking.

Second, steep cliffs inside river valleys require a certain level of rock climbing skills. However, because of the humid environment inside the river valley, some rock surfaces can be very wet and some rocks can be very loose despite appearing solid. To deal with such wet climbing conditions, a pair of professional river-trekking boots are strongly advised.

Safari

A safari is an overland journey, usually a trip by tourists to Africa, traditionally for a big-game hunt; today the term often refers to a trip taken not for the purposes of hunting, but to observe and photograph big game and other wildlife. There is a certain theme or style associated with the word, which includes khaki clothing, belted bush jackets, pith helmets or slouch hats, and animal skins—like leopard's skin.

Touristic Usage

Although the word safari came to popular usage in reference to hunting and touring expeditions in East Africa, it is now also used to mean watching and photographing wildlife in all parts of Africa. The term has also spread to cover other adventurous journeys and expeditions, including whale watching safaris, Arctic safaris, Amazon safaris, eco-safari, etc. The most well known safari areas in Africa include The Masai Mara and Serengeti in East Africa, Kruger National Park in South Africa, Etosha in Namibia, and The Okavango Delta and Chobe National Park in Botswana.

As a Cinema Genre

The safari provided countless hours of cinema entertainment in sound films from *Trader Horn* (1931) onwards. The safari was used in many adventure films such as the Tarzan, Jungle Jim, and Bomba the

Jungle Boy film series up to *The Naked Prey* (1966) where Cornel Wilde, a white hunter, becomes game himself. Also, safaris and the safari genre films were parodied in the Bob Hope comedies *Road to Zanzibar* and *Call Me Bwana.* An instant 15-minute helicopter safari was shown in *Africa Addio* where clients are armed, flown from their hotel and landed in front of an unlucky and baffled elephant. *Out of Africa* has Karen Blixen and Denys Finch Hatton travelling with Denys refusing to abandon home comforts using fine china and crystal and listening to Mozart recordings over the gramophone while on safari.

Fashion and Architecture

Many items worn on safari became fashion statements such as bush hats, pith helmets, bush jackets. These days most tourists will not wear special safari outfits, however it is important to wear neutral colours rather to help blend in with the environment. The 1998 book *Safari Style* by Natasha Burns with photographs by Tim Beddow features interior and exterior design inspired by African safari lodges.

Volunteer Travel

Volunteer travel, volunteer vacations or voluntourism is travel which includes volunteering for a charitable cause. In recent years, "bite-sized" volunteer vacations have grown in popularity. The types of volunteer vacations are diverse, from low-skill work cleaning up local wildlife areas to providing high-skill medical aid in a foreign country. Volunteer vacations participants are diverse but typically share a desire to "do something good" while also experiencing new places and challenges in locales they might not otherwise visit.

There are also other types of travelling that engage people with scientific research and education to promote the understanding and action necessary for a sustainable environment. Participants cover a fee that would include expenses on the different sites worldwide, and engage in projects according to their interest or location.

History

Originally most volunteer vacations were undertaken by people with a direct connection to a particular cause and were considered more as short term, intense volunteer projects rather than vacations. Many of these organizations were long-standing international development assistance organizations which placed short-term volunteers on community development project sites.

1990s

During the 1990s the travel industry developed niche products and firms to provide volunteer vacations to people who had no previous experience with a cause, and to cater to the increasing number of young people taking gap years. These providers expanded the market but also drew criticism for the impact of their methods.

At the same time, the first edition of "Volunteer Vacations" by Bill McMillon was published, featuring under 200 non-profit organizations which facilitated such service opportunities. According to the Travel Industry Association of America, more than 55 million Americans have participated in a volunteer vacation, and about 100 million more are considering taking one.

Controversy

While some experts on volunteering welcome the expansion of volunteer vacations as an opportunity to provide more resources to projects and to encourage a volunteer ethic in people, others have pointed out that the business methods used by tour operators, such as exclusivity deals, and catering to the needs of the volunteer rather than the volunteer project, exploit the communities the projects are intended to help.

Dark Tourism

Dark tourism (also black tourism or grief tourism) is tourism involving travel to sites associated with death and suffering. Thanatourism, derived from the Ancient Greek word *thanatos* for the personification of death, is associated with dark tourism but refers more specifically to violent death; it is used in fewer contexts than the terms dark tourism and grief tourism.

This includes castles and battlefields such as Culloden near Inverness, Scotland, Chernobyl in ex USSR, or Bran Castle, Poienari Castle in Romania; sites of disaster, either natural or man made such as Ground Zero in New York; prisons now open to the public such as Beaumaris Prison in Anglesey, Wales; and purpose built centres such as the London Dungeon. The best-known destination for dark tourism is the Nazi extermination camp at Auschwitz in Poland.

2

Tourism Employment

Introduction

Employment in the travel and tourism industry in Africa

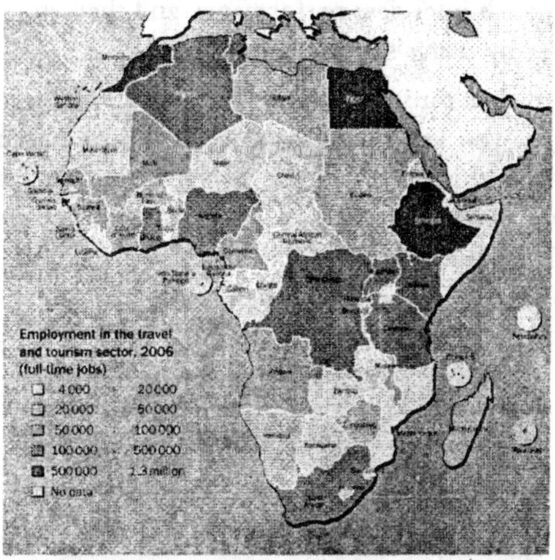

Employment in the travel and tourism industry in Africa. About 6.3 million people work in the travel and tourism industry in Africa, where tourism is highly dependent on natural and cultural environment. However, since travel & tourism touches all sectors of the economy, its real impact is even greater.

Preparing for Employment in Travel and Tourism

Activity

In the last session, work was focused on how recruitment and selection is used in organisations to attract effective people into jobs in the travel and tourism sector. Building on an understanding of how people in the real world make progress through their careers in the sector, you will have learned from completing work on a series of tasks:

- The stages involved in recruiting staff into jobs that you selected.
- That you can produce a flowchart of the process.
- The documents needed, such as a job description and person specification.
- The strengths and weaknesses of your chances of getting into the selected job.

Higher grades were available if you started an action plan for getting the job you want in the industry. In this session, you're going to start looking at the skills you will need to develop in order to promote yourself in a positive fashion during a job selection process. That means analysing someone's interview performance and then showing that you could do better by using self-selling skills.

If you've made it through the initial pre-selection stage to be invited for an interview, you know you stand a chance of getting the job if you perform well at interview. Some people complain that interviews are too highly pressured situations for them to show themselves in the best possible light. But in truth, good interviewing skills are very rarely natural-they have to be learned and then sharpened by experience. Let's see how one individual handled a particular interview.

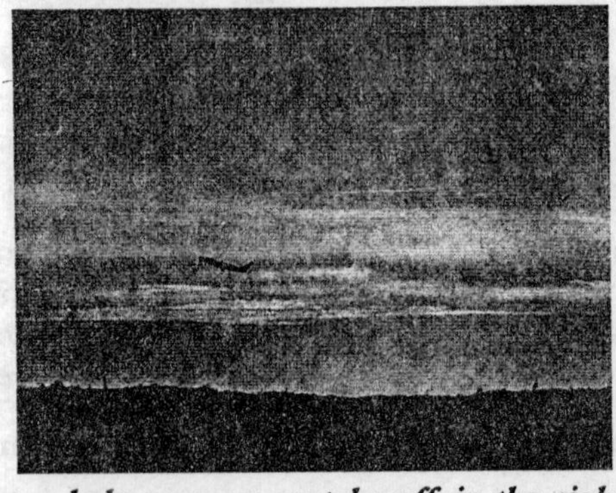

Can you help your career take off in the right way?

A Dream Job and a Nightmare Interview

Tarjani felt nervous. She had been looking at the email she had received from the airline, saying she'd got through to an interview for her dream job: member of cabin crew on the London to Singapore long-haul service. But she hadn't found out much about the airline or the country she would be visiting regularly. Her friend Murali had warned her that she had better be well prepared for the interview, as he knew that the company were pretty hot on getting the right people in as cabin crew. But Murali had gone off with his mates for the evening and Tarjani didn't really know where to start.

Unfortunately, the interview was the next day and she still hadn't done much preparation, expect for rereading the job advert. She hadn't kept a copy of her application, or the documents the company had sent through-the job whatsit and person thingy-as she had been in too much of a rush to get the application sent.

She was still going through her wardrobe, deciding what to wear for the big day tomorrow, when it occurred to her that she would have to catch the bus to the place where the interviews were being held. Murali wouldn't be able to give her a lift-he wouldn't be back at his place until well after she had to leave to get to the interview.

Suddenly, she remembered that she didn't have any credit on her mobile, so couldn't check the bus times or order a taxi if she needed one. That phone box down the road was still out of order, so she'd have to spend all her time this evening going through the timetables online. That took ages, because she always forgot to favourites the right Web site.

She was in a right state and had to stay up really late, as there was no way she could sleep with all the stuff she hadn't done on her mind.

The next day was one that Tarjani would like to forget, but didn't think she would be able to for a while. Later, when she talked to Murali, the sorry tale emerged:

- She'd overslept and missed the bus that would have got her to the office where the interviews were happening.
- Although in the end she was just in time, she was so flustered that she barged into the wrong office, interrupting another interview that was going on. So embarrassing!
- She'd thrown on some clothes which would have been OK if they weren't so creased they looked like she was on her way back from a festival.

- The first question in her interview asked her to say what she knew about the company: doodly squit, as it turned out. She couldn't even get the name of the airline right.
- The other questions weren't much better. She hadn't realised that they would be so in-depth. "What would you do if a passenger was rude to you because for safety reasons you wouldn't allow him to see the flight deck?" She hadn't seen that one coming.
- She thought she was on firmer ground with her answer about her qualifications. But she'd forgotten the name of a couple of modules on her college course. Well, it was nearly a year ago. And surely they'd got it all on her application? That didn't go down too well.
- To cap it all, she caught her heels in the hem of her skirt as she got up at the end of the interview and nearly fell over. She felt such an idiot and the four interviewers all had a good laugh about that. She'd just scowled at them as she left.
- As she left the offices, it started to rain. Disappointed and soaked, she eventually got home after missing another bus.

Murali agreed with Tarjani's analysis: she wouldn't be hearing from them again. "Next time you'll be better prepared," he said. She couldn't help feeling angry with him for deserting her just before her big moment. I mean, if you can't count on your best friend to help you through that, who can you rely on?

Task

Using the experience of Tarjani, who quite clearly blew her big chance at the job of her dreams, write a script for an interview that goes somewhat better. Base the interview on your own choice of job, selected in an earlier session, or one that you have only recently identified.

Track the progress of how you would prepare for the interview, making sure you cover the following important aspects of promoting yourself positively.

About the Organisation

- How is it structured?
- Where are the teams of staff located?

- How is the organisation presented in the media?
- Why do you want to work for them?

Practical Points for the Day

- Have as normal an evening as possible before the interview day.
- Don't stay up late the night before. If you've prepared well, you've got nothing to fear.
- Eat a meal before leaving for the interview.
- How will you get yourself ready for the interview?
- Prepare clean, ironed and appropriate clothes to wear.
- Plan your journey to and from the interview.
- Make sure you get to the interview with plenty of time to compose yourself.

It's your big day-don't miss the bus!

Revise Your Application

- Read through what you said about yourself in your application.
- This means always keeping copies of everything you sent.
- Interviewers only have this information about you, so make sure you know what you said.

Anticipate Questions

- Think about the likely questions you are going to be asked.
- How will you answer them?
- Ask someone beforehand to think up some really tricky questions and work out what you might say in response.

Practice What you will Say

- Practice your interview technique by writing a script of things you might want to say.
- Read these through (in private or with someone you trust!) and listen to how you come across.
- Make sure that you can make your key points fluently, by concentrating on practising them out loud.

Use the Opportunity

- Remember that an interview is not just about an organisation finding out about you.
- It's also an opportunity for you to find out if you'd like to work for an organisation.
- Think up some really good questions, which will show that you've really thought about the job and where it could lead you.
- Practice asking these out loud before the interview itself

Tourism = Employment: Is India Capitalising?

At several trade and global events over the years, the travel and tourism industry has been highlighted as an important economic employment generator. Veterans have voiced their opinion on the same. It is certain that travel and tourism, if properly encouraged can play an important role for economic stimulus and building consumer confidence. Travel fuels business growth, makes entertainment possible and sustains rural destinations.

It also strengthens trade by boosting income for the poorest countries, as well as for global suppliers. Taking all these factors into consideration we need to recognise the value of travel and most importantly its capacity to generate jobs. The tourism sector in India did witness an increase in employment numbers from 44.7 million to 51.1 million during the period 2004-05 to 2006-07 however, we need to cash in more on this potential. Taking India and its cultural diversity into consideration, we have diverse offerings and also the talent of the youth and artisans which need to be tapped. Every state has diverse tourism opportunities but still the focus is on the regular. This gives us an opportunity to augment the much talked about domestic tourism, which certainly needs a short in the arm. Apart from a few players in the industry who have tried to bring a new flavour to domestic tourism, this sector yet needs to be aggressively marketed.

Encouraging domestic travel is good for consumer confidence; international travel has the added value of strengthening trade flows. Action to boost trade promotion, simplify regulation, build infrastructure and rationalise taxes, in turn incites companies to invest, innovate and stimulate demand. This kind of public–private sector collaboration should be strongly commanded within and between all states, as it can help build resilience and buoyancy across economies.

Tourism Employment & Opportunity

CDS' innovative TEMPO model is a collaborative system organized to build the capacity of micro, small, and medium size enterprises to access new markets and B2B linkages, more fully participate in public sector planning, and more convincingly sell the assets they have to offer to the tourism industry.

TEMPO is an 'intrapreneurial' model, and programs that follow it focus on assisting local businesses to provide services demanded by tourists at market rates and international standards. The programs utilize donor funding to build capacity of local businesses and perform asset audits and value chain analyses to determine the goods and services on offer versus market demand from tourists. They then become collaborative non-profit enterprises that link high-performing local businesses into international booking and reservations systems.

This combination of services that provides capacity building for businesses in the tourism industry and facilitates entry into real-time reservations systems is the stand out added value of TEMPO versus other tourism development programs.

Activities within the TEMPO model that create sustainable and sustaining tourism enterprises include:

- Demand Surveys,

- The CDS Inventory and Asset Audit System,
- The CDS Tourism Products Registry,
- Value Chain Analysis,
- Strategy and Action Planning,
- Capacity-building and Partnerships,
- Competitive Grants,
- Product Development,
- Digital Content Development for Marketing and Sales,
- Linkages to Wholesale and Retail Tour Operators and Other Channels.

Tourism Employment

Overall View

On average, 1.1% of persons employed in the EU work in the tourist accommodation sector.

In 2007, more than 9 million persons were employed in the hotels, restaurants and catering (horeca) sector in the EU; this equals 4.2% of all persons employed. The highest number of jobs in this sector was observed in Spain (1.45 million), followed by Germany (1.43 million). However, when taking into account the size of the labour market, the largest shares employed in the horeca sector were found in Malta (8.3%), Spain (7.1%), Greece (6.9%), Austria (6.4%) and Cyprus (6.3%).

About one out of every four persons employed in the horeca sector works in an enterprise providing tourist accommodation (hotels and similar accommodation, campsites, etc.), giving a total of 2.3 million employed in 2007. At the height of the tourist season, i.e. in the third quarter of the year, the number of persons employed climbs by an additional 10 percent to an estimated 2.5 million. In relative terms, this means that 1.1% of all the employed in the European Union work in the tourist accommodation sector.

The Member States showing the highest share of employment in tourist accommodation were Malta (5.3%), Cyprus (3.2%) and Austria (2.3%). Not surprisingly, these are also the top three Member States in terms of tourism intensity, i.e. the number of nights in collective tourist accommodation divided by the number of inhabitants. The sections which follow take a closer look at the pattern of employment in the tourist accommodation sector, compared with the horeca sector and the labour market as a whole.

By Gender

The share of female employment in the tourist accommodation sector is high at 60%.

The share of full-time employment in the tourist accommodation sector is not much different from the share in the EU-27 economy as a whole. About four out of every five persons are employed on a full-time basis. Looking at the hotels and restaurants sector as a whole, this is the case for only 72% of the persons employed (or 69% when excluding the tourist accommodation subsector). Only in the Czech Republic does part-time work tend to be slightly more common in tourist accommodation (8%) than in the horeca sector as a whole (7%).

Looking at the country data, big differences can be seen, ranging from almost no part-time employment in the tourist accommodation sector in Bulgaria or Romania to a rate of 60% in the Netherlands. In general, the figures for this sector reflect the full-time/part-time breakdown in the economy as a whole. Countries with a high share of part-time employment in short-stay accommodation, such as the Netherlands, Denmark (44%), Norway (38%), Germany (32%) or Sweden (30%), also have around 25% or more part-time workers in the whole labour market, compared with the EU average of 18%.

The tourist accommodation sector is a major employer of women. On average, 60% of the EU labour force in this sector consists of female workers, who make up only 45% of the persons employed in all economic activities in the EU. In terms of creating job opportunities for women, the accommodation sector scores even better than the hotels and restaurants sector as a whole – where female employment stands at 56%.

The differences across the European Union are relatively small, although slightly more pronounced than for the economy as a whole, where in nearly every country the share of female employment deviates from the EU average of 45% by no more than a few percentage points. Among the countries for which data are available, more than two out of every three persons employed in the tourist accommodation sector are female in Romania (72%), Norway (71%), Poland (70%), Finland (70%) and Germany (69%). Malta (38%) and Italy (49%) are the only countries where women do not take the majority of the jobs in the tourist accommodation sector. But, together with Greece, these two countries also have the lowest female participation rate in the economy as a whole.

The analysis by gender with the full-time/part-time breakdown. The proportion of women working full-time is much higher in the accommodation sector (75%) than in the rest of the economy (68%) or, more specifically, than in the hotels and restaurants sector as a whole (64%). Among men working in this sector, 90% have a full-time contract, which is slightly less than the overall average for men (92%). Only in the Nordic countries – Denmark (50% versus 36%), Sweden (51% v. 42%) and Finland (27% v. 19%) – are significantly more women working part-time in the tourist accommodation sector than in the economy as a whole. On the other hand, a significantly higher proportion of women are working full-time than in the economy in general in Austria (69% versus 59%), Portugal (96% v. 83%) and Switzerland (59% v. 41%).

The lowest rate of full-time employment in the EU can be observed in the Netherlands, for both male (59%) and female (28%) workers, but this Member State also registers the lowest overall average rate across the EU for both men and women.

The shaded/patterned sections of the pie charts, the share of part-time employment. In both the tourist accommodation sector and in the labour market as a whole, slightly less than 20% of persons employed works on a part-time basis, 19% and 18% respectively. In both cases, women account for around 80% of these part-time jobs. Out of 100 persons employed in the EU, 4 are part-time working men while 14 are part-time working women. For the tourist accommodation sector this is 4 and 15 respectively.

The situation with full-time employment is more pronounced. Women occupy 56% of full-time jobs in the accommodation sector. Indeed, out of 100 persons employed in this sector in the EU, on average 81 work full-time, of which 45 are women and 36 are men. On average in the economy women account for only 37% of full-time employment.

By Age

43% of those employed in the tourist accommodation sector are under 35 years old.

Both the hotels and restaurants sector as a whole and the tourist accommodation sector offer job opportunities to a young work force. Indeed, with 48% of persons employed in hotels and restaurants and 43% in the tourist accommodation sector younger than 35 years, both have a much younger age profile than the rest of the European Union labour market, where only about one in three of those employed is under 35.

This observation at EU level also applies to most of the Member States for which data on the age profile of employment in tourist accommodation are available. In most of these countries, the share of the two youngest age groups taken together lies 10 or more percentage points above their average share in employment in the economy as a whole.

Under-35s make up more than half of the employees in the tourist accommodation sector in Slovakia (58%), the Netherlands (56%), Sweden (56%) and Norway (56%). In all four countries, this share exceeds the average for the whole economy by around 20 percentage points. Cyprus is the only Member State where the age profile of employees in tourist accommodation is less young, with under-35s taking just 28% of the jobs in the tourist accommodation and 33% in the horeca sectors, whereas their share in the economy of Cyprus as a whole stands at 37%.

Only in Greece and Spain, two countries with a big tourism industry, does the age profile in the accommodation sector appear to be not significantly different from the age profile in all economic activities taken together.

At the other end of the age distribution, employment opportunities for persons aged 55 or more tend to be more limited in tourist accommodation (11%) than in the labour market (14%) overall. However, it must be underlined that reliable data are available for only a few countries, partly due to the low probability of including older persons employed in this sector in the sample for the survey used to collect the data.

By Education Level

More than one third of tourism accommodation employees has lower level of education.

The data in the previous sections revealed that tourist accommodation in particular employs younger and female workers. A third socio-demographic group strongly represented in this sector are persons with a lower level of education, i.e. persons who completed lower secondary education at most. That 36% of employees in the tourist accommodation sector did not complete upper secondary education, compared with a general labour market average of 25%.

For all countries where data on employment broken down by educational level are available, the conclusion that the tourist accommodation sector employs relatively more persons with a lower level of education holds true.

The biggest deviations from the average for the economy can be observed in Switzerland, where the share of lower educated persons in tourist accommodation is more than double their share in the whole labour market (36% versus 16%). Other countries where – compared with the entire economy – this sector offers jobs especially to less educated persons are Germany, Sweden, Norway and Denmark. Portugal (71%), Cyprus (24%) and Hungary (14%) are the only countries where there seems to be no noticeable difference (Portugal being the country with the highest share of employees with a low level of education in the European Union).

These findings are in line with the statistics on ICT use in enterprises, which indicate that the tourist accommodation sector does not require a high level of e-skills from most staff. Instead, only 36% of the employees in this sector use computers in their daily work, compared with almost one out of every two employees (49%) when considering all economic activities. Among the branches covered by the Community survey on ICT usage and e-commerce in enterprises, only the construction sector has a lower penetration rate for ICT at the place of work than the hotel and accommodation sector.

By Job Status

A high share of temporary jobs and limited average stay with the same employer.

The accommodation sector does not differ significantly from the rest of the economy in terms of full-time/part-time breakdown.

However, considering the duration of the jobs and the average stay with the same employer, the sector appears to offer less stable jobs than the rest of the labour market.

The proportion of those having a temporary job rather than a permanent job is more than twice as high in the tourist accommodation sector (where 30% of the jobs are temporary) than in the economy as a whole (14%).

In all the countries for which data on the duration of jobs are available, the accommodation sector performs relatively poorly. The largest discrepancies between this sector and the economy as a whole can be observed in Greece (59% permanent jobs v. 89% in the whole economy), Italy, Sweden and Bulgaria.

The more limited availability of permanent jobs can be linked to the seasonal nature of tourism. Indeed, Greece, Italy, Bulgaria and Malta also appear to have the largest variation in number of persons employed between the peak and the trough quarters.

The discrepancy in terms of share of permanent jobs between the tourist accommodation sector and the economy as a whole is particularly small – not more than 3 percentage points – in Hungary, Finland, Denmark and Spain.

The lowest shares of permanent jobs in the tourist accommodation sector can be found in Poland (58%), Greece (59%) and Sweden (61%). In the case of Poland, however, this is not exceptional, as this is also the Member State with the lowest proportion of permanent jobs in the economy as a whole (72%).

Another indicator of stability of employment is the average stay with the same employer. That staff turnover is much higher in the accommodation sector – with an average stay with the same employer of slightly over 6 years (76 months) – than in all economic activities taken together (121 months, in other words more than 10 years).

Comparing the accommodation sector with the rest of the economy at the level of the Member States, the average stay is less than half as long in Greece and Sweden. On the other hand, the discrepancy seems to be smallest in Portugal and Spain.

Seasonal Variation

The tourist accommodation sector has a strong seasonal component.

Tourism activity varies strongly in the course of the year. In every Member State, occupancy in collective accommodation (expressed as number of nights spent by tourists) is at least twice as high in the peak tourism month as in the quietest month.

Logically, the countries with a short tourist season have the highest seasonal variation in nights spent. In Greece and Croatia, the number of nights spent in collective accommodation is respectively 13 and 35 times higher in August than in the low season in January.

The quarterly data, that the number of tourism nights is 2.5 times higher in the third quarter (the peak quarter) of the year than in the first quarter (the trough quarter). With a ratio of "only" 1.2, employment in this sector tends to be far less affected by seasonal influences.

On average, the seasonal variation is only half as pronounced in the hotels and restaurants sector as a whole as in the tourist accommodation subsector. In only four countries (the Czech Republic, Denmark, the Netherlands and Norway) employment in the latter subsector seems to be less volatile over the year than in the horeca sector.

In the economy as a whole, seasonal fluctuation is relatively limited– but this robust aggregate can, of course, hide strong seasonal variations in certain branches of the economy. Within the tourist accommodation sector, the highest seasonal fluctuations in employment are observed in Greece and Croatia.

In both these countries, the level of employment in the peak quarter of the year is nearly double the level in the trough quarter and 30% to 35% higher than the annual average. At the other end of the spectrum, there is no significant seasonal variation in employment in Denmark, the Netherlands and Norway, although the number of nights spent by tourists is two to three times higher in the peak season than in the low season.

Based on data for ten Member States (accounting for 65% of employment in the tourist accommodation sector in the EU), the seasonal variation in employment separately for full-time and part-time jobs. The two types of employment contract tend to have a different seasonal pattern. While both are relatively low in the first quarter, part-time employment seems to be the main contributor to the seasonal needs in the second quarter.

In the third quarter, full-time jobs appear to fill the additional needs on the tourist accommodation labour market (although it is not clear from the data whether these are additional full-time posts or an increase in weekly working hours to bring existing part-time posts up to full-time level).

By Region

Regions with high tourist activity tend to have lower unemployment rates. Tourist activity can have a negative impact on the quality of life of the local population in highly touristic areas. However, the influx of tourists can also catalyse the local economy, including the labour market.

The top regions (at NUTS 2 level) in the European Union in terms of number of nights spent by tourists per capita of the local population and takes a look at the unemployment rates in these regions. In order to take into account structural differences across the EU, the regional unemployment rate is compared with the unemployment rate at national level.

Although tourist activity will, of course, not be the only factor affecting the unemployment figures, That in all but three of the 20 most popular tourist regions listed, the unemployment rate lies below the national average. Two of the three regions where this does not hold true, namely the Canary Islands and Corsica, are island regions relatively remote from the mainland.

The Community statistics on tourism provide no data on occupancy of collective accommodation below the NUTS-2 regional breakdown. However, at a more detailed regional level the number of bedplaces in tourist accommodation in comparison with the local population figures can be used as a proxy for the intensity of tourist activity in the region–assuming the capacity eventually accommodates tourist visitors. That in most of these tourist areas the unemployment rate is lower than the national rate. Two of the most significant exceptions to this finding are the Greek islands Zakynthos (Zante) and Kerkyra (Corfu), both part of the Ionian Islands. As shown above, Greece tends to have a highly seasonal tourism industry.

This seasonal component possibly distorts the comparison as the unemployment figures are an annual average. In Rügen, Germany's number one region in terms of tourism intensity, the unemployment rate is nearly 10 percentage points higher than the German average. In this specific case, the comparison is affected by the fact that Rügen is in Mecklenburg-Vorpommern, the Bundesland with the highest unemployment rate.

Total Employment

Tourism industry in EU occupies about 13 million persons.

The analysis in this paper mainly focused on the tourist accommodation sector, not on the entire tourism industry. In general, the breakdown into economic activities used in official statistics does not single out the tourism sector as a whole.

In particular, apart from a few core tourist activities such as tourist accommodation or the activities of tour operators and travel agencies, most tourist activities can be filed under sectors of the economy of a broader nature. For instance, restaurants can cater for both tourists and locals or transport companies can provide services to tourists but can equally well run freight or commuter operations.

To overcome this measurement problem, the European Union, together with international organisations active in the field of tourism statistics (the UNWTO, UNSD and OECD), has been fostering development of a framework that will allow accurate measurement of the tourism industry and comparison with other branches of the economy.

Taking the concepts, definitions and aggregates of the System of National Accounts as a starting point, this statistical instrument called "Tourism satellite accounts" (TSA) should allow valid comparisons with other industries and also between countries or groups of countries. Part of these TSA cover employment in the tourism industry. Unlike the analysis in this paper, the TSA figures are not limited to the tourist accommodation sector, but also include tourism-related activities of other branches, such as the food and beverage serving industry, passenger transport or culture, sports and recreation.

Currently, national, non-harmonised data are available for a handful of Member States. These estimates for 10 Member States. The contribution made by the tourism industry to total employment ranges from 3.4% in the Czech Republic to nearly 10% in Slovenia. In Spain the tourism industry accounts for almost one out of every eight jobs (12.0%) in the economy.

Based on the aggregate data for these 10 Member States, the share of the tourist industry in total employment appears to be around 6.2%. Employment in the accommodation sector accounts for around 1.1% of the labour market, or approximately 2.3 million jobs. From the TSA estimates, total employment in the tourist industry can be estimated to be five to six times higher, with somewhere between 12 and 14 million employed in the EU. Once again, it must be stressed that these preliminary figures are based on non-harmonised national data from only 10 Member States.

China to Boost Tourism Employment to 100 Million by 2015: Report

China's tourism industry is expected to employ 100 million people by 2015, state media reported Thursday, meaning one in every 14 Chinese will work in the sector then. The government will introduce various policies to help the industry reach the goal, which marks a steep increase from the 60 million currently employed in the industry, the People's Daily said.

Authorities will adopt measures to facilitate job hunting and subsidise training of new staff, according to a statement posted on the National Tourism Administration's website Wednesday.

They also plan to launch a campaign to expand tourism infrastructure in less developed areas, the administration said.

Labour Minister Tian Chengping said earlier this year that the employment;

Employment in the Tourism Industries

- Two possible points of view on Employment.
  - from a perspective of supply (persons employed) and
  - from a perspective of demand (jobs),

- A person might have more than 1 job.
- A job might be occupied by more than 1 person.
- No one to one relationship between jobs and employed Persons.

Tourism Employment vs. Employment in the Tourism Industries

- Labour is a factor of production, and as such, related to a production process, not to a product, and even less so to the consumption of a product by certain category of consumers (a visitor);
- Employment in an establishment, and thus in an industry, can be observed and measured:
- Employment associated with tourism consumption can only be estimated via an explicit or an implicit model.

The basic recommendations: measuring employment in the tourism industries.

The units of measurement

- Number of jobs,
- Number of employed persons,
- hours worked (which should be included???),
- Equivalent full time job.

What do we want to know?

- For each tourism characteristic activity:
  - Number of jobs (monthly? Yearly? Peak and low?) by
- Gender.
- Status in employment.
- Qualification.
  - Number of employed persons,
  - "Quality of the job",
- Permanent.
- Seasonal.
- Direct contract/through an employment agency.
- With/without social insurance.

Sources for measuring employment in the tourism industries;

- From the supply side: household surveys; main difficulties.
  - Significance at the detailed level of activities,
  - Comparability of measurements overtime,
  - Geographical coverage; issue of rural area or small villages,
- From the demand side: surveys of economic activities; main difficulties.
  - Snapshot at a given moment in time,
  - Relationship of this snapshot with supply statistics,
  - Non permanent activities; seasonality,
  - Use of employment agencies.

Tourism Creates Employment Opportunities

Culture

Tourism creates opportunities of employment in the smallest and most remote communities. The Eastern Cape is one of the privileged provinces which has been awarded such an opportunity.

This task of alerting people to the possibilities is led by a non-government organisation called Fair Trade in Tourism South Africa (FTTSA) which is working towards a fairer, participatory and sustainable industry in South Africa.

One of its specific objectives is to contribute towards the Black Economic Empowerment programme and also to assist community-based and other emerging tourism enterprises to access niche markets.

Projects in the Eastern Cape include the Mehloding Community Tourism Trust in the northern Alfred Nzo District Municipality; Pondoland Community Trust and Tshezi Trust in OR Tambo District Municipality; the Kwam Emakana township homestays in Cacadu District Municipality, and the Nqileni Community Trust in Mbashe Local Municipality.

The Mehloding trust is one of the successful projects led by the NGO. The community owns the Mehloding adventure hiking trail and some home-stays for tourists. This was an underprivileged community due to the lack of employment opportunities but FTTSA has sprinkled some nourishing water on the economic and social condition of the community.

Thozamile Xaki, a community tour guide, said: "We learn more about the environment and we gain entrepreneurship skills. This gives us as the community the urge to plough and preserve clean water for our tourists and it encourages us to start our own businesses."

The projects have created job opportunities to impart skills to those who lack them and also recognition for Mehloding but above all the activities draw tourists to Mehloding.

The beautiful nature-preserving community has caught the attention of many tourists throughout the many years of its existence.

Nomthandazo Mnyameni, another community tour guide, said she has witnessed change in her community in terms of recognition and their knowledge on how to approach other NGOs when they need any kind of assistance. Even though this project is alive and advantageous, it does not really cover all the community's needs in terms of giving all of them suitable jobs, nor has it employed all the jobless.

Jabu Manyathi is not employed in this project. She said the project had given jobs to some and imparted skills for those in need. One still has to stand up and do something for oneself in order to survive. Jabu said she was not satisfied with the communication channels between the organisation and the community members that are not employed on the project.

3

Tourism as a Development Strategy

Introduction

Since the Revelstoke Tourism Strategy was developed in 1997, the community has made extensive progress in promoting and marketing tourism opportunities in Revelstoke. The identification of the Chamber of Commerce as the lead tourism marketing and coordinating 'agency', the formation of the Revelstoke Tourism Advisory Committee, the hiring of a full-time Tourism Development Coordinator, and the commitment of the City of Revelstoke and the CSRD to provide long-term funding for tourism marketing activities have all been positive developments. The community has won awards for the quality of the electronic marketing initiatives which have been undertaken, and the quality, variety and distribution of the print-based promotional materials has also improved dramatically over the course of the past six years. The intent of the Revised Tourism Strategy is to identify the opportunities which will further enhance the tourism sector over the next 5 year period.

While the initial Tourism Strategy was prepared several years ago, many of the observations regarding the potential of Revelstoke to capitalize on its tourism assets are still valid today. The 1997 Strategy stated:

> *Revelstoke is very well positioned to take more effective advantage of the community and economic benefits associated with tourism. In addition to a very scenic location on a well travelled highway corridor, Revelstoke is unique among B.C. communities in terms of the range and quality of activity options, the uniqueness and visual appeal of the town itself, and the availability of related support services and infrastructure.*

Since that time, the infrastructure to support tourism has expanded and the quality has improved, increasing the potential for further tourism related development.

Revised Strategy Format

The revised strategy identifies eleven (11) objectives that will set the framework for tourism development over the next five years. These objectives build on the work that has been done since 1997, and have been endorsed by the Tourism Advisory Committee and the tourism industry and wider community through their participation in the Tourism Forum held in October, 2003.

Tourism Strategy Objectives

This has been partially achieved. Following the 1997 strategy, the Chamber of Commerce was identified as the lead agency for tourism development. It is important that the Chamber of Commerce continues to inform the funding agencies and the wider community of the work that it does in coordinating and promoting tourism.

The Tourism Advisory Committee and the Chamber of Commerce will work to secure consistent and stable long-term funding for the position. In addition, to raise the profile of the tourism promotional activities that are underway, the Chamber of Commerce will establish an identity exclusively for tourism promotion.

The Tourism Advisory Committee functions as a communications body between the Chamber of Commerce, the Tourism Development Coordinator, and the community. The committee meets on a monthly basis. The Committee will organize an annual Tourism Forum to facilitate communication with, and to solicit input from, the wider tourism industry and the community. Articles by the Tourism Development Coordinator will also be included in the quarterly publication, Development News.

While several tourism businesses have participated in professional development activities such as the Superhost program since 1997, there is still room for improvement in the level of service offered to visitors. The Chamber of Commerce will initiate a Tourism Service Awards program. In addition, the Tourism Development Coordinator will work on a one-to-one basis to encourage tourism businesses to maintain or develop high levels of customer service.

Many of the recommendations and strategies identified in the 1997 study are still valid, and not all marketing and promotional activities have been undertaken. The role of the Tourism Development Coordinator will be to assist local operators and tourism companies to package and promote winter activities e.g. a weekend visit including cross-country skiing and snowshoeing; a 4-day package including downhill skiing and snowmobiling.

These packages (i.e., getaway and destination) can be marketed via:

- Canadian, American and European tour wholesalers;
- Tour wholesaler fam tours;
- Direct advertising to Canadian, American and European winter sport clubs;
- Ongoing publication of travel articles; and
- The Internet.

Revelstoke needs to do a better job of positioning and marketing itself as a summer destination.

The role of the Tourism Development Coordinator will be to assist local operators and tourism companies to package and promote summer activities e.g. hiking and kayaking; canoeing and bird-watching; trail-riding and visits to local museums; or a combination of any of the above.

Despite improvements to the appearance of the entrances to the community from the TCH, this remains a critical activity for the community to pursue. Further improvements to signage and to areas adjacent to the highway west of town are required to help entice more travellers to visit Revelstoke. In addition, new signs need to be developed to attract more visitors who stop at Woodenhead Park and the fast-food outlets into the community. The Tourism Advisory Committee will continue to provide support to the Enhancement Committee and the City in the highway revitalization efforts. The areas west of town (before the bridge, on either side of the highway) need to be developed and made more attractive.

A specific long-term strategy will be developed by the Tourism Development Coordinator with input from the Tourism Advisory Committee, the City of Revelstoke, and the community. This objective was identified in the 1997 Tourism Strategy, and very little progress has been made over the past six years. The objective and rationale described in 1997 are still relevant today. An Events Committee was formed in 2003, and includes the Tourism Development Coordinator. The Events Committee will ensure that this important objective is pursued during the life of the strategy.

There are excellent opportunities to attract small and medium-sized conferences and conventions to Revelstoke. There are a number of high quality accommodation properties, and the community offers a wide range of recreational and cultural activities which can be packaged to enhance a conference program. The community needs to promote Revelstoke as a Conference Centre and aggressively pursue opportunities that arise.

According to the Tourism Activities and Motivations Study, the Visual Arts, Performing Arts and Heritage Tourism sectors are projected to be the fastest and greatest growth activities in tourism over the next 25 years. Revelstoke has a wealth of cultural and heritage tourism attractions which can be marketed further. A strategy will be developed to increase the promotion of this sector to the appropriate markets.

More initiatives should be undertaken to jointly market with regional and neighbouring communities. For example, preliminary discussions have begun with Nakusp to organize a Kayak the Columbia event, a recreational kayak/canoe race between Revelstoke and Nakusp. Similarly, and the idea of a Peddle the Pass bicycle race between Revelstoke and Golden is being considered. The Revelstoke Golf Club is examining the potential of a TCH golf tour, in partnership with other neighbouring communities on the TCH, Golden, Sicamous and Salmon Arm. These type of events increase the number of visitors to each community and help raise the profile of all communities involved.

The Tourism Development Coordinator will also work with the Tourism Action Society of the Kootenays to seek opportunities for partnering with the Product Club initiative.

It is critical that some objective measures be developed and implemented to try and measure the success of the activities described above. Obviously, the primary measure of success will be increased tourism visitation, resulting in increased expenditures in the community and increased employment in the tourism sector. The Tourism Development Coordinator, with input from the Tourism Advisory

Committee, will work to develop some indicators which can be used to measure success.

Tourism Development Strategy: 2001-2010

The Tourism Development Strategy for the Borough of Coleraine can be downloaded from the link below:

Tourism Development Strategy: The background and objectives of the report can be read here:

Background/Objectives

The Coleraine Borough Council commissioned TTC/Tourism & Leisure Partners to assist it in developing a strategy to develop the area's tourism into the 21st century.

The key aims of Coleraine Borough Council in commissioning this study were:

- to review tourism's role as a vehicle for economic growth;
- to develop a strategy for the future, particularly identifying the constraints which need to be addressed; to set the priorities for the sector, including targets, product development and marketing strategies;
- to identify factors which would improve profitability of the sector and attract investment; and,
- to review the role of government and the commercial sector; to quantify the resources necessary, and support the case for public sector funding where appropriate.

The Terms of Reference for the Tourism Development Strategy clearly defines the key aim of the study as follows:

"To produce a Tourism Development Strategy for the Borough which is soundly market-based-identifies the opportunities and the needs of the Borough-attracts support from the private, public and community sectors; and,-provides a dynamic framework for action over the next ten years".

In meeting the key aim of the study the Council also specified the importance of:

- maximising sustainable economic benefits from tourism; and
- a clear and definite action plan to deliver the economic and social benefits.

The strategic framework is intended to assist a number of different stakeholders involved with tourism. These include policy makers, businesses engaged in tourism, financial institutions and professional advisors to the sector. This report aims to provide information, guidance and direction to all involved in the future development of the industry within the area.

East London Tourism Development Strategy and Action Plan 2004-2006

The completed strategy and action plan for East London aims to support the growth of the east London tourism industry and ensure that the area is firmly on the visitor map. The strategy was launched on 28th September 2004. The plan will make the most of east London's diverse attractions and communities, its rich culture and history and its vibrant new businesses. The plan is an innovative joint venture between the LDA, Tour East London and Visit London and has been completed with input from all key stakeholders. The plan covers the London Boroughs of Barking and Dagenham, Bexley, Greenwich, Hackney, Havering, Lewisham, Newham, Redbridge and Tower Hamlets, plus the Corporation of the City of London.

The plan has a number of priority actions including research to quantify the benefits of tourism to each borough, specific research into the views of visitors to the area, target markets and product clusters in order that the area can be marketed more effectively in the future.

Dcms Sustainable Development Strategy: Sectors Tourism

Tourism is the Fastest Growing Sector in the World Economy

Tourism has a significant input to the economic strand of sustainable development; tourism in rural England alone supports 380,000 jobs and underpins 25,000 small and micro businesses.

Sustainable tourism is about adopting a long-term perspective on quality, competitiveness, impacts on the environment and local distinctiveness.

Tourism's Potential as a Sustainable Development Strategy

This publication contains the proceedings of the 2004 WTO Tourism Policy Forum, organized by the WTO Education Council and held at the George Washington University in Washington, D.C. It includes over thirty speeches and academic papers from Tourism Ministers, development agency representatives, WTO officials, academics, and other tourism experts who presented at the main session of the conference. Also included are summaries of the parallel sessions in which case studies were presented.

The Forum was organized with the aim of exchanging views with bilateral and multilateral donor organizations, as well as representative recipients; discussing sustainable tourism development policies in relation to the MDGs; reporting on WTO general initiatives in relation to sustainable tourism and development and particularly the WTO STEP program to bring sustainable tourism development into the service of poverty elimination; sharing promising practices for sustainable development and considering lessons learned from exemplary tourism projects supported by donors; and formulating recommendations for utilizing tourism as a sustainable development tool for achieving MDG outcomes.

Fifteen years ago, a group of university professors, professionals and public tourism officials gathered together at The George Washington University to attend the first Tourism Policy Forum (TFP), which was held at the initiative of Professor Donald Hawkins. Some of us in attendance were seriously concerned about the exhaustion of the tourism paradigm of the 1970s and 1980s, the so-called mass tourism model, which we later renamed Fordian tourism. The externalities of this tourism business paradigm were already threatening the very sustainability of tourism activity, and called into question tourism's capacity to contribute to development.

The 1990 TPF made it possible—I believe for the first time ever—to carry out a deep, collective reflection at the global level regarding (i) tourism scenarios in the 1990s (taking into account economic, technological, sociocultural and environmental aspects), (ii) Tourism Policy objectives going beyond simply maximizing the number of tourists and/or tourism revenues, and (iii) the instruments of this sectoral policy.

Using today's terminology, it could be said that 1990 TPF was an international exercise in knowledge management in tourism, which had a considerable influence on the development of tourism policy in the 1990s. Indeed, some of the key tourism policy documents of the 1990s (e.g.: Australia's Passport to Growth: A National Tourism Strategy, 1992; Futures: Plan Marco de Competitividad del Turismo Espanol, 1992; or White Paper: Development and Promotion of Tourism in South Africa, 1996), it seems to me, show the impact of many of the concepts discussed at 1990 TPF, whether due to the direct participation of their authors in the TPF, or thanks to the dissemination of such concepts through the academic and governmental publications and forums of the time (e.g.: meetings of the International Academy for the Study of Tourism, academic activities and research work supported by the European Union's DGXXIII, General Assemblies and knowledge management activities of the WTO, etc.).

In September 2003, on the occasion of the awarding of the WTO's Ulysses Prize to Professor Hawkins, and the tribute event held in his honour in Andorra by the WTO. Themis Foundation, the idea arose to revive the TPF, this time as a permanent programme of the WTO under its Department of Education and Knowledge Management (WTO.EKM) and in close collaboration with the WTO Education Council (WTO.EdC). As everybody knows, the WTO.EdC is composed of some fifty educational and research institutions from around the world, which have received the WTO's TedQual Certification through a quality audit. The WTO.EKM, for its part, carries out the Programme of Work of the WTO in the areas of research, education and training, and the application of knowledge to tourism policy and governance in tourism.

Introduction

For one thing, it was decided to make it a biannual event, thus allowing constant interaction with the WTO's deliberative bodies and decision-making organs (the Executive Council and the General Assembly). For another, the new WTO TPF was to place greater emphasis on practical results and encourage the active participation of public bodies, both national and international, as well as of civil society entities with the capacity to support and implement the conclusions reached by the forum.

It remained only to decide the subject areas to be tackled by this new WTO TPF, and this task was made relatively easy in view of the full integration of the WTO in the UN system in December 2003, and its consequent dedication to the Millennium Development Goals, and especially to the issue of development and poverty reduction (e.g., ST-EP Foundation, WTO. Scholars programmes in collaboration with the cooperation agencies of Italy and Mexico, etc.). Thus, the 2004 TPF took shape with a focus on the issue of tourism as an instrument of development.

This issue is both old and new at the same time. Tourism's capacity to generate income and wealth, to consolidate cultural and environmental assets and to transmit knowledge and information has been discussed and analysed from very diverse perspectives-academic, professional, and governmental-over the past several decades. And yet, actual tourism policies have paid much more attention to the purely promotional and microeconomic/entrepreneurial aspects of tourism.

For this reason, the WTO, in organizing the 2004 TPF, had two great hopes from the outset: (i) that it would contribute to clarify the methods and instruments of tourism as a motor of development, and (ii) that it would lead to broad consensus among governments, institutions of the United Nations, development agencies, educational and knowledge management institutions, NGOs, and the private sector regarding best practices, initiatives and recommendations.

We believe that the results have lived up to expectations, although it is clear that we have a huge task ahead of us. The 2004 TPF, which was held at The George Washington University (Washington D.C.) in October 2004, drew some 200 participants representing the upper echelons of decision-making in tourism, plus another 200 highly qualified observers. In my view, the event constituted a milestone in the WTO's Programme of Work, and a high point in the effort to tackle the issue of tourism as an instrument of development. Someone once said that humanity's development has been a race between knowledge and chaos. I believe that the 2004 TPF has given a substantial lead to knowledge-and I trust in its concrete application as well.

Tourism Development Strategies

Recognising its importance, the Lao government has declared tourism to be one of the top three priority areas for socioeconomic development, with a target of 1.2 million tourist arrivals by 2010. Significant investment has already been committed to the upgrading of the tourism infrastructure and plans are currently being prepared for the establishment of a tourism marketing and promotion board and the adoption of a master plan for tourism development. At the present time by far the greatest proportion of foreign tourists visiting Laos are those from neighbouring countries of the Asia Pacific region. In 2004 this group made up 81.59 per cent of the total number, incorporating the two largest visitor groups from Thailand (489,677, 54.72 per cent of the total) and Viet Nam (130,816, 14.62 per cent of the total). Other major national groups visiting the country in 2004 included Americans (37,181, 4.16 per cent of the total), Chinese (33,019, 3.69 per cent of the total), French (27,806, 3.11 per cent of the total), British (27,402, 3.06 per cent of the total), Japanese (20,319, 2.27 per cent of the total), Australians (15,149, 1.69 per cent of the total) and Germans (14,009, 1.57 per cent of the total). At present few figures are available for domestic tourism, but this is also believed to be on the increase.

Market research of recent years has shown consistently that the cultural heritage scores highly amongst the country's visitor attractions – in 2004 56 per cent of the 1,417 international visitors surveyed at Wattay International Airport claimed to have been drawn to Laos mainly by its culture, 39 per cent by its temples and monuments, 54 per cent by its natural beauty and 23 per cent by its ethnic minorities. The consequence for tourism has been that to date around 80-90 per cent of all tourism has focused on relatively short visits to the country's two main cultural centres of Vientiane and Luang Prabang.

In practice, the main focus of cultural tourism to Laos has been the former royal capital of Luang Prabang, which was awarded World Heritage status in 1995 for its 'exceptional example of fusion' between traditional architecture, Lao urban design and the structures built by colonial authorities in the 19th and 20th centuries. In the years which followed that award the town's tourist infrastructure expanded exponentially. Many local people were displaced as hotels, guest houses, restaurants and souvenir shops sprang up everywhere, often in contravention of building regulations, while at the same time numerous historic buildings were renovated with little regard for authenticity.

Realising that urgent action was required to deal with the unplanned and inappropriate development in Luang Prabang, the government established a National Inter Ministerial Coordinating Committee for the Protection and Development of Cultural, Historic and Natural Heritage by Prime Ministerial Decree in 1996. This was followed in 1997 by the

Presidential Decree on the Preservation of Cultural, Historic and Natural Heritage, which outlined regulations and measures for the management, conservation, preservation and use of the national heritage, including the upgrading of movable and immovable assets with historical or cultural or natural value into national heritage.

In Luang Prabang itself an inter-institutional body known as the Provincial Committee for the Protection and Development of Luang Prabang Heritage was also set up in 1996 with support from UNESCO to bring together the key stakeholders in the Luang Prabang World Heritage site, namely the Luang Prabang Provincial Government, the Luang Prabang Provincial Service of Information and Culture, the Luang Prabang Provincial Tourism Office and the Luang Prabang Service of Construction, Transport, Posts and Communication. Since that time all construction work carried out within the protected area-whether for new structures or for renovation of old buildings-has required its agreement. In the same year the Maison du patrimoine (Heritage House) was established under the auspices of the Luang Prabang-Chinon (France)-UNESCO World Heritage Centre Cooperation Project as a technical office within the Luang Prabang Provincial Service of Information and Culture; this now acts as the Committee's executive arm and secretariat, offering advice on all building permit requests and developing regulations and plans for safeguarding and developing the Luang Prabang World Heritage protected area and buffer/support zones. A parallel initiative, UNESCO's Cultural Survival and Revival in the Buddhist Sangha Project, is currently training monks in the traditional arts and crafts skills needed to properly care for, preserve and conserve their temples.

Similar measures are currently being implemented for the heritage sites of Wat Phu Champassak and the Plain of Jars, regulating construction and requiring all new buildings in those areas to conform with regulations in respect of size, style and building materials used.

However, with 105,513 foreigners and an unquantified but undoubtedly substantial number of Lao tourists visiting Luang Prabang (a tiny city of 30,000 inhabitants) in 2004 and visitor numbers at Wat Phu Champassak and the Plain of Jars also showing significant increases in recent years, the Lao authorities recognise the urgent need to diversify the tourism sector in order to take spread the load more evenly. As a result, the LNTA is currently placing the development of ecotourist attractions at the core of its official tourism development strategy.

In 1993 the government identified and designated 20 locations as National Biodiversity Conservation Areas (NBCAs). These areas now fall under the jurisdiction of the Division for Resource and Development of the Ministry of Agriculture and Forestry's Department of Forests. Zoning, management and safeguarding guidelines and regulations for both the environment and people living within the protected areas are in the process of being created.

The LNTA's National Ecotourism Strategy and Action plan 2004-2010, produced with advice from the SNV Netherlands Development Organisation, sets out the framework for the development of ecotourism in Laos by: strengthening the institutional arrangements for planning and managing ecotourism growth; supporting training, capacity building and the promotion of good practice; supporting environmental protection and nature conservation; providing socioeconomic development and cultural heritage protection for host communities; and developing ecotourism research and information.

One particular Lao ecotourism project has been operating with success for several years. The UNESCO Nam Ha Ecotourism Project in Luang Namtha Province is being implemented by the LNTA in cooperation with the Lao Ministry of Agriculture and Forestry, the Luang Namtha Provincial Service of Forestry Resource Conservation and the Luang Namtha Provincial Service of Information and Culture. The UNESCO Office of the Regional Advisor for Culture in Asia and the Pacific is the project's executing agency and provides technical assistance and monitoring. The project itself is funded by grants from the government of New Zealand and the International Finance Corporation (IFC).

The objectives of the project are: to ensure that tourism contributes to the conservation of Laos' natural and cultural heritage; to involve local communities in the development and management of tourism activities; to use tourism as a tool for integrated rural development; to provide training and human capacity building skills to tourism providers and local communities; to integrate public and private sector investment in culturally and environmentally sustainable tourism; and to assist communities to establish cultural and nature tourism activities in and around the Nam Ha National Biodiversity Conservation Area (NBCA). The UNESCO Nam Ha Ecotourism Project has received the UNDP Award for Poverty Alleviation and the British Airways Tourism for Tomorrow Award.

Promotion of community-based ecotourism is also an important focus of the four-year US$14.2 million Mekong Tourism Development Project, currently the LNTA's flagship programme, which was launched in 2003 in partnership with the Asian Development Bank. This project, which also covers Cambodia and Vietnam, seeks to improve tourism-related infrastructure, support pro-poor, community-based sustainable tourism in rural areas and strengthen sub-regional cooperation with a view to facilitating the flow of tourists in and between the three countries.

An important component of the Mekong Tourism Development Project is the Pro-poor Community-based Tourism Development programme, which is similar in format to the Nam Ha project but covers four provinces-Luang Namtha, Luang Prabang, Khammouane and Champassak.

This programme aims to assist local communities with distinctive rural lifestyles or living in areas with pristine ecosystems to manage and determine their limits to tourism growth, to increase control over the selection of tourist types and modalities, and to equitably distribute tourism benefits. It is envisaged that it will develop pilot ecotourism and village-based tourism projects, foster the conservation and improvement of the cultural and environmental heritage of selected areas, monitor social impacts, promote the role of women, and establish mitigation measures to minimise negative impacts due to increased tourism.

Development Strategy to the Challenge of a "Plan de Excelencia"

History, Context and Background of the Cultural Tourism in Cáceres

The city of Cáceres is located in the mid western part of Spain, about 300 km from Madrid, at an altitude of 459 m. above sea level. It is the capital of its province, and belongs to the *Extremadura* region. According to the population services, the town counts 90.930 inhabitants, of which 60% is comprised between 20 and 60 years old, and 20% under 20. To these figures we have to add an extra population of 15.000 nonresidents, most of them students.

The economy of the city has been traditionally based on the primary sector, though in the last half century Cáceres has evolved into a third sector city, with a small presence of textile and food industries. Nowadays it is the main commercial, economic and administrative centre of its province, and the most important tourism destination of the region.

Cáceres was founded as colony by the Romans in 25 B.C., with the name of Norbensis Caesarina (Home-page of the Municipality of Cáceres), close to an important way of communication that will be later known as "The Silver Route". The settlement is destroyed by the Visigoths in the 5th Century, and the city remains abandoned until the arrival of the Muslims from the north of Africa in 8th Century. This population takes advantage of the strategic position and transforms the ruins into a military base to face the Christian kingdoms of the north during the first centuries of the reconquest.

Part of the walls are rebuilt under the rule of Almoarab leader Abu Ya'qub. In 1229 the town is definitively occupied by the troops of Alfonso IX, monarch of the Leon Kingdom. The city is granted a free status, and is ruled by 12 *Regidores* (Rulers) elected by the citizens. This status makes the city prosper, and new churches and palaces rise on the foundations of previous mosques and Muslim palaces. The 15th, 16th and 17th century are the most important centuries from the built heritage point of view, since the fortunes brought back from America by adventurers and emigrants transform the downtown into the monumental city we see nowadays. Palaces and sumptuous residences spread around two focuses:

Santa Maria Square and San Mateo Square. The most impressive palaces are built by the powerful families between the 15th and 16th century. In the following centuries Cáceres evolves into a quiet, forgotten province's capital. The situation essentially remains the same until the 1950's when immigration from the countryside starts to make its economy shift from the first to the third sector. In 1986, following a gradual growth of tourism, Cáceres was included in the list of World Heritage Cities.

Tourism Development Strategy: Plan de Excelencia (Excellence Plan)

The tourism vocation of the city has developed at the end of the 20th century: the number of beds grew of almost 50% in the last decade.

However, it is difficult to calculate the average number of tourists per year, since the indicators we have are partial or can't be compared between them. For example, the "Institute de Estudios Turisticos" of the Ministry of Industry Tourism and Commerce provide figures related to the whole region, and can vary from the first available estimation of 1.562.000 Spanish tourists in year 2001 to the 1.227.000 in year 2002. Other indicators, provided by the Municipality, are the number of visitors of different cultural attractors in Cáceres in the year 2003: 20.791 visitors to the Museo de Historia Cultura "Casa Pedrilla"; 34.677 to the Sala de Exposiciones permanente municipal "Ciudad de Cáceres"; 28.505 to the Museo Vostell; and 68.813 to the Centre de Interpretacion "Torre de Bujaco".

We will have to wait until the launch of the planned Tourism observatory before we have reliable estimations of the number of tourists that arrive to Cáceres every year. The offer of tourism in Cáceres has traditionally been related to Hunting, and thus concentrated in the autumn season. The progressive increase of city-breaks and of cultural tourism in general opened an interesting perspective of development. This lead the local authorities to try to develop a tourism of quality (in terms of purchasing power of the visitor), and improve the ratio of overnight stays rather than just the number of visitors.

However, in the late 1990's the lack of a defined strategy was evident: the offer was a monothematic, un-structured, and initiatives were taken mostly by private actors. The chance to put some order and to exploit the sector according to sustainable and also rational criteria came with the *Plan de Excelencia* started in 2000. In Spain this kind of plan comes out of a series of national framework plans for tourism competitivity: FUTURES (1992-1995) and PICTE (2000-2006), launched in the early nineties by the Ministry of Industry, Tourism and Commerce. The first framework plan was created to reduce and correct the negative impacts (mainly ecological and in terms of town planning) of thirty years of wild tourism development, and the second one was created after assessing the success of its predecessor, with the same goals. The *Planes de Excelencia* are the operative tools developed to accomplish these goals: they are addressed to "mature" destinations: mostly traditional "sun & beach" destinations, but also to cities of great historic value, where the main issue is to rise or control the tourism capacity. The investments, financed equally by a Collective Agreement of local, regional and national administrations, are distributed over three or four years. The objectives of the *Planes de Excelencia* are usually focused on the diversification of the tourism seasons and the development of a care for details in the offer: improvement of marketing strategies to attract tourists in low-season, embellishment of historical centres, renovations and reforms of infrastructures, and adaptation of hotels and restaurants to quality standards.

In the specific case of Cáceres, the *Plan de Excelencia* was launched by a collective agreement between the Ministry of Economy, the Region of Extremadura, the Municipality of Cáceres and the representatives of the private sector of the city. Its planned length was of three years, from 2000 to 2003, and the total budget amounted to 2,7 Millions of Euros. The generic goal of the *Plan* was to transform the city in a tourism benchmark at national and international level, but developing a tourism of quality, different from the mass-tourism models of the sun & beach offer.

Concrete Actions Within the Cultural Tourism Strategy

A series of objectives were defined, in order to achieve the generic goal source: Ministry of Industry, Tourism and Commerce):

- Urbanistic rehabilitation of the downtown.
- Improvement of the management.
- Recovery of the Historical built Heritage.
- Construction and development of infrastructures.
- Promotion.
- Equipment.
- Definition and diversification of the tourist offer.

The objectives generated a series of actions, presented in a publication of the Municipality of Cáceres in 2003 and 2004. Regarding the urbanistic rehabilitation, it involved restoration of facades, from specific and isolated cases to whole districts in close cooperation with the urbanism councillor. This objective also lead to the creation of a limited traffic area in the downtown, equipped with sophisticated access monitoring systems. Another action issued from this objective was the creation of a pneumatic system for the automatic collection of the rubbish in the downtown area. Concerning the improvement of management, it meant the provision of the funds needed to have a full-time staff devoted to the accomplishment of the Plan, and development subventions to the tourism-related enterprises of the city.

The Historical built Heritage recovery activities consist in the lighting of historical buildings, as well as the rehabilitation of representative places for its public use (for example, the transformation of Torre de Bujaco into a visitors centre with a viewpoint, and the enhancement, in different phases, of several stretches of the city walls). Regarding the construction and development of infrastructures, the actions undertaken have been the improvement of the streets of the downtown, and the construction of a bus parking area. The promotion actions, varied from the organisation of fairs and seminars, to the advertising of the city in newspapers and specialised magazines, as well as the publication of a *Plan de Excelencia* bulletin.

Concerning the equipment objective, it entailed the installation of street furniture, as well as urban and tourism signpost, and information panels on the facades of representative built heritage elements. Finally, the definition and diversification of the tourist offer entangled the preparation of strategic plans and the development of cultural tourism offer: the most relevant actions in this context were the preparation of tourism routes in cooperation with the Church administration, the inauguration of two visitor centres (in the Parking Galarza and in Torre de Bujaco), and the creation and/or promotion of events in low season, in order to increase the number of visitors (i.e., the medieval market, the "Semana Santa", theatre festival).

The *Plan de Excelencia* expired in 2003 but some actions have been achieved in the following years. In October of 2006 according to a press note released by the Municipality to *El periodico de Extremadura*, the *plan* isn't still fully accomplished (98%). Beside the concrete actions awaiting to be completed (mainly the enhancement of the Wall and a second tower for visit purposes), the strategic plans and the objectives fixed by the plan are still defining the policies of the municipality. For example, there is the idea, presented in the second issue of the Plan de Excelencia's publication, of launching a "Tourism Observatory", as the one in Avila, a platform devoted to the monitoring of Tourism flows, to visitor studies and to macroeconomic studies that will show the incidence of tourism in other productive sectors of the city. This will also analyse the offer of the sector and the national and foreign demand, in terms both quantitative and qualitative, providing info to establish coherent future strategies.

The Tourism Observatory, which hasn't been launched yet, is the result of a mature and professional approach to audiences management issue, and arrives in due time, since one of the gaps in the tourism policy of Cáceres detected by PICTURE surveys was precisely the absence of monitoring tools. In this sense, the Tourism Observatory, if organised as the one of Avila or the one of Cordoba, will probably be very close to the Cultural Offer Quality Monitoring Tool developed by the UAM team. The techniques and methodologies are different, but both tools are conceived as part of the whole process of management of cultural resources. They do not just complement the management process and strategies, they are integrated into it. The main difference between a Tourism Observatory and our (UAM) tool is that our tool provides more qualitative analysis of the city's cultural offer quality, while other Observatories aim more to statistical results. This is why the testing of our tool offers complementary information suitable to improve the cultural offer of the cities, and Cáceres in this particular case. The detailed survey and conclusions of our tool can be found in the final report.

However we would like to mention here the most remarkable outcomes in relation to the strategies of the *Plan de Excelencia.* Regarding the urbanistic rehabilitation of the downtown, and the recovery of the Historical built Heritage, the results proceed adequately, gathering the visitor's full appreciation of the value of the downtown's built heritage; however, there seems to be a problem with the promotion, because our tool has detected a mismatch in the perception of Cáceres between real and potential visitors. The first group is already aware of the rich tangible and intangible heritage of Cáceres, and comes to the city for that reason, while the second group has an idea of the city as a place with little or no cultural offer at all. This means that the efforts in promotion must continue and strengthen the image of Cáceres that the municipality wants to export.

Concluding Comments and Transferable Key Lessons

The experience of Cáceres is for many reasons a reference model in the management of Heritage cities. Here are the main keys that have contributed to its success.

- Holistic approach: understanding that the dynamics of Tourism are not separate from the dynamics of other domains (social, economical, environmental...), they all are interconnected parts of a system where any action may alter the inner balance;
- Existence of a strategic plan where the tourism policies are integrated into the general policies of the administration;
- Tight cooperation and coordination between different departments (Culture, Urbanism, Environment);
- Integration of assessment and evaluation tools in all the stages of the strategic plan;
- Investment of external funds (*Plan de Excelencia*) not only in short-term and isolated actions (i.e., built heritage conservation and embellishment) but also defining and launching development strategies that will survive after the aid is over.

National Sustainable Development Strategies

The United Nations Conference on Environment and Development (UNCED) held in Rio de Janeiro in 1992, recognised the pressing environment and development problems of the world and, through adoption of Agenda 21, produced a global programme of action for sustainable development into the 21st century.

Agenda 21 states that countries should adopt national strategies for sustainable development, which "should build upon and harmonize the various sectoral economic, social and environmental policies and plans that are operating in the country".

The 1997 Special Session of the UN General Assembly set a target date of 2002, for "the formulation and elaboration of national strategies for sustainable development". It confirmed the approach and purpose of national sustainable development strategies as "important mechanisms for enhancing and linking national capacity so as to bring together priorities in social, economic and environmental policies". It also reaffirmed that "all sectors of the society should be involved in their development and implementation".

The Millennium Declaration was signed in September 2000. The associated Millennium Development Goals includes onerelating to environmental sustainability, to "integrate the principles of sustainable development into country policies and programmes and reverse the loss of environmental resources". Activities towards developing and implementing national sustainable development strategies will, thus, contribute to the achievement of this goal.

Finally, the World Summit for Sustainable Development (WSSD), held in August 2002, urged in its Plan of Implementation that "States should take immediate steps to make progress in the formulation and elaboration of national strategies for sustainable development and begin their implementation by 2005". Since UNCED, governments have made extensive efforts to integrate environmental, economic and social objectives into decision-making by either elaborating new policies and strategies for sustainable development, or by adapting existing policies and plans. To assist in this process, an International Forum on National Sustainable Development Strategies was held in Ghana in November 2001. The Forum adopted a guidance document containing a number of recommendations on approaches for integrating the principles of sustainable development into policies and programmes of both developed and developing countries. The Forum agreed that a national sustainable development strategy is a tool for informed decision-making that provides a framework for systematic thought across sectors and territory. It also helps to institutionalize processes for consultation, negotiation, mediation and consensus building on priority societal issues where interests differ.

Development of a strategy empowers countries to address interrelated social and economic problems by helping them to build capacities, develop procedures and legislative frameworks, allocate limited resources rationally and present timetables for actions. It was strongly reiterated, that countries would benefit from formulating strategies both directly (as a result of making development more sustainable) and indirectly (from the process itself).

United Nations Department of Economic and Social Affairs Division for Sustainable Development

"The next 50 years could see a fourfold increase in the size of the global economy and significant reductions in poverty but only if governments act now to avert a growing risk of severe damage to the environment and profound social unrest. Without better policies and institutions, social and environmental strains may derail development progress, leading to higher poverty levels and a decline in the quality of life for everybody."

Tourism Development Strategy (2006 – 2010)

Vision

By 2010 Linden has become a tourist destination topping 10,000 visitors per year. More than 300 beds are offered by hotels and bed & breakfast providers. Linden and Region 10 offer attractive events and particularly Linden serves as a hub for tourists to other destinations in the interior.

Tourism has developed into the third biggest industry in the Region after mining and forest production. The enterprises working in the tourism sector are well-trained and developed into hospitable entities serving satisfied clients. The Region 10 Tourism Development Association (RTTDA) offers professional services, avails of a well-functioning office and counts more than 100 members. The Region 10 tourism industry is well integrated into national efforts to attract even more tourists to Guyana.

Summary

The Tourism Development Strategy centres around three axes:

1. Development of Region 10 into a genuine tourist destination (identification of destinations, creation of events),
2. Improvement of services through local enterprises (training, information),
3. Institutional strengthening of the Region 10 Tourism Development Association (organisation, coordination).

The three axes are accompanied by an aggressive marketing of Region 10 as a tourist destination (external marketing) and of the RTTDA as the major platform for local enterprises earning their livelihood from tourism (internal marketing of the association). Logic of this strategy: the creation and identification of tourist events and destinations trigger a higher influx of visitors who will be professionally hosted and catered for by the local tourism industry to make them come back again in future. RTTDA is the institutional backbone ensuring organization, coordination, promotion and services to its members.

Target Market

Given the comparatively low attraction of Region 10 destinations and events to foreign tourists at present, focus will be laid on national and Caribbean visitors. Some potential for European and American tourists is identified in bird watching possibilities, Linden as a transition to more attractive destination in Region 9, and in linking Linden to other cities during flight hopper tours (such as Bartica – Linden–Georgetown on a day tour). Greatest market potential lies in the Diaspora Lindeners having keen interest in revisiting their birth town while some are expected to resettle and invest in Linden after retirement. The influence of this target market became clearly visible with the announcement of 300 Diaspora Lindeners visiting the Linden Town Week 2006 celebrations with the dedicated assistance of the Linden Fund/USA.

Tourist attractions (events + nature)

New tourist attractions will be created if the tourism industry is to grow. The starting point is the successful operation of singular events (such as the Kashif & Shanghai Football Tournament and the Linden Town Week). More events preferably stretched over several days will be identified to improve the influx of tourists. The Rockstone Fish Festival planned for August 2006 is the first step into this direction. Other ideas emitted so far are: Jazz Festival, Cycling race Georgetown – Linden with finish in Linden, extended carnival festivities (LICA = Linden Carnival), and regattas. It is evident that developed event ideas need to be marked by a great uniqueness.

Apart from the event attractions, other destinations and related services will be offered. Some have already been identified and will be further explored: bird watching and *Victoria Regia* on Gluck Island *(ecotourism niche for short one-day* visits, and possibilities of setting up larger tourist facilities such as a guest-house *or professional boat services*), museum, fishing and hunting tours around Rockstone, visits to reclamation activities in the mined-out areas with scientific guidance, regular weekend visits of the bauxite mine, etc.

Events and nature will be accompanied by a comprehensive signage system leading tourists to and guiding them in Linden. A huge signboard at the Soesdyke-Linden junction will indicate the way to Linden. Arriving in Linden a tourist signboard with map and important destinations of relevance for tourists in Linden will be established (another one for visitors coming from the South). In collaboration with the Town Council traffic signs will be placed in Linden and on the routes to Kwakwani, Ituni, Rockstone, Lethem and other destinations in Region 10. In Linden itself, buildings of relevance for tourists (such as the waterwheel, museum, etc.) will be indicated by special boards explaining the history in brief. Differently coloured sign posts will guide the tourists to these destinations.

Tourist services

Existing and new tourist attractions and events can only be marketed successfully if the clients' needs are satisfied. Hence, we favour competition and we welcome any investor in the tourism sector from abroad or from other areas in Guyana. Tourist services will be provided through the "Linden Office for Visitors" (LOV) as the most important entry point for client information and through individual service providers being members of the association.

a. The "Linden Office for Visitors" (LOV) is the executive branch of the association where contacts with clients are made. Hard copies of all promotion material are made available to incoming visitors. Email queries are answered and the association's activities are coordinated by an executive secretary. More personnel might be hired if the financial situation allows for that. The office is located in the museum; it is equipped with PC, printer, photocopier, display shelves. LOV serves as a facilitating and mediating agency linking customers to the Region 10 tourism service providers. It will concentrate on association members in the first place, hence creating a need for service providers to join.

b. Individual service providers: existing hotel accommodations in Linden, Ituni and Kwakwani will be inspected and rated according to existing standards. A four-tier categorization will be applied as this is currently done with the B&B providers.

The rating (stars for hotels and restaurants, diamonds for B&B providers) will be officially acknowledged through specifically designed signs (size: 1x1 ft) which can be fixed on the walls of the establishments. These signs carry high promotional value and may also attract other service providers to join the association.

Assessments and inspections will be done on a yearly routine basis providing room for all members to improve their standards and services. Tourists can easily locate recommended establishments. While rating criteria exist for hotels and B&B providers, a similar rating system for restaurants will be elaborated and applied.

Service providers will be trained in areas common for all such as client reception, customer care, monitoring of customer satisfaction, pricing of services, importance of insurance systems, safety regulations and cleanliness issues. These training offers will be binding for the association's members in order to maintain and eventually improve their grades. Furthermore, there will be sector-specific training arrangements on a needs basis such as cooking of speciality dishes, accommodation standards and design, kitchen hygiene, etc. The needs of the different tourism sectors will be analysed during meetings with the committees to be established under the umbrella of the RTTDA.

Institutional Strengthening

RTTDA is a certified and recognized institution under the Friendly Societies Act. However, in the past the internal functioning was based entirely on the voluntary work of dedicated members who were never asked to pay any fees.

The newly developed fees structure distinguishes between a general admission fee of $2,000 for all and sector-specific yearly fees which have been developed in accordance with income prospects. In future, only those individuals and enterprises are considered members who have paid their dues and will be eligible to vote and to decide during the internal meetings.

At the end of each fiscal year, RTTDA will conduct "Certificate Award Functions" during which members who provided excellent services and other personalities and institutions which contributed significantly to the tourism development in Region 10 will be awarded with certificates and plaques. These functions are also meant to enhance visibility of the association and the sector. Increase in (paid) membership will be achieved through the provision of services which consist primarily of marketing, training and lobbying. The services will be organized according to our members' needs and in cooperation with the regional and national bodies in which RTTDA is organized. Sector-wise committees (for example: B&B providers, restaurant owners, etc.) will be established whenever desired by the members in order to make sure that specific questions can be professionally dealt with by the concerned business people. Chiefs of committees will be elected who report to the RTTDA General Assembly during its official meetings.

RTTDA will become a paying member of the Linden Chamber of Commerce, Industry and Development to ensure the best representation of its interest on the regional level. Interests on the national level will be defended through membership in THAG and close cooperation with the Ministry of Tourism, Industry and Commerce (MINTIC) and particularly the Guyana Tourism Authority (GTA). We will develop special relationships to identified sponsors and donor agencies because it is acknowledged that the membership fees will hardly suffice to pay for overhead costs and association staff. A particular relationship exists with the Linden Fund representing the largest tourism target group at the time being, GTIS and LEAP which provided valuable assistance in the past. Inputs in institutional strengthening are required in the following areas: preparing requests for external assistance, internal functioning of the association and membership care, linkage to potential visitors overseas, tourist product development, assistance in design of marketing devices.

Marketing

The printing of the "Discover Linden" glossy magazine will serve as a starter in Region 10 tourism marketing efforts. The Linden Town Week is the catalyst to get more diversified marketing efforts on stream.

The RTTDA Web Page is the central long-term marketing tool informing customers about tourist destinations and accommodation facilities. The office in the museum building is centrally located; it will be staffed with at least one competent person who answers questions on the telephone, replies to email inquiries, links visitors to accommodation facilities, distributes tourist brochures and sells tourism articles and literature.

Brochures on the following issues are circulated per hard copy: B&B facilities, hotel accommodation, restaurant and catering services, travel-, boat and fishing tours, Linden tourist map, other tourist services such as bars, taxi and other transport services, offer of handicraft products, and a general flyer summarizing key information of interest to tourists.

To attract visitors from Georgetown, regular ads are published in national newspapers, particularly in conjunction with the different events to be organized. On very special occasions, TV ads will be made on the national TV station. All published information material will also be accessible to interested persons at the "Tourism & Hospitality Association of Guyana" (THAG) of which RTTDA becomes a member. National seminars and workshops on tourism will be used as a platform to attract visitors and investors in the tourism industry to Region 10.

Tourism Development Strategy

In 1993, a detailed community survey of Revelstoke was conducted and a Vision Statement prepared. The Vision Statement, which provided direction and a statement of community values, is being used to guide Revelstoke's growth and development. In 1995, this vision statement served as the basis for the development of a Community Economic Development Strategy.

As recommended in this Strategy, a Tourism Development Strategy was prepared during 1996-97, and has served to guide the development of tourism over the past 6 years. In 2002, the members of the Revelstoke Tourism Advisory Committee recommended that the strategy should be revised to better reflect changing conditions in the local tourism industry. It was decided that revisions to the Tourism Development Strategy could be carried out 'in house' by the local Community Economic Development Department, and that the Revelstoke Tourism Advisory Committee would act as the Steering Committee for the development of the revised Tourism Development Strategy.

During 2000, as part of the development of a new Revelstoke Community Development Strategic Action Plan, an extensive community survey was undertaken to determine the priorities and concerns of Revelstoke residents. Over 68% of those surveyed identified tourism and hospitality as the highest priority sector of the economy for the community to develop. This was by far the most important sector for development identified by the community.

The revision to the Revelstoke Tourism Development Strategy was undertaken during 2002-03. The Revelstoke Tourism Advisory Committee acted as the steering committee for the project. During this time, Revelstoke had undertaken an initiative to develop a strategy to determine how best to market the community to outside investors. As part of this initiative, external consultants reviewed the state of the local economy and met with several business and civic leaders to determine community economic priorities and the most effective ways of promoting the community to international investors. The consultants recommended a focus on tourism development as the best way of attracting investors and of improving the local economy. It was decided to utilize the same consulting team to interview local tourism operators to obtain their input regarding the state of the Revelstoke tourism industry. This information (included in Appendix I) was used to assist in determining tourism priorities for the next five year period.

Objectives

The overall goal of this study is to prepare a tourism strategy that provides the community of Revelstoke with clear direction relative to the development of the community's tourism industry for the period 2003 to 2008. The specific objectives of this project include preparing a tourism development strategy which supports the following:

- Achievement of a sustainable economy in keeping with the community's Vision Statement;
- Promotion of tourism growth and development to ensure economic stability;
- Enhancement of the growing tourism and outdoor recreation sector; and,
- Diversification of the local economy and creation of job opportunities.

Study Process

The steering committee felt that the existing (1997) strategy provided a solid base. The intent of the revised strategy project was to update the existing strategy i.e. identify what has been accomplished, what still needs to be done, and establish priorities for the next 5 years.

The following activities were carried out:

1. Update baseline data (including a review of strengths and weaknesses),
2. Identify gaps/review tourism strategies from other communities,
3. Consultation with the tourism industry,
4. Compile information/identify priorities,

5. Prepare draft strategy/circulate for comment,
6. Prepare final strategy.

The Development Strategy For Ecotourism in Wolong

Wolong Natural Reserve (WNR), known as a shining pearl in the southwest China, is the largest national-level natural reserve specializing in protecting giant pandas and natural ecological system. With respect to protection and development, active efforts were made in the 1990s but failed. It was widely acknowledged that tourism should be given the top priority for the development and protection of WNR. Therefore it is of great necessity to re-consider the tourism development strategy so as to make it more efficient and more compliant with market rules.

Advantages in Resources & Marketing Orientation

Famed as the "Hometown of the Giant Panda" and with a total area of 2000 km^2, WNR is located in the Aba Tibetan and Qiang Nationalities Autonomous Prefecture, and is just 120 km from Chengdu.

Advantages in Resources

Nature has richly endowed in tourism resources, including natural resources such as wild animals and plants, forests, mountains, lakes and pleasant weather conditions. WNR boasts abundant cultural resources from the religious traditions of Taoism & Buddhism, customs of Tibetan and Qiang nationality and local house styles. WNR accommodates over 100 Pandas in the wild, 10% of the total wild population, and 64 Pandas in its breeding centre.

Moreover, WNR has a complicated land ecology system with 7 vertical ecology system belts resulting in tremondous biological diversity. There are 1989 higher plants varieties and 450 kinds of vertibra, of which 57 under key state protection. WNR has a world-class panda protection research centre, the only-one panda museum, and the largest trial park for training animals back to the wild.

Wild animals and rare birds can be easily observed in various places within WNR. Flocks of blue sheep and Takins in Yinlonggu, thousands of swifts in Guanyingya and rare birds including the Tibetan Eared Pheasant, blood pheasants and Chinese Monals in Pengsheng Gaur Valley can all be seen in WNR. It has the largest primitive Davidia forest in China and two highland grasslands, Huangcaoping and Niupingzhi.

Market Orientation

The development of tourism in WNR should be aimed at an international, high-quality ecology tours oriented to domestic and foreign markets, featuring by giant pandas and the beautiful scenery of their natural habitats.

Products Patterns & Strategic Targets

Stress will be laid on the following four tour product patterns. 1. Forest holiday-making. With comfortable weather conditions, fresh air, and sufficient sunshine and, tour products such as forest recuperation, travels, conference tours, and health-making tours can be developed. Villas and hotels for holiday-seekers can be constructed accordingly. 2. Unique eco-tour.

Its waters, large areas of virgin forests, wild animals, numerous snowcapped mountains and waterfalls are extremely suitable for ecotours. 3. Panda image products. The image resources of pandas should be turned into actual resources by constructing a panda ecology valley where people can go directly to see pandas in the wild. This would allow WNR to produce tour souvenirs for tourists and videos of the giant pandas for tourists. 4. Ethnic culture products.

Generally, the development of tourism in WNR will concentrate on creating a world-class ecology tour attraction and China's national park by 2005; bidding for world heritage, serving as a model for sustainable development among national reserves and world natural heritages, and enjoying an important position among tour sites in Sichuan as well as in China.

Principles & Measures for Development

The following principles should be observed in the tourism development of WNR: 1. Protection of unique and irreplacable resources; 2. Market-oriented, sustainable development; Harmonious co-existence between humans and nature. Based on the ideas and development principles above, and practical experiences in developing eco-tour sites at home and abroad, the development of WNR must follow the principle of "Tour inside, lodge outside". A "For-ecology Moving-out" Project will be implemented, that will move all residents in Wolong Township to Gengda Township, merging Gengda and Wolong Township to create a new township with strong ethnic flavours so as to make it a reception centre for tourists. An ecology protection system that is much stricter than other reserve areas should be established and implemented in order to have ecology-friendly protection regulations.

Operation & Management Measures

The reserve should be strictly administered in accordance with the management rules of national park and natural heritage regulations. A new method of "Separation of Rights" will be introduced, namely separating the rights of ownership, management and operation. The ideas above have been included in the just-completed WNR General Plan of Ecotourism. By now the preparatory works for merchant-invitations and project-bidding have already been started. We firmly believe that in near future China's national Yellow Stone Park or a World-Class Eco-tour Attraction will emerge in southwest China.

2008 Economic Development Strategies-Agritourism Industry

Background

With New Jersey farmers facing rising costs and stagnant commodity prices, agritourism offers an important opportunity to generate additional farm income and keep farms economically viable. Agritourism presents opportunities for New Jersey growers seeking to add value to their crops and/or capture more of the market price of their products by directly accessing consumers. Many residents consider agriculture a novelty and something to be explored and enjoyed. They desire to share the agricultural experience while increasing farm income at the same time. New Jersey's agritourism industry provides for a great introduction to the agriculture of the Garden State. The educational and economic contributions of agritourism to the state's agricultural economy are many.

A National Agricultural Statistics Survey (NASS) study conducted this year determined that the economic impact of agritourism upon New Jersey's economy was $91 million in 2006. This quantitative information confirms the qualitative recommendations of a 2005 Rutgers University study that examined farmers' and farm leaders' perceptions of the opportunities and challenges associated with agritourism.

There are other states that have comprehensive agritourism programs and these will be studied as work moves forward to more closely cooperate with the various agencies that share a common interest in promoting tourism in New Jersey. A new interactive, GIS-based, agritourism industry website, "visitnjfarms.org", allows for easy consumer mapping based on products, services and location, within a specified town or county, or within a specified driving radius of a user-defined beginning point. It also allows farmers password access to the site to provide updates to their own listing.

To assist in the development of the agritourism industry, the Department will be focusing on three major objectives: developing strategic partnerships, consumer promotion and industry education.

Develop Strategic Partners

Strategy – Continue to support the New Jersey Agritourism Industry Advisory Council in their charge to develop, support, and market this sector of the agricultural community.

Strategy – Continue working with the N.J. Office of Travel & Tourism (T&T) to develop and market agritourism. Develop three agritourism based travel tours for each of the state's six tourism regions. Encourage T&T to integrate an agritourism press familiarization tour into their work.

These tours acquaint the regional travel and tourism media with New Jersey agritourism. Encourage T&T to incorporate agritourism research into their established travel industry research program. Market agritourism to the travel and tourism trade through participation in the annual Governor's Conference on Tourism, cooperative advertising, and other industry opportunities.

Strategy –Publicize the National Agricultural Statistics Survey (NASS) study that assessed the economic impact of agritourism upon New Jersey's economy.

Consumer Promotion

Strategy – Produce and distribute an inexpensive agritourism brochure with industry websites and contact information. This brochure would promote seasonal events, special attractions, and direct farm marketing opportunities. Create and disseminate regular press releases promoting the agritourism industry and related websites. Work to expand the promotion of the agricultural fairs in New Jersey.

Strategy – Continue to develop and promote the "visitnjfarms.org " website.

Industry Education

Strategy-Coordinate an Agritourism symposium to address common opportunities and challenges and to provide some basic tourism and hospitality industry training. Work with Rutgers Cooperative Extension to develop and implement this training.

Strategy-Conduct tourism industry outreach activities for agritourism operators. Promote listings in the N.J. Office of Travel & Tourism's "Calendar of Events". Promote participation in "The 2007 New Jersey Governor's Conference on Tourism". Promote the use of the "Tourism Cooperative Grant Program" to organizations representing various facets of the New Jersey's agritourism industry.

Strategy – Continue to review, comment, and support work towards the adoption of agritourism Agricultural Management Practices (AMP's) as proposed by the State Agriculture Development Committee. Compliance with the agritourism AMP's will aid grower protection under the Right to Farm Act.

Introduction

The success of tourism in Cambodia depends in Fart on the country's ability to develop a knowledgeable and skilled work force. Meeting the wide range of education and training needs must therefore be seen as essential for d l sectors of the industry. Failure to embrace all of the training issues will result in an imbalance within the travel product. Visitor satisfaction can diminish in a number of ways, and destinations that fail to recognize and address the needs and expectations of their tourists place the tourism industry at risk.

There are a number of different dimensions in beginning to understand a human resource development strategy. It cannot be assumed that classrooms are the only settings for education and training but rather that training and education can occur in a number of different ways. Given new technology and means of delivery, significant number of Cambodians can develop new skills and knowledge that are essential in ensuring the quality of the country's tourism industry.

There are a number of new providers in the country that have shown entrepreneurial skills in beginning to address some of the important training and education needs in tourism. It is essential that the public and private sectors come together and the research work behind the strategy clearly recognizes the importance of this partnership. The document is divided into three parts: An assessment of public sector training and education needs.

The Ministry of Tourism

In assessing the training needs for each of the departments, there appears to be overlap in responsibilities. In many cases the tasks within a particular department would logically be the responsibility of other departments within the Ministry of 'Tourism. In some instances, the responsibility would be that or other government ministries where the appropriate expertise would be more readily available.

As of October 2000, the registered number of staff at MOT based in Phnoin Penh is approximately 450. It is believed that 30%-40% of the registered employees are actually active. This is derived from interviews as well as advice from consultants assigned to M01. The percentage of active staff to registered staff will serve as basic data necessary for determining the scale of staff training and capacity to perform daily duties. In other words we arc not dealing with 450 staff members who require training but rather a much singular subset that actually are working within the Ministry.

A number of staff have participated in overseas training, a high percentage being university graduates which reflects the practice of donors to impose requirements for overseas training such as the need to possess a University degree or equivalent qualifications, three years of' employment in a related field and language competener; (English) before training is provided. While there has been a satisfactory level of international training there has not been any formal evaluation from the point view 01' quality and relevance of that training. It is recommended that all international training exercises require baronial report both of the individual as well as of the individual supervisor.

Domestic Training

Domestic training carried out in the past five years can be categorized as "introductory training the training for tour guides", "basic training" (tourism development and management) "skill training" for MOT staff, and "hospitality training related to tourism awareness".

The majority *of* the training was related to % wiliness". Though this can appraised from the viewpoint of broadening the tourism base one cannot help but say that this activity only covers a small part of the training and education gap. There is no evidence that a needs survey was conducted before deciding on the content, hereby indicating that the is no assurance that the desirable level of training was necessarily provided.

MOT and other Ministries' Training Needs

Through a series of questionnaires and several meetings has identified a nu iber of training requirements that need to be met if the government bureaucracy in Cambodia is to meet the country's tourism objectives. However, until staff is paid a living wage much of the training will not necessarily! increase the capacity of staff given their need to seek additional forms of livelihood. A possible solution might be in job sharing where two persons share the responsibility for specific objectives and outputs. The working day could be split into two time units, with a handover period, e.g., 7.30 to 12.30 and 12.00, 17.00 hours. Staff would then be officially free to undertake secondary employment. This strategy relieves office space increases motivation, and allows employees to supplement their income until such time as the Government is in the position to enhance the Fasic wages of civil servants.

Ministry of Tourism

Introduction to Basic Tourism Planning and Development Concepts

There is an urgent need for staff at all levels to understand what is meant by 'tourism'; to appreciate that it is basically the sale of a shared experience, based on physical comfort, providing a visual experience and a service component. The expectations of the tourists need to be clearly understood, in order to create a positive growth environment. Within this context the Ministry can then embrace its responsibility to provide guidance and support to a growing industry.

Basic General Skills

The following training needs have been identified. Private sector training organizations offer courses covering all of' these topics. Selected staff can be enrolled on an individual basis, or group rates can be negotiated for larger numbers.--

* Language skills-Basic, Intermediate and Advanced.
* Report writing.

* Keyboard skills.
* Word processing.
* Computer literacy.
* Numeracy skills.
* Basic accounting.
* Database management.
* Stock control.

Statistical Analysis: In the report on the development of an economic base study for Cambodia carried out by the need for such training is well illustrated and discussed. A basic introduction to economic analysis should be included. When the tourism law is enacted there will be an urgent need to train inspectors in a wide range of teclmical and jurisdictional issues if they arc to be effective in carrying out their important tasks.

Basics of Small and Medium-Sized Enterprise Creation

Staff must begin to understand how to support small and medium-sized enterprises if poverty reduction is to occur. It is important that staff move from the rhetoric that is now becoming common about the importance of small and medium-sized enterprises to actually beginning to understand the dynamics behind the creation of such initiatives.

Training Needs for MOT and Other It event Ministries

Information Officers

It is evident that the staff of various ministries interacting with tourists needs assistance to develop its tourist information services. Information should include communication and courtesy skills, care and presentation of information desks, collection and filing of' information display of promotional materials, etc. Interpretation, design of exhibits and publications and the development of multimedia presentations also need to be trained. This will have to be at various levels and directed at specific staff.

Marketing and Promotion

Staff should be exposed to the basics of market research and promotion in order to allow them to participate effectively in the research process and to interact with marketing and promotion professionals. There should be no attempt to train a large number of skilled people but it is clear that market research skills are an important need in Cambodia. Relevant Ministries: Ministry of Tourism. Ministry of Cultural and Fine Arts and Ministry of Environment.

Managing Service Excellence in the Cambodian Tourism Industry Knowledgeable travellers are demanding the best quality the tourism industry can provide. A competitive hospitality or tourism organization or business requires employees who (a) arc committed to exceeding industry standards for quality service. (b) can perform effectively in a multicultural environment. and (c) can contribute creatively to addressing service challenges in the work place. Consistent, predictable service quality translates into customer satisfaction and increased revenues from positive referrals to potential customers and repeats visits. Quality service training can also heighten employment satisfaction and positively influence employee retention.

The Management of Ecotourism

Such a course would allow the participants to understand the basic elements of ecotourism, evaluate market trends, assess the potential of individual and group ecotourist speciality markets use green guidelines for operating a successful ecotourism business, analyse and address the special needs of ecotourists and local communities, establish an ecotourism planning process at the local and regional levels, develop trip circuits and travel packages that are safe and offer a wide variety of experiences and understand the vital role of interpretation and education in adding value.

Ecolodge Development

Such a course would allow the participants to assess the market demand for ecolodge types and the experiences they provide, estimate realistic cost projections/revenue potential and develop pricing strategies, and understand how to find the best locations and evaluate site development opportunities and constraints.

Coastal & Marine Ecotourism

Such a course would allow the participant to integrate coastal zone management and mariners conservation into a sustainable tour ism development strategy identify the special characteristics of marine ecotourists, use innovative resource planning techniques and coastal zone management best practices, establish zoning and visitor tracking methods, educate visitors and staff about low-impact forms of recreation, monitor and assess more accurately the long-term effects of tourism on local resources and increase government's commitment in marine park protection and effective coastal management.

Historical Site Management

Observation of activities within the Angkor Wat complex would indicate that site management would need to be urgently improved. While the present ad-hoc arrangements may have been acceptable for love volume traffic, there is an urgent need for staff to be trained to deal with ever larger number of visitor numbers.

Project Management

Staff must be exposed to leading-edge project management skills and knowledge areas. It is becoming increasingly important, as transparency and good governance are required that team leaders and managers understand how to manage large-scale projects in a financially responsible manner. There is increasing concern within the donor community about the level of project management in Cambodia. It is clear that this is age skill and knowledge area that will be urgently required as donors and others become more demanding.

Poverty Reduction through Tourism

As we discover more and more about the role that sustainable tourism can play in alleviating poverty, staff must be provided with the opportunity of developing their skills and knowledge in poverty reduction initiatives. The training should range from simple awareness raising to sophisticated training for small numbers in developing policies and programs designed to deal with the poverty issue in a comprehensive manner. Relevant Ministries: All ministries dealing with tourism.

Recommendations for Travelling and Education For the Private Sector

The Private Sector is made up of a number of different organizations and activities as illustrated by Figure 4. The challenge is to ensure. That the relevant actors are trained and educated to support the overall tourism development and management process. From the beginning it is important to stress that the Ministry of Tourism is only one of many government actors responsible for delivering:! quality tourism product. There are therefore a series of other ministries that require capacity building. The assessment used the following list of private sector occupational activities as a means of organizing its work:

* Adventured Outdoor Tourism Guide.
* Advertising Manager/Assistant.
* Amusement Park Employee.
* Amusement Park.
* Operation/Management.
* Bartender.
* Beverage Services Manager.
* Campground Operator.
* Casino Dealer.
* Casino Slot Attendant.
* Catering Manager.
* Director of Sales and Marketing.
* Door Staff.
* Food & Beverage Manager.
* Food Sr. Beverage Server.
* Food Service Counter Attendant.
* Front Desk Agent.
* Golf Club Manager.
* Guest Services Attendant.
* Housekeeping Room Attendant.
* Human Resource Management.
* Hunting Guide.
* Kitchen Helper.
* Leisure Centre Manager/Assistant.
* Line Cook.
* Marketing Manager/Assistant.
* Promotion Manager/Assistant.
* Reservations Sales Agent.
* Retail First level Manager.
* Retail Sales Associate.
* Sales Manager.
* Small Business Owner/Operator.
* Special Events Coordinator.

* Special Events Manager.
* Taxicab Driver.
* Tour Bus/Vaii Driver.
* Tour Director.
* 'Tour Guide.
* Tour Operator.
* Tourism Small Business Owner.
* Tourism Trainer.
* 'Travel Counsellor.
* Wine Service.

Survey of Training Needs In 'the Cambodian Travel and Tourism Sector

In order to better understand the needs of the travel and tourism sector several initiatives were taken. In addition to the significant number of interviews and meetings with many members of the tourism industry, the project worked with Rege: it College in Phnoni Penh in a study that was intended to provide a snapshot of the current human resource capacity in the travel and tourism industry.

This included not only the hospitality sector, but also related industries of international and domestic travel services and other support services. The key objectives were to provide a clear and relevant overview of the current level of skills among personnel working in the hospitality and travel industry and, by analysis of current recruitment practices, human resource and training policies, to identify clear areas where a skills gap exists.

In addition the study aimed to assess the commitment and capacity of owners. Managers and currently existing training institutions 10 address these questions. To achieve these objectives.

Primary data was collected from a Closs section of accommodation services restaurant and catering services, and travel and tour operators. Secondary data was provided by the hospitality. Travel and tourism sectors, the Ministry of Tourism and Ministry of Education. 'The project team wishes to thank Regent College for its cooperation and professionalism in completing the survey.

Methodology

Due to the necessarily limited nature of the time and financial resources available to carry out a survey. Three key sites were selected as representing the current focus of tourism activity in Cambodia. These were: Phnom Penh, the capital city and principal port of entry for the Kingdom.

Despite a significant decrease of growth in arrivals, a< a result of the government's Open Skies policy, 56.75% of all visitors to Cambodia in 2000 still arrived through Pochentong International Airport. Siem Reap, home of Angkor Wat and the principal centre for tourism development.

In 3,000, 18.66% of all visitors to the kingdom arrived through Siem Reap Airport a figure that has shown an enormous increase in the year to date, with a 110.98% rise in the first quarter alone. Sihanoukville (formerly Kampong Som), Cambodia's principal seaside resort town located 230km south of Phnom Penh one of four international border checkpoints and a popular destination for domestic holidaymakers.

Primary research in each of these locales consisted of questionnaires, scheduled interviews and, in the case of Phnom Penh, follow-up felcus group discussions (FGD's). Potential respondents were drawn from PADECO's comprehensive listings of hotels, guesthouses, restaurants and travel and tour operators.

PA1 IECO's categories were further subdivided based on considerations of price. Facilitics, site, ownership and location. Subsets in each locale were identified using these four criteria, md from these subsets a random sample was made, proportionate to the size/number of each location. A total of one hundred respondents were selected across the three locations.

Questionnaires focused on current recruitment and HR policy, the current educational and skill levels of management and staff, recent experience of, or participation in internal or externally conducted training, management commitment to staff development perceived constraints or obstacles to the provision of training and the prioritization of specific skills for enhancement or development. In addition to the quantitative data obtained, the questionnaires contained a qualitative component in the form of brief interviews based on a set of prospected questions.

'The questionnaires were administered in face-to-face interviews with owners or managers of hotels, restaurants or travel and tour operators. Questionnaires were available in English or Khmer as required and each interview team consisted of one native speaker and one Khmer interviewer to minimize problems of comprehension. Secondary information sources consisted primarily of the Ministry of Tourism Statistical Report for 7000.

The 1999 MPDF report on Developing SMEs in the Tourism Industry and the 1996 National Human Resource Strategy developed by WTO/UNDP. Immediately following completion of the formal questionnaires, respondents were invited to colour issues which had atisen in the course of the interviews in an informal setting, and to provide a more personalized insight into the topics covered.

Following completion of all primary data collection, two focus group discussions were conducted to further explore the issues raised by the study, involving respondents from the training and education field, and owners and mangers from the private sector. 'This report provides information on the most important findings.

Findings

Recruitment Policy

It was discovered across each of the sample groups (hotels, guesthouses, restaurants, travel and tour operators) that recruitment in the main depended on either the employment of relatives of owners or managers or on word-of-mouth from current staff as can be seen. A clear majority 01' all companies interviewed expressed a preference for this lorni of internal recruitment, usually citing simple issues of trust as the principal criteria.

Outweighing other considerations of specific skills or suitability. Although this was true for all groups and in each location, it was particularly marked in the restaurant sector and in Category 2 and Category 3 hotels. While newspaper advertising, usually in Reaksmey Kampuchea was the second most popular form of locating new staff this was still relatively minor.

At the opposite end of the scale as predicted there was a reluctance to consider staff with more than basic. Qualifications due to the necessarily low wages paid and the. Perception that better qualified staff would either seek higher salaries or would not remain in place long. Attitudes Towards investment in Training One of the recurring concerns stated when discussing recruitment or training was the impression that investment in training or in recruitment based on merit or achievement was undesirable due to the mobility of employees.

Repeatedly owners and managers stressed that if staff were not family members, or were trained to higher standards, they would either leave. For better employment or would establish their own business in competition.

Indeed, when asked the most common reason for staff changes it is true that 40% were due to employees finding better positions, but when asked about staff turnover. The results showed a relatively high degree of stability with 72% of companies securing a minimum of six months' employment from staff: and almost 62% retaining staff for over a year.

Given the seasonal nature of the industry, and the rate of hotel and restaurant development in Phnom Penh and Sictn Keap, this suggests that even in those businesses not employing family members. The situation is less volatile than one would expect.

Following on from the above data, the questionnaire then focused on what training was provided to staff, either internally or externally following recruitment.

Respondents were questioned about specific positions to provide a detailed insight into the relative importance placed on training of management, front-line and back-office staff.

In the case of hotels and guesthouses, those employed in management or supervisory positions ordinarily received little more than orientation. Primarily due to being perceived as already qualified or experiment. Only *5%* of respondents offered a structured training plan For these positions and less than *90/0* of respondents sought outside training for management or supervisory staff.

In the case of front-of-house staff results were broadly similar with again only *5%* of companies having a structured training programme, relying instead on the previous experience of new staff members or limited in-service training to achieve the results required.

Cost of Training

Respondents were questioned regarding a range of options to assist with the cost of training. An earlier question had established that the level of fees most respondents willing to sponsor training were prepared to pay was in the US$20-50 range, based on an average ten-week part-time course of 40 hours.

Preferred Training Providers

Another key question concerned the preferred training provider should external training be required. Interestingly, in Siem Reap and Phnom Penh a clear majority preferred private sector providers to a Ministry-run training institution, with 48.6% in favour of a private institution against 37.5% in favour of a Ministry Training Centre. Most respondents were very receptive to the ideas of the Ministry adopting a {supervisory and licensing role rather than a direct training role.

Conclusions

It is clear from the bulk of respondents surveyed that while skills levels remain 10\+ across the tourism industry. Training represents a low priority for most owners and managers, whether of medium sized hotels. Small guest houses, restaurants aimed at the tourist market or family-run travel and tour operators.

While a few companies interviewed showed an impressive commitment to training and staff development, as well as a keen awareness of the areas where i improvement was most needed. These were clearly exceptions.

Of course significant variations exist between the three locales, with a sense of despondency to be found among some owners in Phnom Penh and Sihanoukville, compared to the bullish mood found in Siem Reap. At several of the mid-range hotels in Phnom Penh owners or managers bemoaned low levels of occupancy and commented that their income and staff levels were actually lower now than four years ago.

Some other hotels quite openly discussed the level and extent of their financial losses. Although few hotels have declared bankruptcy in the last year (three in Phnom Penh in 2000) it seems that many of the interviewers encountered businesses in Phnom Penh and Sihanoukville with few positive signs of growth.

In Sihanoukville, the situation is acute with a clear oversupply to rooms in the $10-25 range. The inexperience of many hotel and restaurant owners is apparent firm the moment of arrival, with little attention paid to customer service cleanliness or presentation. The vulnerability of many smaller operators to better-organized or better-finded competitors is also evident.

While this is true in all countries in such a small and concentrated area it is surprising to be able to go from a clean, modern hotel with facilities such as a swimming pool tennis courts, restaurants, hairdresser etc. to a hotel with extremely basic room facilities, no additional facilities a very poor standard of cleanliness and customer service, and to be offered the same rate (lJS$30) at both. It is clear that managers and staff of such hotels could benefit from training in the expectations of being tourists regarding decor.

Furnishings etc., as well as service considerations, but there is little awareness of the importance of these issues. In Sicm Reap the contrast with Sihanoukville is obviously striking.

Whereas Sihanoukville in low season is a quiet, almost moribund setting, with little activity evident on the streets and rows of empty or sparsely populated restaurants, hotels and bars, Siem Reap continues to display vibrant signs of life.

More than one business commented that low season now is similar to high season in previous years. While this is clearly cause for optimism, in the case of some of the respondents interviewed this clearly leads to a sense of complacency in that it is clear that tourist numbers arc growing at a rate unprecedented in the history of the town and that seasonally at least business is booming with little effort necessary on their part. As has been noted elsewhere, Siem Reap is not a budget location. Prices are cospensive compared with neighbouring countries while the quality of service remains low. Consideration of this among owners arid managers however is limited.

Correspondingly while there was a greater proportion of owners and managers who expressed a commitment to training, particularly in languages and improved customer service., there were many more who clearly felt that business was proceeding well enough without the additional expense of training staff. As stated in the MPIIE' report from 1999. "many managers have a short term vision in conducting their business and are not willing to enlist in improving the quality of their services and facilities."

Perhaps the most significant findings of the surveyor that despite the fluctuating fortunes of recent years, the majority of owners and mangers persist in a short-term view of tourism development, lacking the business experience and vision to consider the impact that future market changes could have on their businesses.

Issues of quality are seldom addressed or wen considered, and the result is that trained stair is perceived as a luxury rather than a necessity. Perhaps due to inexperience, the connection between training, education and productivity is not often made.

In line with a recent study by Merrill Lynch showing that companies employing a work force with a 10% higher than average educational attainment level enjoyed an 86% higher-than-average productivity, the message that training pays off is one that must be stressed if the industry is to embrace any future proposals. In line with this, it seems clear that left to their own devices few businesses are likely to take a pro-active approach to training.

Existing Training Programs

Training and education is provided at various levels ranging from certificates diplomas, and Bachelor and Master degree programs. The Royal University of Phnom Penh currently offers a Masters program in Tourism Development, while the National Institute of Management and four other institutions offer undergraduate studies 4 in tourism.

Also several private schools provide technical training. Approximately IOC students per year graduated from these institutions seeking tourism related employment in both the public and private sectors. However, the demand for people with technician training is very high making technical education and training a major issue.

As indicated above there are several institutions. Providing tourism education and training. Given the lack of national standards there is a concern about the quality of students/people who are trained from these tourism providers. This is due to several reasons.

Lack of cooperation among tourism equation providers including government. NGOs, private sector and domestic and international institutes. Teaching staff that does not have the necessary qualifications and experience. Inadequate resources and materials of villous kinds to assist students in their classroom as well as private study.

The private sector teaching establishments are keel to develop programs specifically for the tourism industry. While most of these institutions would favour topics which are an extension of their existing teaching fields, i.e. hotel front office and tour guiding Techniques, some have already investigated the possibility of working in partnership with hotel operators to provide practical training venues for the training of lousemaids and waiting staff.

Most employers would be happy to see operational standards improve, arid would contribute more to in-house training if they had the ability. Most operators experience problems recruiting staff competent at basic skills level, let alone find trainers capable of upgrading the skills of others.

With the exception of the lop hotels, few have ever carried out ii training needs analysis, mainly because they themselves are unable to define desirable standards of performance or to relate these to guest expectation. Any further developments in in-house training by the private sector will be dependent in part on the availability of training materials and the opportunity for their heads of department to attend a skills under relationship techniques workshop.

Defining Training and Education Needs

Developing a learning experience is at times a complex process that requires the participation of a number of individuals. This short chapter attempts to identify some of the major steps and issues to be considered when designing a learning experience. It is not designed to replace the need for trained and experienced course designers. Rather it is aimed at identifying the nature of the issues and the process that are normally followed in course design and delivery. There is certainly no one route to the development of a course or learning experience and no magic formulas to rely.

Very often after an idea for a course has been identified an expert is hired to deliver a course without any planning occurring. While this may be cost-efficient it is not effective in actually meeting the needs that will have been identified through the research process. At a possible process for designing a learning experience. The course designer should ideally be somebody with a sound knowledge of adult education and preferably with a good grasp of the subject material.

In many cases it is message to combine the skill of the educator with the subject specialist. When we refer to the term course designer it can either be an individual or in some cases a group of people. Increasingly with the introduction of interactive information technology there is a need to have a specialist in this area as part of the design process.

Is important that the designers start off with an pen mind on how best to meet the need identified. 'Too often it is an automatic assumption that the only way to train people is to develop a course or learning experience in the standard classroom fashion. Delivering knowledge in a classroom may at times be the least efficient and effective way of attempting to raise the knowledge and skills of a group of participants from the tourism industry.

With our increased knowledge of how people learn it is becoming increasingly clear that the standard classroom experience may in fact be the least effective way of imparting knowledge and skills. In this short discussion the term course could mean a number of different types of learning experiences that will be discussed later in this chapter. The following steps can be followed in determining the nature of learning experience.

Identification of the Training or Education Need

The need for a particular skill or knowledge to be developed into a course can come from a number of sources. In the case of Cambodia a staff person of the Ministry of 'Tourism in his or her work could observe the need for knowledge and skills to be developed and then transmitted to a particular group responsible for particular tourism planning or development issues.

The need can come from a community group seeking help in addressing issues in their community or a group of professionals could collectively define a gap in their training or knowledge set. 'The need could also come from an overall human resource development strategy such as the one that has been developed for Cambodia. Whatever the source of the need identification it is important to start with clear identification of the need and the establishment of the priority of that particular need.

Defining Capacities and Needs

Depending on the nature of the identification process there then must be a clear definition of the actual need. This requires that the eventual provider or sponsor carry out a careful research process in order to determine the actual dimensions of the training need. Too often a wry general concept is quickly turned into a course that never meets the actual needs of the participants.

Normally within the course development process the designers will use existing data from a human resource development research process or at times must carry out their own investigation. Depending on budget and the complexity of task the following sources may be consulted: Representatives from within the particular sector where the need has been identified.

People actually carrying out the task. Employers in the particular sector identified as requiring training. The providers of training to determine their views on the need itself and the actual learning experience. Consultations with institutions or organizations offering similar types of courses either in Cambodia or elsewhere in the world.

In order to systematically collect information the designer can employ a range of techniques including questionnaires, surveys and focus groups.

It must be remembered that the survey process simply collects information and cannot replace the need for the skill and judgment of the course designer. The course designer will bring to the process the knowledge of how best to meet the needs of a particular group given a set of realities. This process should allow the designers to identify the following factors within the overall course design process:

The nature of the audience (level of education nature of their experience, language skills, previous training opportunities etc.) 'The number of people who could be trained given the opportunity. (It is important in this case to define not only the existing number of potential participants but the anticipated demand for a learning experience in the future.

In some instances there is a significant pent-up demand that must be met for that need only to find that after that demand has been met there is little potential for the ongoing delivery of the course experience). The level of training needs to be addressed which can range everywhere from the imparting of basic awareness creation to establishing a sound basic skill or knowledge set to professional development experiences. The length of the course must be determined based on the course objectives and the length of time participants will be in a position to spend in the learning experience.

The nature of the certification is certainly always an important issue and in some cases it may be determined that the particular skill or knowledge must be met within the context of a group of courses that can take the form of a certificate, diploma or in some cases a university degree.

The location of the people requiring the training and their ability to travel is especially important. Do they exist in one central location or are they in fact scattered over the entire country? 'This issue becomes particular important from a financial perspective.

Assessing the Interest and Capacity of Providers

Depending on the nature of course determined by Step 2 it is important to then work with providers to *sec* how the course can be delivered. If the course is to be complicate, subsidized then this step becomes less important but more open than not the delivery process depends on sonic form of market response. Is important that discussions he held on: The cost of' delivering such a Earning experience.

It is important to remember that the course development process has to be factored into the eventual course delivery fees unless it is subsidixt.

The capacity of the local or national providers to deliver the course must be determined. In other words do they have the experience and the trained personnel to deliver the course experience? Does the institution have the necessary reputation to enable the participants to obtain a job or for advancement in an agreement once the learning experience has been completed. The sustainability of the provider *must* be assessed especially if 'an ongoing set of courses is being contemplate.

Determining Learning Objectives

At this point the course can be more clearly understood and the factors discussed earlier determined. It is particularly important at this point that a series of course objectives for the Incurring experience be determined and agreed to by the relevant stakeholders. In effect these objectives now become the guiding principle for the detailed course development process.

Detailed Course Learning Design

Is not possible within this document to describe the detailed design process but as identified, there are number of issues to be considered:. This includes the following factors: Hie identification of instructors and facilitates and whether they themselves require training either in the from to' subject specific development or in training methods. There are times when there are people whiting the industry who may have the necessary knowledge but not the ability to treatment that knowledge in a professional and effective way.

'The nature of the subject material and the lacks to be delivered should then be identified in sufficient detail that a course instructor can deliver the required objectives. It should be determined whether any form of prerequisite is necessary for the learning experience. This can he as basic as language skills or can be more complex requiring a participant to have participated in one or more previous courses. The delivery methods arc then carefully identified and as suggested in figure there are a series of ways of delivery methods available always renumbering that the classroom is but one specific response domestic and out of country delivery methods include:

Developing the Course Package

'The course package that includes the information from the steps described above can then be produced. In the ideal situation it is then possible to select the instructor and/or facilitator based on the material that is produced. This material would include such things as the detailed course objectives, the learning sequences. The nature of the group work to be carried out: books: video or CDs, the evaluation methods to be used and a well-designed course evaluation technique.

Evaluating and Monitoring the Learning Experience

There must be an ongoing process of assessment both while the course is being delivered and certainly once the experience has been completed. It is not sufficient to rely on an evaluation form that is often hastily completed at the end of the course. If one is truly interested in understanding the effectiveness of a learning experience the respondents.

Their employers, fellow employees and most importantly in the tourism industry customers should be carefully surveyed in order to determine whether the course objectives have been met. This information of course is important in terms of redesigning or reformatting the nest offering of the course experience.

In a world that is quickly changing. It is often necessary to update material on a regular basis and to adapt delivery methods to new and more accessible technology.

Major Recommendations and Conclusions

Cambodia is faced with a number of significant human resource development challenges.

As an emerging economy there are a number of demands placed on the country to meet a series of needs necessary to allow the country to achieve its full potential. It is very important that national authorities recognize the need to place a high-priority on human resource development at all levels.

There is a need to ensued that children in schools are made aware of tourism as an activity and its role in the national society, there must be clear information available on opportunities in all classes of tourism activity, vocational schools must provide opportunities for obtaining basic skills especially in the hospitality industry graduate level programs must conform to international standards and there is an extreme urgency for professional developments and skills and knowledge development for those already working in the industry. Faced with this challenge the country must seriously address its human resource needs in the tourism industry given its importance in the overall development of the society. It is important to recognize that training and education must be available to all sectors of the society and in particular the poor and women who,) have an opportunity of benefiting from tourism activity if they have the necessary skills and knowledge. It is clear that human resource development is an essential element in an overall poverty reduction strategy related to tourism.

As discussed earlier in this document the role fought Ministry of tourism and in particular the 'Training and Education Department is crucial in helping to ensure consistent human resource not be to act as a provider but to contribute advice and direction on crucial issues within the overall tourism planning and development process.

This will require that the Ministry staff is trained in human resource development in order to measure that needs and requirements can be professionally identified and that the Ministry staff can effectively work with the range of public and private sector providers that now exis in Cambodia. It is also important that Ministry staff is in a position to design funding proposals that will meet international standards as they relate to human resource development.

The Ministry is in a unique position given its presence in all parts of the country to be arvare of problems within all sectors of the tourism industry. Through its human resource development staff it can identify specific needs and work with the essential providers in meetings kill and knowledge gaps.

Cambodian Tourism Human Resource Development Commission

Recognizing the challenges identified in this strategy it is recommended that a public/private Cambodia Tourism Human Resource Development Commission be created that would be responsible for both needs assessment as well as helping to bring together the necessary public and private resources to meet the significant tourism capacity building requirements 01' the country.

The Commission would be made up of representatives from the tourism industry, the Ministry 01 'Tourism and other government ministries. It is recommended that the Commission be made up of equal numbers of public and private numbers. Private sector participants would be representatives of various groups including the hotel industry, the restaurant sector, travel companies and the tour and travel areas of activity. Training institutes and universities would have both public as well as private representatives. It is further recommended that in addition to the Ministry of 'Tourism the Ministry of Education.

The Ministry of Culture and Fine Arts and the Ministry of the Environment have membership on the Commission. The Commission would also be responsible for establishing national standards for all occupational groups. In addition, the Commission would be responsible for working with colleges and universities in designing degree programs that meet international standards.

The Commission would be established in such a way that it would monitor various educational programs and on a regular basis assess these programs using both Cambodian as well as international experts to ensure that Cambodians have access to international level training and education that is adapted to the Cambodian contest.

The Ministry of 'Tourism would act as the secretariat for the Commission and provide all necessary administrative support in order to ensure the effective functioning of the Commission. It is recommended that a task force be established immediately made up of representatives from the essential sectors to further define the nature of the Commission. The approach used by the Canadian government could serve as a useful model for development.

Establishing Professional Associations

There is a need to further encourage the private sector to from and support professional associations i.e., hotels and restaurants, tour operators and tour guides. Such associations can then speak with one voice to influence the content of training programs and to moderate the examination and testing procedures. In addition, professional associations can present specialist workshops on a cost-sharing basis by bringing in experts to meet specific objectives.

Conclusions

The Human Resource Development Strategy for Cambodia outlines the principal needs thing the country as it attempts to use tourism as a major tool of societal development. It is essential that the needs identified for the public sector be seen as priority areas for action.

Unless there are trained government employees working in various areas of cultural and natural resource development and protection with a sound understanding of market issues there is a distinct possibility that the important opportunities facing tourism in Cambodia will be lost.

Given the very rapid growth of the hospitality sector there are significant needs to he fulfilled to help position Cambodia as an international destination. It is of concern that the private sector appears place a high priority on training and education and the Ministry of Tourism along with other sectors of the industry must establish a climate were training and education is seen as essential as Cambodia continues to enjoy significant tourism growth. It is clear that without further opportunities achieving international status will be impossible. However, given the realities of the private sector it is important that be Commission adopts innovative techniques for delivering skill and knowledge development. It is stressed that innovative techniques are used to meet the market realities.

4

Priorities of Tourism Policies and Plans

Mexican Priorities: Gaming, Tourism and Energy

Since early in January 2007 three issues have been highlighted as priorities, so that Mexico will be able to attract foreign investment and to create promised jobs that are currently nonexistent.

First is a ruling on gaming permits that were granted by officials during prior administrations, the legality of which will depend on a forthcoming judgment by Mexico's Supreme Court. This ruling will relate to the validity of the 2004 Regulation of the Federal Gaming and Raffles Law, and whether or not permits issued under that authority in 2005 by former Secretary of Government, and now Senator Santiago Creel, are valid. Permits that well may have cost Creel the National Action Party (PAN) presidential candidacy.

According to most expectations, this proceeding — that is being handled by Justice Olga Sanchez Cordero, and that the Court as a whole must rule on — will favour and uphold the issuance of the permits. And by doing so, the Secretariat of Government will be able to grant future permits for Bingo-type numbers game parlours, remote betting centres called "Books," and electronic gaming machines.

Still, casinos per se, with gaming tables and the like, cannot be authorized until the 1947 law itself is amended. Yet if the aforementioned permits are allowed, surely reforms to the law will become more likely in the near term so that the next steps can be taken, as casinos and the gaming industry should be important development opportunities and attractions for many Mexican cities.

The Mexican Congress can also be expected to take up this matter in the near future. And based on the agreement strategy on economic matters that has been reached by the National Action Party (PAN) and Institutional Revolutionary Party (PRI), advances could come about quickly on this issue that should not be allowed to lag behind.

The second matter, that has been the subject of considerable debate for years, deals with crude oil and its derivatives. It has been made clear that the privatization of Petroleos Mexicanos, PEMEX, will not be proposed due to difficulties in reaching agreements to change the Mexican Constitution in order to allow foreign investment in the state owned petroleum conglomerate.

In other words, the exploration and exploitation of oil and gas will continue to be activities reserved for the state. Nonetheless, predictions are that advances will be made towards allowing private sector national and foreign investment in the refining or transformation of hydrocarbons, as well as in their storage and distribution.

What will be important is to plan modifications based on the Mexican Constitution, and not to try to find novel interpretations of the Constitution that provoke opinion and debate but will not resolve the problem nor provide greater security for this investment.

The subject of economic sovereignty in deciding amounts of exploitation of oil and gas fields, along with exploration, can continue to be safeguarded by the Constitution, but too new resources in the areas of oil and gas refining, storage and distribution should be promoted and empowered.

By continuing an indiscriminate exploitation of crude oil in order to maintain exportation levels, and by not making investments needed in other development areas, in just a few years Mexico will be out of the oil export business. And soon thereafter it will become an importer, with the sovereignty over energy resources that is being defended today lost. Therefore this is an urgent matter.

The final subject that is to be a priority is tourism.

Mexico has yet to take full advantage of its tourism opportunities and possibilities, and to thus become one of the leading tourist destinations in the world. Certainly it is an attractive destination, but it still comes up short in its potential for greater visitor industry income.

During this sexennial tourism must become a true and stronger source of foreign exchange, on a par at least with crude oil exports and revenue from remittances sent home by Mexicans living abroad. And to do so, even more legal reforms will have to be made to allow outside capital in the tourist industry, part of which would be invested and brought to Mexico once casinos are authorized and opened. These three issues and areas are indeed important — and addressing them as immediate priorities is not only needed but also overdue.

Tourism Development Priorities in North East England

Understanding which niches, products and services are currently being developed and which areas of product development are being prioritised in the region, will help to identify whether a proposed project is likely to receive support and backing

In North East England there are five organisations responsible for driving and developing sustainable tourism. They are One North East Tourism (the regional organisation) and the four Area Tourism Partnerships: Visit County Durham, Northumberland Tourism, Tyne and Wear and visit Teesvalley. Collectively they are known as Tourism Network North East and they work together to provide a coherent set of services to promote and develop tourism in North East England. Through extensive research, the regional and area priorities for tourism have been identified, and strategies have been developed to meet these priorities. Priority areas and current projects around the region are:

Northumberland Tourism

Priority areas/niches: Northumberland priorities for activity are divided into three overlapping – not mutually exclusive – approaches:

- Activity to realise plans for the key Destination Management Areas.
- Delivery of the prioritised Capital Projects.
- Actions delivering to agreed Programme Activities.

The priority Destination Management Areas for Northumberland are:

- Towns in the Market Town Welcome Programme (Berwick, Wooler, Seahouses, Alnwick, Amble, Haltwhistle, Morpeth & Hexham).

- Hadrian's Wall corridor.
- Kielder Water and Forest Park.
- Northumberland National Park.
- The Northumberland Coast and North Pennines Areas of Outstanding Natural Beauty.

(Druridge Bay is also developing with potential to emerge as a future priority).

Priority Capital Projects are:

- Alnwick Garden (completion of cherry orchard).
- Hadrian's Wall Central programme projects (Vindolanda, Housesteads & The Sill).
- Kielder Water and Forest Park 'Big Picture'.
- Seaton Delaval Hall acquisition.
- Hexham Abbey Christian Heritage visitor facilities.
- Market Town Welcome capital programme.
- Northumberlandia at Blagdon.

A list of priority Programme Activities to develop the visitor economy of Northumberland – to improve the marketing and branding of the sub-region, the information available to visitors before, during and after their visit, and the whole visitor experience whilst they are in the area – is available in the Northumberland ATMaP.

Tourism Tyne & Wear

Priority areas:

- Business Tourism-supporting the development of an International Convention Centre and Exhibition Centre in Newcastle Gateshead.
- Events-delivering a world class events programme.
- Online and E-commerce-increasing the online visibility and capacity of tourism businesses.
- Coastal Tourism-enabling coastal regeneration.
- Visitor Information-transforming the provision of visitor information.
- Quality-improving the quality of the tourism product.
- Marketing-delivering effective marketing.

- Attractions-providing great attractions and new reasons to visit.
- Partnerships-strengthening tourism partnerships.

Priority projects:

- Convention Centre/events space in Newcastle Gateshead.
- Wearmouth Jarrow World Heritage Site.
- Development of visitor focused coastal infrastructure.
- Legible Cities projects.

Visit County Durham

Priority areas/niches:

- Optimise the potential of Durham city to attract visitors to the county and region, particularly through the development of Durham as a short stay destination and through investing in key attractions that will have a national profile and appeal.
- Improve the quality and service of visitor-facing businesses to improve the national appeal and attract higher-spending visitors.
- Develop local distinctiveness in line with the image and identity of the county utilising the name 'Durham' and its brand themes-history and innovation, people and location and connectivity.
- Tackle seasonality, particularly through focusing on high profile, off-peak events and on business tourism to increase visits in the shoulder season and midweek.
- Raise the profile of the county regionally and nationally, particularly by developing the product. Specifically to grow events that have potential national pulling power.
- Extend the stay of visitors, particularly by helping rural town centres to develop services and facilities to draw visitors. Specifically develop destination development plans and ensure their implementation.

Visit Tees Valley

Priority areas/niches:

- Improve the physical product to local, national and international visitors. Our four key physical product elements are:
    - o The urban playground experience of Stockton and Middlesbrough.

- o The coastal stretch from Hartlepool to Redcar, Saltburn and onto Staithes.
- o The countryside and towns including Guisborough, Yarm, and Darlington and the outdoor experiences to be enjoyed there.
- o Heritage and innovation – a celebration of industrial heritage into the 21st century.

- Develop and promote Tees Valley as an events destination of local, national and international significance.
- Upskill the tourism and hospitality sector work force-the aim will be to give both visitors and residents a quality experience that meets and surpasses their expectations.

Tourism and the Imperatives of Sustainable Development

Statement of the Committee for Sustainable Development

The Committee for Sustainable Development;

Recognising: That the tourism industry has an increasingly important economic, social, cultural and environmental impact, both globally and on the national scale, and that the continuing growth of tourism and tourism-related activities has diverse implications for the achievement of sustainable development,

Recalling: That issues of tourism were addressed by IPU on several occasions in recent years, such as the Inter-Parliamentary Conference on Tourism held in 1989 in The Hague and the two International Fora "Parliaments and Local Authorities: Tourism Policy-Makers" organised by the World Tourism Organization with the support of IPU respectively in Cadiz (Spain) in 1995 and Bali (Indonesia) in 1996,

Believing: That the tourism sector is a major driving force behind the economic advancement of many countries, including developing ones, where it fosters job creation, stimulates economic diversification and boosts foreign exchange earnings,

Realising: At the same time that over-reliance on tourism, especially mass tourism, entails significant risks for tourism-dependent economies,

Noting: That demand for new forms of tourism, including ecotourism, is growing in many parts of the world and presents new challenges for the tourism industry, national governments, parliaments and the international community,

Recognising: The important role played by the World Tourism Organization in shaping the future of the global tourism industry, and *recalling* in this regard the rich record of cooperation between IPU and this body,

1. Believes that projected sustained growth of the tourism industry will present serious challenges to environmental protection unless policy-makers develop effective regulatory policies and systems of economic incentives and disincentives and address the issue of promoting awareness of tourists, the tourism industry and the public at large of the importance of safeguarding the natural and cultural environment;
2. Emphasises that linkages of tourism with other economic sectors necessitate its full integration into national development plans as well as the provision of adequate legislative support, for which parliaments bear primary responsibility, so that tourism develops in harmony with overall economic, social and environmental goals;
3. Considers that an integrated policy framework for sustainable tourism development should include a mechanism ensuring that investment, employment, operational and other business decisions of tourism enterprises take full account of the wider implications of these actions for the long-term development and economic sustainability of the destinations in which they operate and that the carrying capacity of sites visited by tourists should be respected even if this implies restricting access to sites at certain periods or seasons;
4. Supports the development of new and alternative forms of tourism, including ecotourism, which favour closer contact and understanding between tourists and receiving populations, respect cultural identity and preserve distinctive and original tourist products and facilities;
5. Urges the international community to enhance and strengthen international coordination and relevant monitoring systems through liaison among governments, parliaments, the private sector and concerned parties with a view to promoting the positive aspects and minimising the negative impacts of tourism;

6. Is convinced that national parliaments should show increased concern for tourism development and review existing laws on tourism, consolidate them into comprehensive legislation and codify national policy and priorities for tourism including such aspects as safety and security of tourists, spread of epidemic diseases such as AIDS, and elimination of terrorism, in particular by addressing its root causes;

7. Energetically supports the view that the promotion of ecotourism should be given priority within overall tourism development planning and that effective mechanisms should be introduced to prevent and control tourism-related abuse and exploitation of people, particularly women and children;

8. Urges national parliaments and other tourism policy-makers to support the objectives of the International Year of Ecotourism-2002;

9. With a view to deepening its reflection on the issue of tourism and sustainable development and in order to produce comprehensive recommendations for the Union's governing bodies in this regard, *resolves* to include a relevant item on the agenda of the session of the IPU Committee for Sustainable Development to be held in the year 2000.

Mekong Tourism Office Defines Priorities

The Mekong Tourism Office has announced its new marketing plan, 2008-2011.

The MTO's Senior Advisor, Mr. Peter Semone (pictured), told GMS member countries that the priorities would be to consolidate resources, build credibility and win the confidence of the private sector over three phases of activity. Addressing delegates of the GMS Tourism Working Group Ad-hoc Meeting in Vientiane on December 3, he recommended that phase I of the plan should include:

1. Appointing a country coordinator for Mekong activities in each member NTO.
2. Upgrading the MTO's website.
3. Creating a Mekong Travel Planner for travel agents.
4. Presenting MTO at international events.
5. Facilitating subregional networking activities.

6. Enhancing the MTO member database.
7. Improving monthly updates to all stakeholders.
8. Holding regular private sector advisory meetings, and
9. Carrying out market research.

Mr. Semone told the 35 delegates that it was important for the MTO to get the basics right. "Later phases should include GDS engagement, social website capabilities with search engine optimization, media familiarization trips, reestablishing the Mekong Tourism Forum, and a visit GMS year," he said.

About the Mekong Tourism Office

The MTO was established in February 2006. Its four key objectives are to:-

- Develop and promote the Mekong as a single destination, offering a diversity of good quality and high-yielding sub-regional products that help to distribute the benefits of tourism more widely.
- Add to the tourism development efforts of each GMS country.
- Contribute to poverty reduction, gender equality and the empowerment of women.
- Promote sustainable development, while minimising adverse impacts.

Tourism bosses from national tourism agency Visit England were in the region yesterday (TUES) to meet with key businesses and organisations including Regional Development Agency One North East.

Lady Cobham, chair of Visit England and James Berresford, chief Exec of Visit England, met with a number of tourism businesses to find out more about what the North East has to offer and how the region's public and private sector have worked together to help support tourism businesses in the region.

Businesses such as Hadrian's Wall Heritage, Newcastle International Airport and the Arts Council North East attended the event at Newcastle's Theatre Royal which was hosted by Geoff Hodgson, chairman of the North East Tourism Advisory Board and Stacy Hall, Director of Communications & Tourism at One North East.

Visit England was officially launched in April this year following consultation which identified the need for a distinct body responsible for tourism in England. It works in partnership with Visit Britain, the Regional Development Agencies, local authorities, and the private sector, creating a national tourism strategy, optimising marketing investment, and developing the visitor experience across England.

The visit was part of an England-wide tour by Visit England bosses to introduce the new organisation to businesses and discuss its key role and objectives.

Stacy said: "To continue to promote North East England as a major tourism destination we need to work in a coordinated way with national organisations such as Visit England and VisitBritain, as well as private and public organisations in the North East.

"Today's meeting has been vital in developing this relationship and has given the region a chance to share its priorities for tourism and to find out more about Visit England's future plans.

"Tourism is a major part of the region's economy, contributing almost £4bn and employing more than 60,000 people."

This year the region has taken advantage of more people holidaying at home with occupancy levels for the first six months up on last year. And 63% of attractions have seen a rise in visitor numbers for the first six months of the year.

Lady Cobham said: "It has been an absolute pleasure to be in North East England today. The region is a great example of partnerships working together to enhance the visitor experience and to provide a coordinated service for both visitors and businesses alike.

"Visit England looks forward to working closely with Regional Development Agencies such as One North East to drive forward the tourism strategy for England."

Tourism Planning

Tourism is one of many activities in a community or region that requires planning and coordination. This bulletin provides a simple structure and basic guidelines for comprehensive tourism planning at a community or regional level. Planning is the process of identifying objectives and defining and evaluating methods of achieving them. By comprehensive planning we mean planning which considers all of the tourism resources, organizations, markets, and programs within a region. Comprehensive planning also considers economic, environmental, social, and institutional aspects of tourism development.

Two Sides of Tourism Planning

Tourism planning has evolved from two related but distinct sets of planning philosophies and methods. On the one hand, tourism is one of many activities in an area that must be considered as part of physical, environmental, social, and económic planning. Therefore, it is common to find tourism addressed, at least partially, in a regional land use, transportation, recreation, economic development, or comprehensive plan. The degree to which tourism is addressed in such plans depends upon the relative importance of tourism to the community or region and how sensitive the planning authority is to tourism activities.

Tourism may also be viewed as a business in which a community or region chooses to engage. Individual tourism businesses conduct a variety of planning activities including feasibility, marketing, product development, promotion, forecasting, and strategic planning. If tourism is a significant component of an area's economy or development plans, regional or community-wide marketing plans are needed to coordinate the development and marketing activities of different tourism interests in the community.

A comprehensive approach integrates a strategic marketing plan with more traditional public planning activities. This ensures a balance between serving the needs and wants of the tourists versus the needs and wants of local residents. A formal tourism plan provides a vehicle for the various interests within a community to coordinate their activities and work toward common goals. It also is a means of coordinating tourism with other community activities.

Like any planning, tourism planning is goal-oriented, striving to achieve certain objectives by matching available resources and programs with the needs and wants of people. Comprehensive planning requires a systematic approach, usually involving a series of steps. The process is best viewed as an iterative and on-going one, with each step subject to modification and refinement at any stage of the planning process.

There are six steps in the planning process:

1. Define goals and objectives.

2. Identify the tourism system. a) Resources b) Organizations c) Markets
3. Generate alternatives.
4. Evaluate alternatives.
5. Select and implement.
6. Monitor and evaluate.

***Step One*:** Defining Goals and objectives. Obtaining clear statements of goals and objectives is difficult, but important. Ideally, tourism development goals should flow from more general community goals and objectives. It is important to understand how a tourism plan serves these broader purposes. Is the community seeking a broader tax base, increased employment opportunities, expanded recreation facilities, better educational programs, a higher quality of life? How can tourism contribute to these objectives?

If tourism is identified as a means of serving broader community goals, it makes sense to develop plans with more specific tourism development objectives. These are generally defined through a continuing process in which various groups and organizations in a community work together toward common goals. A local planning authority, chamber of commerce, visitors bureau, or similar group should assume a leadership role to develop an initial plan and obtain broad involvement of tourism interests in the community. Public support for the planning process and plan is also important. Having a good understanding of tourism and the tourism system in your community is the first step toward defining goals and objectives for tourism development. The types of goals that are appropriate and the precision with which you are able to define them will depend upon how long your community has been involved in tourism and tourism planning.

In the early stages of tourism development, goals may involve establishing organizational structures and collecting information to better identify the tourism system in the community. Later, more precise objectives can be formulated and more specific development and marketing strategies evaluated.

***Step Two*:** Identifying Your Tourism System When planning for any type of activity, it is important to first define its scope and characteristics. Be clear about exactly what your plan encompasses. A good initial question is, "What do you mean by tourism?" Tourism is defined in many ways. Generally, tourism involves people travelling outside of their community for pleasure. Definitions differ on the specifics of how far people must travel, whether or not they must stay overnight, for how long, and what exactly is included under travelling for "pleasure". Do you want your tourism plan to include day visitors, conventioneers, business travellers, people visiting friends and relatives, people passing through, or seasonal residents?

Which community resources and organizations serve tourists or could serve tourists? Generally, tourists share community resources with local residents and businesses. Many organizations serve both tourists and locals. This complicates tourism planning and argues for a clear idea of what your tourism plan entails.

You can begin to clarify the tourism system by breaking it down into three subsystems:

(1) tourism resources,

(2) tourism organizations, and

(3) tourism markets.

An initial task in developing a tourism plan is to identify, inventory, and classify the objects within each of these subsystems.

Tourism Resources are any: (1) natural, (2) cultural, (3) human, or (4) capital resources that either are used or can be used to attract or serve tourists. A tourism resource inventory identifies and classifies the resources available that provide opportunities for tourism development. Conduct an objective and realistic assessment of the quality and quantity of resources you have to work with. A suggested classification to help obtain a broad and organized picture of your tourism resources.

Tourism Organizations combine resources in various proportions to provide products and services for the tourist. A partial list and classification of organizations that manage or coordinate tourism-related activities. It is important to recognize the diverse array of public and private organizations involved with tourism. The most difficult part of tourism planning is to get these groups to work toward common goals. You should develop a list of these organizations within your own community and obtain their input and cooperation in your tourism planning efforts. Setting up appropriate communication systems and institutional arrangements is a key part of community tourism planning.

Table 1. Tourism Resources

Natural Resources

* Climate-seasons.
* Water resources-lakes, streams, waterfalls.
* Flora-forests, flowers, shrubs, wild edibles.
* Fauna-fish & wildlife.
* Geological resources-topography, soils, sand dunes, beaches, caves, rocks & minerals, fossils.
* Scenery-combinations of all of the above.

Cultural Resources

* Historic buildings, sites.
* Monuments, shrines.
* Cuisine.
* Ethnic cultures.
* Industry, government, religion, etc.
* Anthropological resources.
* Local celebrities.

Human Resources

* Hospitality skills.
* Management skills.
* Seasonal labour force.
* Performing artists-music, drama, art, storytellers, etc.
* Craftsman and artisans.
* Other labour skills from chefs to lawyers to researchers.
* Local populations.

Capital

* Availability of capital, financing.
* Infrastructure-transportation roads, airports, railroads, harbours & marinas, trails & walkways.
* Infrastructure: utilities water, power, waste treatment, communications.

Table 2. Tourism Management Organizations and Services

Off-site: Coordination, planning, technical assistance, research, regulation:

* Federal & state departments of commerce, transportation, & natural resources.
* Federal, state, regional, & local tourism associations.
* Educational organizations & consultants, e.g., Travel & Tourism Research Association; U.S. Travel Data Centre; Travel Reference Centre, Univ. of Colorado, Boulder; Travel, Tourism, & Recreation Resource Centre, Michigan State University.
* Travel information & reservation services.

On-Site: development, promotion and management, of tourism resources:

* Federal agencies, NB. departments of commerce, transportation, & land management agencies.
* State agencies, NB. departments of commerce, transportation, & land/facility management agencies.
* Local government organizations, e.g., visitor information, chamber of commerce, convention & visitor's bureaus, parks.
* Businesses:
  - Accommodations: Hotels, motels, Lodges, resorts, bed & breakfast cabins & cottages, Condominiums, second homes, Campgrounds.
  - Food & Beverage: Restaurants, Grocery, Bars, nightclubs, Fast food, Catering services.
  - Transportation: Air, rail, bus; Local transportation: taxi, limo, Auto, bicycle, boat rental; Local tour services.
  - Information: Travel agencies, Information and reservation services, Automobile clubs.
  - Recreation Facilities & Services: Winter sports: ski, skating, snowmobile areas; Golf courses, miniature golf; Swimming pools, water slides, beaches, tennis, handball, racquetball courts, bowling alleys; Athletic clubs, health spas; Marinas, boat rentals and charters; hunting & fishing guides; Horseback enterprises; Sporting goods sales & rentals.

- Entertainment: Nightclubs, amusement parks, spectator sport facilities; Gambling facilities: casinos, horse racing, bingo; video arcades; art galleries and studios, craft shops, studios, demonstrations; performing arts: theatre, dance, music, film; historic & prehistoric sites; museums: art, history, science, technology; arboreta, zoos, nature centres,
- Special festivals and events.
- Support services: Auto repair, gasoline service stations; boat & recreation vehicle dealers and service; retail shops: sporting goods, specialities, souvenirs, clothing; health services: hospitals, clinics, pharmacies; laundry and dry cleaning; beauty & barber shops; baby-sitting services; pet care; communications: newspaper, telephone; banking and financial services.

Tourism Markets: Tourists make-up the third, and perhaps most important subsystem. Successful tourism programs require a strong market orientation. The needs and wants of the tourists you choose to attract and serve must be the focus of much of your marketing and development activity.

Therefore, it is important to clearly understand which tourism market segments you wish to attract and serve. Tourists fall into a very diverse set of categories with quite distinct needs and wants. You should identify the different types of tourists, or market segments that you presently serve or would like to serve. This may involve one or more tourism market surveys. A visitor survey identifies the size and nature of the existing market and asks the following questions:

* What are the primary market segments you presently attract?
* Where do they come from?
* What local businesses and facilities do they use?
* What attracted them to the community?
* How did they find out about your community?
* How satisfied are they with your offerings?

A market survey (usually a telephone survey) also can be conducted among households in regions from which you wish to attract tourists. This type of study helps identify potential markets, and means of attracting tourists to your area.

Tourism market Segments

In a general tourism plan, some clear target tourism market segments should be identified. You might begin by defining the market area from which you will draw most of your visitors.

The size of your market area depends upon the uniqueness and quality of your "product", transportation systems, tastes and preferences of surrounding populations, and your competition. Identifying the market area will help target information and promotion and define transportation routes and modes, competition, and characteristics of your market.

Next, divide your travel market into the following trip length categories:

* day trips from a 50 mile radius,
* day trips from 50 to 200 miles away,
* pass-through travellers,
* overnight trips of 1 or 2 nights (most likely weekends), and
* extended overnight vacation trips.

After you have an idea of your market area and kinds of trips you will be serving, begin defining more specific market segments like vehicle campers, downhill skiers, sightseers, family vacationers, single weekenders, and the like. These segments can be more clearly tied to particular resources, businesses, and facilities in your community.

What kinds of products and services are likely to attract each of these groups? Tourist needs as well as their impact on the local community are quite different for day tourists versus overnight tourists.

Areas catering primarily to weekend traffic will experience large fluctuations in use. In deciding the relative importance of these different segments, communities need to assess both their ability to provide required services (do you have enough rooms?), as well as the demand for different types of trips relative to the supply and your competition.

The Environment: A tourism plan is significantly affected by many factors in the broader environment. Indeed, one of the complexities of tourism planning is the number of variables that are outside of the control of an individual tourism business or community.

These include such things as tourism offerings and prices at competing destinations, federal and state policy and legislation, currency exchange rates, the state of the economy, and weather. These factors are discussed more fully in Extension bulletin E-1959 as part of the market environment analysis.

Local populations also must be considered in tourism planning. As they compete with tourists for resources, they can be significantly affected by tourism activity, and they are an important source of support in getting tourism plans implemented. A survey of local residents can be conducted to assess community attitudes toward tourism development, identify impacts of tourism on the community, and obtain local input into tourism plans. Public hearings, workshops, and advisory boards are other ways to obtain public involvement in tourism planning. Local support and cooperation is important to the success of tourism programs and should not be overlooked.

Table 3. Tourism Market Segments

I. Geographic market areas.

II. Trip categories.

Day Trips:

* short-within 50 miles.
* long-up to 200 miles.

Pass through traffic:

* day visitors.
* overnight stays.

Overnight Trips:

* weekend.
* vacation.

III. Activity or trip purpose.

Outdoor Recreation:

* Water-based Activity:
  - Boating: sail, power, cruise, row, canoe, water ski.
  - Swimming: pool, beach, sunbathing, scuba.
  - Fishing: charter, sport, from pier, boat, shore, ice.
* Land-based Activity:
  - Camping: back packing, primitive, developed.
  - Hiking: climbing, beachcombing, spelunking.

- Hunting.
- Skiing: downhill, cross country.
- Snowmobiling.
- Bicycling.
- Horseback riding.
- Picnicking.

* Air-based Activity:

- Aeroplane rides, hang gliding, ballooning, parachuting.

* General:

- Nature study.
- Photography or landscape painting.
- Viewing natural scenery.

Sightseeing & Entertainment:

* Visiting particular sites or areas:

- historic or prehistoric.
- cultural.
- amusements.
- scenic.

* Attending particular events, shows, or demonstrations:

- ethnic festivals.
- sporting events.
- performances.
- agricultural fair or festival.
- boat show.
- shopping.

Other Primary Purpose for Trip:

* Visiting Friends & Relatives.

* Convention & Business/Pleasure.

Step Three: Generating Alternatives. Generating alternative development and marketing options to meet your goals requires some creative thinking and brainstorming. The errors made at this stage are usually thinking too narrowly or screening out alternatives prematurely. It is wise to solicit a wide range of options from a diverse group of people. If tourism expertise is lacking in your community, seek help and advice outside the community.

Tourism planning involves a wide range of interrelated development and marketing decisions. The following development questions will get you started:

* How much importance should be assigned to tourism within a community or region?
* Which general community goals is tourism development designed to serve?
* Which organization(s) will provide the leadership and coordination necessary for community tourism planning? What are the relative roles of public and private sectors?

Tourism marketing decision questions include:

* Segments: Which market segments should be pursued; geographic markets, trip types, activity or demographic subgroups?
* Product: What kinds of tourism products and services should be provided? Who should provide what?
* Place: Where should tourism facilities be located?
* Promotion: What kinds of promotion should be used, by whom, in which media, how much, when? What community tourism theme or image should be established?
* Price: What prices should be charged for which products and services. Who should capture the revenue?

Step Four: Evaluating Alternatives. Tourism development and marketing options are evaluated by assessing the degree to which each option will be able to meet the stated goals and objectives. There are usually two parts to a systematic evaluation of tourism development and marketing alternatives:

(1) Feasibility analysis, and

(2) Impact assessment.

These two tasks are interrelated, but think of them as trying to answer two basic questions:

(1) Can it be done?, and

(2) What are the consequences?

A decision to take a specific action must be based both on feasibility and desirability.

Feasibility Analysis: First, screen alternatives and eliminate those that are not feasible due to economic, environmental, political, legal, or other factors. Evaluate the remaining set of alternatives in more detail, paying particular attention to the market potential and financial plan. Make a realistic assessment of your community's ability to attract and serve a market segment or segments. This requires a clear understanding of the tourism market in your area and how this market is changing. Also carefully identify your competition and evaluate your advantages and disadvantages compared to the competition.

Plan toward the future because it takes time to implement decisions and for your actions to take effect. Therefore, look at the likely market and competition for several years to come. Review forecasts for the travel market in your area, if available. Careful tracking of tourism trends in your own community can help identify changes in the market that you will have to adapt to.

Impact Assessment: When evaluating alternative development and marketing strategies it is important to understand the impacts, both positive and negative, of proposed actions. Table 4 presents a classification of economic, environmental, and social impacts associated with tourism development. The types of impacts and their importance vary across different communities and proposed actions. Generally, the size, extent, and nature of tourism impacts depend upon:

* volume of tourist activity relative to local activity.
* length and nature of tourist contacts with the community.
* degree of concentration/dispersal of tourist activity in the area.
* similarities or differences between local populations and tourists.
* stability/sensitivity of local economy, environment, and social structure.
* how well tourism is planned, controlled, and managed.

Look at both the benefits and costs of any proposed actions. While tourism development can increase income, revenues, and employment, it also involves costs. Evaluate benefits and costs of tourism development from the perspectives of local government, businesses, and residents.

Table 4. Impacts of Tourism

Economic Impacts:

* Sales, revenue, and income.
* Employment.
* Fiscal impact-taxes, infrastructure costs.
* Prices.
* Economic base & structure.

Environmental Impacts:

* Lands.
* Waters.
* Air.
* Infrastructure.
* Flora & fauna.

Social Impacts:

* Population structure & distribution.
* Values & attitudes.
* Education.
* Occupations.
* Safety & security.
* Congestion & crowding.
* Community spirit & cohesion.
* Quality of life.

Impacts on Local Government Local government provides most of the infrastructure and many of the services essential to tourism development, including highways, public parks, law enforcement, water and sewer, garbage collection and disposal. Evaluate tourism decisions with a clear understanding of the capacity of the local infrastructure and services relative to anticipated needs, and take into account both the needs of local populations and tourists.

A fiscal impact analysis evaluates the impact of tourism on the community's tax base and local government costs. It entails predicting the additional infrastructure and service requirements of tourism development, estimating their costs, deciding who will pay for/provide them, and how. Will tourism generate increased local government revenue through fees and charges, local sales or use taxes, increased property values or property tax rates, or larger local shares of federal and state tax revenues?

Impacts on Business and Industry Businesses that are directly serving tourists benefit from sales to tourists. Through secondary impacts, tourism activity also benefits a wide range of businesses in a community. For example, a local textile industry may sell to a linen supply firm that serves hotels and motels catering primarily to tourists. A local forest products industry sells to a lumberyard where local woodcarvers or furniture makers buy their supplies. They in turn sell to tourists through various retail outlets. All of these businesses benefit from tourism.

If most products and services for tourists are bought outside of the local area, much of the tourist spending "leaks" out of the local economy. The more a community is "self-sufficient" in serving tourists, the larger the local impact.

Impacts on Residents Local residents may experience a broad range of both positive and negative impacts from tourism development. Tourism development may provide increased employment and income for the community. Although tourism jobs are primarily in the service sectors and are often seasonal, part time, and low-paying, these characteristics, are neither universal nor always undesirable. Residents may value opportunities for part time and seasonal work. In particular, employment opportunities and work experiences for students or retirees may be desired.

Residents may also benefit from local services that otherwise would not be available. Tourism development may mean a wider variety of retailers and restaurants, or a better community library. It may also mean more traffic, higher prices, and increases in property values and local taxes. The general quality of the environment and life in the community may go up or down due to tourism development. This depends on the nature of tourism development, the preferences and desires of local residents, and how well tourism is planned and managed.

Steps Five And Six: Implementation, and Monitoring and Evaluation. We will not attempt a complete discussion of decisionmaking, plan implementation, and monitoring, but these are critical steps in the success of a tourism plan. A set of specific actions should be prescribed with clearly defined responsibilities and timetables. Monitor progress in implementing the plan and evaluate the success of the plan in meeting its goals and objectives on a regular basis. Plans generally need to be adjusted over time due to changing goals, changing market conditions, and unanticipated impacts. It is a good idea to build monitoring and evaluation systems into your planning efforts.

Concluding Remarks

Successful tourism planning and development means serving both tourists and local residents. The bulletins in this series stress the importance of a market orientation for attracting and serving tourists. This market orientation must be balanced with a clear view of how tourism serves the broader community interest and an understanding of the positive and negative impacts of tourism development.

Remember, tourism should serve the community first and the tourist second. Tourism development must be compatible with other activities in the area and be supported by the local population. Therefore, the tourism plan should be closely coordinated with other local and regional planning efforts, if not an integral part of them.

Abu Dhabi Races Ahead with Tourism Plans

With events such as The Formula One Grand Prix on the docket, Abu Dhabi is rapidly emerging as a world-class tourism destination and is threatening to overtake Dubai as the top tourism hot spot in the UAE.

The capital of the UAE has long taken a back seat to Dubai on the tourist map, preferring to take a more low-key approach and focusing on business tourism rather than the leisure market.

However, in the wake of the global financial crisis the two emirates have seen the fortunes of their tourism industries go in opposite directions.

Dubai's high-flying hotel sector, like much of the rest of the world, witnessed declines in occupancy and revenues throughout the downturn, while Abu Dhabi has risen to new heights.

In the first half of 2009, average daily room rates in Dubai fell 24% while rates in Abu Dhabi rose 5% from the same period the year before, said a report by Hogg Robinson. And with room rates averaging $275 a night in the first half of the year, Abu Dhabi replaced Dubai as the most expensive major destination in the world, according to Hotels.com's hotel price index.

Detailed Strategy

Abu Dhabi's rise as a tourist destination is the by-product of a carefully thought-out strategy by the government that involves billions of dollars of investment in infrastructure, marketing, and tourism developments.

In the immediate future, the emirate is expecting to receive a large influx of visitors for two high-profile events: the Abu Dhabi Grand Prix-the UAE's first-ever Formula One race-which will take place in the first week of November on Yas Island, and the FIFA Club World Cup UAE 2009, which will be held the following month.

In addition to attracting race fans, the F1 event will also serve as a showcase for the $36bn island development, whose offerings when completed will include high-end resorts, golf courses, and a Ferrari theme park.

Seven new hotels will open this month on the island in time for the race, including the 500-room Yas Hotel from real estate developer Aldar, two Rotana-managed properties, two IHG hotels, a Radisson Blu by Rezidor, and the UAE's first Park Inn.

Diversified Growth

In addition to hosting the up coming sporting events, the capital is also hoping to gain a reputation as a cultural hub with the development of Saadiyat Island, which will be home to the Guggenheim and Louvre museums.

The emirate's tourism efforts are being aided by the rapid growth of Abu Dhabi International Airport, which is now directly linked with 69 destinations and served by 32 airlines. Passenger traffic at the airport has grown significantly over the past five years, almost doubling from five million a year to nine million.

Abu Dhabi is on target to receive 1.5 million hotel guests in 2009, which would be on par with last year's performance, Ahmed Hussein, Deputy Director General, Abu Dhabi Tourism Authority (ADTA) told AME Info.com. 'Next year we are looking for a 10% increase with a 15% increase slated each for 2011 and 2012, so that by the end of 2012 we will reach our goal of receiving 2.3 million hotel guests,' he noted.

To help meet these ambitious targets, approximately 10,000 rooms are under construction in the emirate to be delivered in the remainder of this year and through 2010, with a further 7,000 to come on line in 2011. Overall, the emirate hopes to have 24,000 available rooms by 2012.

Infrastructure Milestone

Last week Abu Dhabi achieved a milestone in its infrastructure with the opening of a bridge that links Saadiyat Island with the city for the first time. The city also opened a 27km expressway which stretches from Port Zayed on the Abu Dhabi mainland to the Shahama District, passing through Saadiyat and Yas islands.

Abu Dhabi also recently launched a new hotel rating system aimed at raising hospitality standards in the emirate and providing accurate and consistent information for tourists. All hotels and hotel apartments in the emirate will have to display their rating by the end of October.

Two years in the making, the rating system will also give tour operators 'increasing confidence in selling the destination and being able to recommend suitable accommodation to their clients', Hussein said. 'Everyone will now know what to expect from hotels with specific star ratings-it gives us added product integrity.'

Oversupply Risk

Currently Abu Dhabi is very much undersupplied, hence the steep rise in price of its hotel rooms, said John Podaras, associate director at TRI Hospitality Consulting. 'Whereas a year ago people doing business in Dubai were staying in Abu Dhabi where hotels were cheaper, now the reverse is true,' he said.

With so much supply coming on board, there is a risk that the emirate will be temporarily oversupplied, but since most of these projects are geared around major government initiatives, they should generate their own demand, he noted.

'Their master plans maps out a strategy for the future that is quite comprehensive and is very much vested in the development of Abu Dhabi as a capital city, with these various other developments all working with each other to provide a demand synergy which is not only targeting tourism but also the complete industrial and social framework of Abu Dhabi,' Podaras said.

Hotel room supply is rising much more rapidly in Dubai, where inventory is expected to reach 54,000 in 2010, up 40% from 2008. With so much being invested in the tourism industries in Abu Dhabi and Dubai, is it realistic to expect that both emirates, which are just one hour's drive apart, can sustain this growth?

Podaras believes the answer is yes. 'Dubai and Abu Dhabi coexist well because Dubai has chosen a different path. They are more focused on foreign investment and bringing private developers in to develop what it is going to actually be. And they are looking at a bigger market.'

'Abu Dhabi is looking at a much tighter integration between each of the districts they are developing across the whole of the emirate. It is a different strategy and the positioning is different, so they should complement each other very well,' he said.

Kerala Tourism plans 'Onam Road Show'

Kerala Tourism is teaming up with leading players in the tourism industry to organise a four-day road show covering Thiruvananthapuram and adjoining Kollam districts from Sunday.

This has been designed as a strategy to beat the 'recession blues' likely to get reflected in fall in tourist arrivals in the State during the peak season starting concurrently.

According to sources, projections are that the beach destination of Kovalam stands to suffer the worst during the peak season kicking off in October, signalling at large the dire fortunes of centres of tourist importance in the southern districts.

Titled 'Onam Road Show,' the event will feature at least 150 tour operators from across the country, including from Delhi, Mumbai, Kolkata, Hyderabad and Chennai, and second-tier cities such as Nagpur, Pune and Ahmedabad.

At least, 35 properties in Kollam and Thiruvananthapuram districts will be part of the four-day jamboree.

Houseboat operators and homestay owners are also expected to pitch in.

Tourism Caravan

The South Kerala Hoteliers' Forum (SKHF) and the Association of Professionals in Tourism (APT) will combine with 'Incredible India' and Kerala Tourism to host the caravan that will travel from Thiruvananthapuram variously to Kovalam, Poovar, Chowara, Varkala and Kollam. Besides calling at the properties in Kovalam, Poovar, Chowara, Kollam and Varkala and taking time off for a backwater cruise in adjoining Kollam, the tour operators will sit down for business-to-business ('B-2-B') session.

With the State Government-sponsored Onam celebrations set to roll out in Thiruvananthapuram city, the organisers have made arrangements to take the tour operators to the Kanakakkunnu Palace grounds, the hub of the celebrations, on Tuesday.

South African Tourism Plans to hold in-country Road Show in India in August 2009

Successfully Completes Road Shows in Mumbai, Ahmedabad, New Delhi

South African Tourism (SAT) plans to hold an in-country road show in India in August this year and is planning to invite around 100 agents from India and South Africa. This was informed by Medha Sampat, Country Head India, South African Tourism, who said that the idea behind holding an in-country road show is to spread awareness about South African and Indian tourism's products mutually among agents of both countries. The in-country road show will be held in a five-star hotel; however, the exact venue and date are not yet decided.

SAT, last week, concluded its three-city road show in New Delhi. The other two cities were Mumbai and Ahmedabad. A delegation of 25 companies showcased their products to the travel trade in these three cities. The delegation companies comprised various travel and tour operators, game parks, hoteliers etc. from South Africa. "The response has been amazing and the delegates have been busy highlighting the products to the travel trade. This clearly shows that India is an important market for South Africa. The tourism board is looking at educating the travel trade through interactive workshops and presentations at our various events like road shows and Incountry Famil," said Sampat.

The tourism board will soon launch a luxury and indulgence guide and adventure sports guide as a supplement with a leading Indian magazine, which will act as a ready reckoner for travel agents and end consumers to plan their holidays. These guides will cover various aspects of Luxury Tourism and Adventure Sports Tourism. In addition to this, South Africa will host FIFA World Cup in 2010, which will further boost tourist arrivals to the country. This year, SAT has active promotional strategies wherein it will advertise on billboard, television and on the web. It will also advertise in children's magazines such as Robin Age published in Pune and Mumbai for special distribution in schools. Sampat believes that children can have greater influence in their families for building awareness about South Africa whereby the country will receive large number of tourist from India. Commenting on the total number of Indian tourists visiting South Africa, Sampat said about 60 per cent of travellers are form northern India while the remaining 40 per cent are from western India and southern regions of India

CR-T1021: Tourism Plans and Investment Designs in Wild Protected Areas

Project Description: Out of the 10 Protected Areas benefited with the Program currently under development by the Bank, only 3 of them have Sustainable Tourism Plans with their corresponding priority investments identified. Furthermore, even for these three Areas, the priority investments are only listed and located on a map, while they lack a detailed design of the corresponding works. Since such detailed designs and environmental permits are required to execute the investments financed with the Loan, the present technical cooperation (TC) will help develop Sustainable Tourism Plans for the 7 Protected Areas that don't have such Plans and produce detailed designs and environmental assessments for the investments already identified in the three Sustainable Tourism Plans already finished. The implementation of this TC to develop the mentioned products will be carried out during the period before approval of the Loan Program by the Costa Rican parliament, and will be very useful to assure a fast start-up of the Program, to help execute the Loan within its scheduled execution period.

Tourism Plans Road Show in Middle East

Seychelles will host a road show around the Middle East countries in November to promote our archipelago as tourism destination.

Alain St. Ange, the director of tourism marketing at the Seychelles Tourism Board (STB) said this on Monday after taking part in the Arabian Travel Market (ATM) tourism trade fair held in Dubai from May 5 to 8.

He said the road show will help consolidate what his delegation launched during the fair.

"We will go with groups of people from the private sector here. The airlines flying to Seychelles will join us to go right round this part of the world to ensure Seychelles is perceived as a destination that is ready to receive clients. We will meet tour operators and the press," he said.

He said STB will invite Vice-President Joseph Belmont who is the Minister for Tourism to launch the show, "so as to set the tone that it is an official event".

Seychelles delegation at the ATM was headed by the STB chairman Maurice Lousteau-Lalanne.

Also present at the ATM were members of the local trade – 7°South, Creole Travel Services, Select Seychelles, Starwood Hotels in Seychelles, the Fisherman's Cove and the Barbarons Beach Hotel and Berjaya Hotels and Casino.

Saying their mission was successful, the delegation said it is now evident the Middle East remains a potential market for Seychelles "with virtually daily flights coming to Seychelles from that region".

"A large number of travel agents visited the Seychelles' stand, asked about our country and established contacts with our destination management companies.

The delagates met with many tour operators including Emirates Holidays, Qatar Holidays and DNATA. They also met with the two major airlines flying to Seychelles from the Middle East – the Emirates Airline and Qatar Airways.

"Our meetings with the media were attended by representatives of magazines, newspapers and radio stations who showed keen interest to learn about Seychelles and to feature it" said Mr. St. Ange.

"The trade fair reconfirmed what we knew about the possibilities existing for Seychelles in the Middle East. This part of the world remains the area with the biggest growth potential."

"We must not sit and wait for business to grow by itself because that will be a long process, we need to be pro-active and the new STB will be spearheading a revamped marketing strategy for that market to ensure we get our fair share of that market."

Tourism Plans for Andamans go on, Tsunami Notwithstanding

The Andaman and Nicobar Islands are still seen as tourist havens, even after being ravaged by the tsunami in December 2004. The tourism policy of Andaman and Nicobar Island 2003 listed its objectives as large-scale, resource-intensive tourism, opening more islands for tourism, attracting private investment for high-end eco-tourist resorts and obtaining relaxation of the Coastal Regulation Zone (CRZ) rules. The model is still followed, with minor modifications, after the December 2004 disaster.

The question, however, is: can islands like the Andamans, vulnerable to tsunamis and other natural disasters, depend exclusively on tourism? In 1996, the Commission on Sustainable Development warned small island states in the Caribbean and Pacific about the perils of over-reliance on tourism.

Their warnings ring true for the Andaman and Nicobar Islands as well.

But the island's administration continues to milk dry the tourism cow. Of course, post-tsunami there were neither tour operators nor tourists. Souvenir, handicraft and small hotel businesses—the mainstays of an island economy dependant on tourism—were destroyed.

Take Murugan's experience for instance. The tides devastated his hotel and house in Wandoor, a south Andaman island. The family of six adults and a child got refuge in a temporary shelter.

The roadside coffee shop they built fetched them a pittance. "Only revival of tourism could save our living," were Murugan's mother's words back then. Tourism had admittedly become important for local communities. But Murugan's story also holds another lesson: in islands prone to natural disasters, the vulnerability of the tourism economy is several fold higher.

This is a lesson that's not yet been learnt. "The hotels here violate CRZ rules. It is only in some cases in Havelock that locally available materials have been used," says Samir Acharya of the Port Blair-based Society for Andaman and Nicobar Ecology (SANE).

Lip Service

Of course there is a master plan for the islands that speaks of enabling environmentally sustainable tourism. But it needs closer scrutiny.

Consider one proposed by the Union ministry of tourism in association with the World Tourism Organisation. It envisages lowering the limits of coastal development prohibition zones in areas earmarked for development for tourism. The threshold will be down to 50 m behind the high-tide line (HTL) if this UN Environment Programme funded plan gets underway. It is currently 200 m behind HTL. The plan also calls for de-reserving forest lands in areas marked for tourism.

All this contravenes the Supreme Court order of 2002 directing that tourism be low impact and sensitive to the ecological context of the islands. This master plan was, of course proposed before the tsunami, but continues to remain on the anvil. Plans to link Port Blair in the Andaman and Nicobar Islands with Phuket in Thailand is also on the anvil. This, despite the fact that tourism development in Phuket has cost the country its reefs, forests and subsistence agriculture dearly.

Various tourism development plans for Andamans dating to the pre-tsunami days stress the need to improve air connectivity. Experiences from across the world have, however, shown that contrary to boosting the tourism industry, over-connectivity has deepened the tourism crisis during natural disasters and contributed to the rapid downfall of tourism dependant economies.

No Regulation

Post-tsunami, there is a sense of urgency to continue what was planned for the islands before the catastrophe. The Parliamentary Standing Committee on Home Affairs prepared a background note on developmental activities in the Andaman and Nicobar Islands. Among its objectives is: "Promotion of resorts preferably by private sector." It recommends that more islands with tourism potential need to be opened for investment by the private sector.

Even as the islands struggle to recover from the devastation wrought by tsunami, the administration has selected 50 sites on 15 islands to set up "eco-friendly" hotels and resorts. SANE says these plans violate CRZ rules on Havelock and other islands. It has recommended banning backpackers during the revival stage.

The tsunami showed how catastrophic the impacts of unplanned and unregulated development could be. But the lesson, obviously, has not yet been learnt.

Madhya Pradesh Lines up Big Tourism Plans

The Madhya Pradesh government is considering a proposal to launch 'Malwa Odyssey', a luxury train on the lines of 'Palace on Wheels' in Rajasthan, linking its tourist destinations with Bhopal. A suggestion in this regard was first made by the Indian Heritage Hotels Association which submitted a detailed report to Chief Minister Shivraj Singh Chouhan last week on ways to boost tourism in the state.

The association has stressed on the need for running such a train, to attract domestic and foreign tourists, connecting Ujjain, Indore, Shivpuri, Gwalior, Satna, and Jabalpur with Bhopal.

The association in its Annual General Meeting (AGM) held in Bhopal also submitted a list of heritage sites to be developed as hotels and resorts, saying it would open a huge tourism opportunity for the state. Chouhan, who met Railway Minister Lalu Prasad and Tourism Minister Ambika Soni in New Delhi some time back, has sought Central assistance to boost tourism in Madhya Pradesh.

He also requested the railway minister for a rail ink for the historical sites in the state to provide easy access to places of tourist importance in Madhya Pradesh which are either untapped or did not get prominence due to lack of connectivity.

Chouhan, however said the state government was doing its best to connect the destinations through road to facilitate entry of tourists, both Indian and foreigners, by road.

Efforts were also being made to connect major tourist attractions including Sanchi, Khajurao, Gwalior, Pachmarhi, Datia, Jabalpur, Rewa, Tikamgarh, Mandu and Maihar (Satna).

The state government was also planning a Son-et-Lumiere (light and sound) show at Mandu fort, Ujjain temples, old Taj Mahal at Bhopal, Islam Nagar fort near Bhopal in conjuction with Indian National Trust for Art and Cultural Heritage (INTACH) or India Tourism Development Corporation.

Initiatives have also been taken to improve visitors' management system at Mandu Fort, as well as at Sanchi, Orchha, Bhimbetka, Gwalior on the lines of Ajanta and Ellora caves, the official said.

The state government was also considering to form a state level Tourism Advisory Board, consisting of government departments and tourism industry stake holders, to promote tourist destinations through marketing and publicity materials, tourism friendly literature and signages in different languages.

The government also plans to establish better connectivity to these places through train and air, by air taxis and helicopter services. Apart from this, the state's tourism ministry has identified 16 private properties owned by the erstwhile royals to convert them into heritage tourism destinations. The objective is to promote tourism and protect the heritage sites, the official said. The list of 16 heritage sites were forwarded by the Indian Heritage Hotels Association to the chief minister in its recent meeting in Bhopal. These include assets at Berasia (Bhopal), Chhatarpur, Gwalior, Datia, Jabalpur, Mandu, Tikamgarh and Maihar (Satna). These sites were selected by the Madhya Pradesh Tourism Ministry after a survey to convert them into heritage hotels, lodges and resorts.

Association president Maharaja Gaj Singh told *PTI* that the chief minister has invited them in November for a detailed discussion on the development of these sites. The 16 sites identified by the state government are Alipura Garhi (Chhatarpur), Datia Qila, Pili Kothi and Narayan Singh Mahal (Datiua), Raja Gokul Ballabh Mahal (Jabalpur), Jamnia Gaddi (Mandu), Tikamgarh Palace, and Maihar Qila (Maihar, Satna).

At present, Welcome group has six heritage hotels at Bhopal, Jabalpur, Kanha, Bandhavgarh, Pachmarhi and Ujjain. Rakesh Mathur, President, ITC Welcome hotels group told *PTI* that we are looking at the proposals on whether these sites could be developed or not, as per our system but emphasised that the government should develop proper infrastructure first. Madhya Pradesh has every thing except necessary infrastructure for the development of tourism in the state Maharaja Gaj Singh said. Pushparaj Singh, Maharaja of Rewa and a member of the Heritage Hotels Association told PTI that he was in favour of developing museum hotels besides adventure, health and educational tourism for foreigners and provide them detailed information and recreation with regard to India adventure, herbal healthcare and history.

Puerto Rico Tourism Plans Major European Expansion

The Executive Director of the Puerto Rico Tourism Company (PRTC), Terestella Gonzalez Denton, along with the Secretary of the Department of Economic and Commercial Development, Ricardo

Rivera Cardona, recently travelled to Europe to launch an aggressive strategic plan aimed at further developing Puerto Rico's presence in Europe.

Their visit initiated an agenda of meetings and presentations by PRTC representatives that included visits to six cities and four countries with very high potential for tourism and economic development in Puerto Rico.

"The development of the tourism industry is intricately linked to the economic progress that our people enjoy. In connection with the economic policies designated by our Governor, PRTC is working toward short-and long-term goals defined by our Strategic Tourism Plan to enhance Puerto Rico's tourism offering, providing substantial economic impact to the Island, said Gonzalez Denton. "One of our priorities is strengthening the Island's presence in Europe, a region which has the potential to increase visitors to Puerto Rico, and in turn economic growth to the Island."

PRTC meetings were held in London, Madrid, Naples, Rome, Genoa and Frankfurt with airlines, cruise lines, wholesalers and travel agents to grow relationships and establish partnerships between Puerto Rico and the European tourism industry to increase the number of European visitors and their length of stay on the Island.

A key objective for Puerto Rico was to enhance air access and introduce direct flights from diverse European destinations, making Puerto Rico a more attractive vacation and business destination for Europeans. PRTC met with British Airways, Princess Cruises, Virgin Holidays, Delta Airlines, Iberia, MSC Cruises, Top Cruises and several wholesalers and travel agents, among others.

Gonzalez Denton explained that at the beginning of the current term, there existed a certain distance between the European and Puerto Rican markets. Consequently, PRTC has begun to implement a number of strategies to amplify the presence of the Island in this market by actively participating in tourism trade shows, investment forums and meetings with industry leaders to better understand their needs and to promote Puerto Rico's extensive tourism offering.

PRTC held a successful meeting with its long-term partner, Iberia, who reaffirmed its commitment to work together with PRTC to develop additional traffic on its San Juan route. The plan includes trying to attract European tourists to experience the Caribbean through multi-destination packages which would include a connection in San Juan as part of the roundtrip ticket.

Dubai World scraps most of its Rwanda Tourism Plans

According to the Rwanda Development Board (RDB), which promotes foreign investment in the east African state, Dubai World has pulled out of all but two of its ambitious tourism schemes, citing the impact of the global financial crisis.

The planned portfolio had included a sprawling luxury hotel and golf course in the capital Kigali, and an eco-lodge in Akagera national park, but these projects have been shelved, said Clare Akamanzi, deputy CEO at RDB.

Banahaw Ecotourism Plans Studied

Research activities are now being conducted to boost the ecotourism potential of mystical Mt. Banahaw in the Southern Tagalog Region.

The studies are being done under the project "A Comprehensive Diagnostic Assessment to Enhance Eco-Tourism in Barangay Kinabuhayan and Taytay in Mt. Banahaw-San Cristobal Protected Landscape (MBSCPL)." The project is implemented by the Department of Environment and Natural Resources-Ecosystems Research and Development Bureau (DENR-ERDB) headed by Director Marcial Amaro Jr.

Funding it is the Department of Science and Technology-Philippine Council for Agriculture, Forestry and Natural Resources Research and Development (DOST-PCARRD) headed by Executive Director Patricio Faylon. Both DENR-ERDB and DOST-PCARRD are based in Los Banos.

Supporting the project are the DENR-Region 4-A; DENR-Protected Area and Wildlife Bureau (PAWB); Quezon Provincial Government Environment and Natural Resources Office; South Luzon State University (SLSU) in Lucban, Quezon; the local government units of Dolores Quezon, Majayjay, Laguna, and San Pablo City; Department of Tourism – Region 4; and Laguna Lake Development Authority.

"Our goal is to provide scientific knowledge that will serve as a basis in establishing an eco-tourism management plan for the MBSCPL," said Dr. Lope Calanog, ERDB senior science research specialist who is project leader. "We also intend to encourage stakeholders to support and strengthen the project," he said.

ERDB recognizes the area's vital role in the economy, religious belief, culture, and health of the people. It is also a habitat for plants and animals.

However, the ERDB research project team noted the alarming condition of the area. Tons of garbage have been dumped and left everywhere because of the increasing number of tourists and pilgrims, most especially during the Lenten season.

India: Sikkim to Expand Tourism Plans

The resurgence of the campaign for Gorkhaland in Darjeeling in the last few years has diminished tourism to Darjeeling but increased interest in the neighbouring state of Sikkim, which has seen so much tourism growth that it is embarking on a plan to become a year-round destination. The Himalayan state has many natural attractions to make it an adventure sports haven, including the world's third highest mountain, Kanchenjunga. Its mix of Buddhist and Hindu beliefs gives it strong cultural appeal as well. Earlier this year, general strikes in Darjeeling by Gorkhaland supporters kept tourists out of the area for long periods of time, which also affected travel to Sikkim because the road there from the plains passes through the Darjeeling hills. The Gorkhaland campaign remains active and could affect travel to Darjeeling for some time to come.

Confident of LTTE rout, Sri Lanka Draws Tourism Plans

The Sri Lankan government plans to turn the country's war-torn northeastern region, which boasts of some of the island's most scenic beaches, into a tourist attraction as the decades-old conflict with the Tamil Tigers seems to be nearing its end.

'The battle between the Sri Lankan forces and the LTTE (Liberation Tigers of Tamil Eelam) is nearing its end, paving way for long awaited peace and development in these areas. Against this backdrop, Sri Lanka Tourism is gearing up for a post conflict strategy focusing on development of the tourist potential in the northeast,' said an official statement issued here.'The development of the east is of specific focus for the government as the beaches there are some of the best in the island.

Arugam Bay is famous as one of the best surfing destinations in the world,' the statement said.

The tourism department is making plans for development of other locations such as Passikudah and Trincomalee, which have excellent beaches for recreation.

The strategies on the anvil include a marketing blitz for Sri Lanka Tourism, promoting the area as an 'off the beaten track' vacation, promotional activities with hotels and the national carrier Sri Lankan Airlines. The primary markets are the French, German and British tourists, the statement said.

Nearly 250,000 post cards will also be distributed among visitors while a discount booklet will be distributed with over 50 discount offers for a range of hotels and shopping malls.

The statement said that in 2005, the LTTE had over 16,000 sq km under its control.

But within two-and-a-half years of start of a military campaign in 2006, the government has managed to squeeze the rebels to 8 sq km area in the northeastern part of the country.

'As the conflict is drawing to an end in the north, there is a sense of relief among all citizens that peace, prosperity and development is close at hand.'

5

Tourism Human Resources

Overview and Objectives

Tourism sector industries generate a large number of highly diversified jobs in different branches of activities such as hotels, restaurants, travel agencies, tour operators, leisure activities and passenger transport. Human resources are a key element in ensuring the quality and content of tourism products. There is a growing need for skilled manpower able to meet the needs of a changing environment and to maintain the competitiveness of tourism enterprises. In a competitive labour market, the tourism sector suffers from a relatively poor image and finds it difficult to retain employees on a long-term basis.

In the light of these changes and challenges, strategies for managing and promoting human resources have a central role to play in a sustainable development approach to tourism. The understanding of labour markets in the tourism sector remains inadequate.

The effects of the new practices introduced by certain governments and the industry to improve skills and enhance the competitiveness of the sector in the labour market have not been widely shared and assessed. The pursuit of strategies to promote the skills needed in a globalizing tourism industry must be continued. Lastly, in a context of liberalisation and globalization of tourism services, the possibility of harmonising the differing regulatory approaches to the labour market in the tourism sector should be discussed in depth with all actors on national and international labour markets.

The conference on "Partnership in Vietnam's tourism human resources development" was the second annual conference held by the

Vietnam Human Resources Development in Tourism Project at the Furama Resort, Danang.

The conference on "Partnership in Vietnam's tourism human resources development" was the second annual conference held by the Vietnam Human Resources Development in Tourism Project at the Furama Resort, Danang. It took place on 30th November 2006 and followed the conference on "Vietnam tourism human resources development and regional integration", held in Hanoi during December 2005. Among the 150 participants (international and local) were representatives from Vietnam National Administration of Tourism, the National Steering Committee for Tourism, representatives from ministries, the Delegation of the European Commission to Vietnam, the Secretariat and National Tourism Organisations of ASEAN, provincial tourism departments, representatives from hotel and travel enterprises, tourism training institutions, etc. By attending the conference, regional tourism representatives viewed the activities of Vietnam's tourism human resources development at first hand, and Vietnam's tourism administrators and experts gained further insights into regional practice.

After the introduction by Mr. Jozef W.M. van Doorn, the Co-Director of the Project, presenting the Project's outputs to date, Mr. Jaap Funnekotter, Chairman of the conference, reviewed outcomes from last year's conference. Conference 2006 followed the same format as last year's edition in order to create continuity, so speakers from both public and private sectors presented their experience of partnership in tourism human resources development. After the presentations, there was a panel discussion on the topic: "Has any synergy between the educational institutes and the hotel and tourism enterprises taken place in the last year?" along with some further discussion of best practices.

Attending the Gala Dinner, participants were introduced to a training DVD on housekeeping according to the Vietnam Tourism Occupational Skill standards (VTOS). This is one of 14 videos that will be developed by the Project as support for training. It is designed to be used in conjunction with the Project's Trainer Development Programme training manuals, or for entry-level staff training within enterprises.

The second day of the conference was spent on a field trip to My Son and Hoi An, two of the World Cultural Heritage sites.

UNWTO Summit Discusses New Reforms for Human Resources in Tourism

According to the January 2009 issue of the UNWTO World Tourism Barometer, in 2008, international tourist arrivals worldwide increased by 2%. The Middle East registered the best performance among all world regions with 11% growth in international tourist arrivals in 2008 over the previous year. Based on passenger traffic data from worldwide airports for the first two months of 2009, it appears that of all the world regions, the Middle East is the least affected the global crisis thus far. It was the only region with a positive traffic growth of 3.1%.

The Summit has demonstrated the complexity of labour markets in the region and constantly returned to the fact that the rapid growth of tourism in the region brings with it issues of labour supply gaps and skills shortage. The Qatar Summit identified a range of human resource challenges for tourism.

Tourism employment comes in the shape of a broad spectrum of roles and varied tasks, across all sectors benefiting in particular women, the young and the unemployed. Tourism is well known as a generator of employment, so a well-trained tourism labour force will both anticipate and remedy such economic crisis.

Longer-term challenges include the poor image and lack of understanding of tourism jobs, and the fact that availability of labour and skills is highly variable across the region.

The Summit addressed these issues into four key pillars of reform:

> *The first one is the need to change the mindset of both governments and communities towards employment in tourism, as well as the need for the industry to change its view of human resources to one that values peoples, their skills and knowledge, develops them and treats them as valued resources.*

The second pillar means the necessary understanding of labour markets. With the Tourism Satellite Account (TSA) methodology, it is now easier to understand and measure labour markets, diagnose the problems and act. Governments will be able to plan for future labour and training needs.

Re-engineering education and training, the third pillar of reform, will demand national standard setting in partnership with industry and the development of articulated and legible pathways to allow students to gain qualifications, and ensuring that programmes are creatively packaged, innovative and utilize edge technology for lifelong learning.

The final pillar of reform relates to the work and leadership of both the UNWTO and Qatar in addressing these challenges and engaging stakeholders to craft new strategies. The solutions demand the forging of effective partnerships and working together to implement the recommendations of the Summit, as well as the findings of the Bali conference and the ILO's Decent Work Agenda.

Professor Chris Cooper, summit moderator, commented:

'The message of this summit is clear-tourism is a people-centred industry, the sector must invest in the education, training and development of the labour force to secure the future." Alongside the Qatar Summit, the 32nd meeting of the United Nations World Tourism Organisation commission for the Middle East took place on April 22nd and 23rd.

Dr. Taleb Rifai, Secretary General of the UNWTO, presented to the members of the Commission a snapshot analysis of the current economic downturn's impact on tourism in the Middle East and North Africa. Country briefs and response measures were also discussed in a regional perspective. The Secretary General presented the research programme: "Tourism towards 2030", as well as regional training programmes and possible adjustments in the light of the global economic downturn. This meeting of the UNWTO commission for the Middle East reviewed the preparations for the eighteenth session of the General Assembly of UNWTO, that will take place in October 2009.

On the occasion of the conclusive press conference, Mr. Ahmed Al Nuaimi, Chairman of Qatar Tourism and Exhibitions Authority, declared, "I am really pleased Qatar Tourism and Exhibitions Authority hosted this UNWTO conference. With 250 participants, we shared different experiences and had very fruitful discussions that enabled us to create a roadmap with four pillars of reform. Tourism is a key economic pillar and we need to ensure the future of the region."

Tourism Human Resources in Shortage, Weak

Weakness in Foreign Languages

According to statistics of the Vietnam National Administration of Tourism (VNAT), the total number of workers in the tourism sector is around 850,000 at present, including 250,000 workers who directly serve tourists. However, only around 50% of them are trained.

The tourism sector needs an additional around 35,000 trained workers each year but training centres can provide only about one-third of the volume.

Besides weakness in terms of professional knowledge and skills, the largest disadvantage of Vietnamese tourism workers is foreign languages. Besides English, the major foreign language, Vietnamese tourism workers are also weak in other languages like Japanese, Chinese and Korean.

Specifically, the number of Korean travellers coming to Vietnam is increasing fast (ranking second after Chinese) but Vietnam currently has only 50 tour guides who can speak Korean. For the Japanese market, the third potential market of Vietnam, just 8% of tour guides speaking Japanese can fluently speak this language.

English: Below Standards

As part of a programme to raise the quality of the tourism human resources of Vietnam, the Test of English for International Communication (TOEIC) Vietnam has currently made a survey to test the English ability of some occupations in the tourism sector.

Based on the need of using English in each position, TOEIC Vietnam performed nearly 400 surveys of the need for English skills of nearly 200 hotels of three-to five-star standard and travel agents throughout the country. The major subjects of those surveys are directors, human resource managers and direct managers like team leaders who clearly understand the need for English of their staffs.

Random surveys of 1,000 workers at tourism companies reveal that the English skills of most of them are low and below the standards required by their employers.

The survey also points out that hotels of higher standard have high percentages of staffs that don't meet standards in English.

According to Doan Hong Nam, director of the TOEIC Vietnam, the standards that we apply to evaluate the English skills of tourism workers is to ensure the minimum quality of service so the survey results show that the English skills of surveyed tourism workers is even lower than the low standards.

This is not only a hindrance for the development of the tourism sector but others as more and more foreign tourists are coming to Vietnam to seek business opportunities. Mr. Nam said that Vietnam needed to quickly improve the quality of the current tourism services by issuing common standards for foreign languages for each position in the tourism sector. This is a necessary foundation for the training tasks of training centres and tourism firms.

Philippines: DoT holds 1st Tourism Human Resources Congress Today

In line with the Department of Tourism's (DoT) "Gandang Pilipinas, Galingng Pilipino" GP2 campaign which aims to further develop tourism services, DoT Secretary Roberto "Obet" M. Pagdanganan will lead the launch of the 1st Tourism Human Resources Congress today at The Peninsula Manila Hotel.

Pagdanganan said the activity, which will be held until tomorrow (June 18), will further enhance the industry's manpower resources enabling them to meet the international standard of tourism service.

"In order to cope with the global challenges in the tourism industry, we must arm ourselves with the changes in the international market. Quality services and products are fast becoming a norm in the new global economy. We must make precedence by introducing speed, innovation and customization," he added. The Tourism Industry Board Foundation, Inc. (TIBFI) organizer of the event, is a non-stock, non-profit institution composed of representatives from the government (which include the DoT as founding member), private and labour sectors.

The foundation aims to provide manpower development, ensuring an adequate supply of trained workers who will match the skills of the labour force with the manpower requirements of the tourism industry.

TIBFI invited distinguished guest speakers including World Tourism Organization (WTO) representative Professor Chris Cooper to talk about the TedQual Programs, which focuses on quality service assurance and the WTO products and services standard.

Human resources directors and heads of various tourism sub-sectors, associations, industries and government agencies (TESDA, CHED, Government Training Institutions), tour guides and the academe including state colleges and universities are invited to participate in the two-day assembly. Registration fee is R1,500.

Tourism Human Resources

The Tourism Industry

* Tourism is the largest earner of foreign exchange in Antigua & Barbuda.
* It is estimated to be the largest employer when all enterprises providing direct and indirect services to the sector are combined.

Tourism and The Labour Force

* Though there are no definitive statistics on the labour force involved in tourism in Antigua & Barbuda, a recently produced Antigua & Barbuda Tourism Strategic Plan (2005-2009) stated that surveys suggest that approximately 8,000 workers or 26% of the total labour force could be employed in the accommodation sector: hotels, guests houses, apts., villas, with other sectors of the industry creating a further 3,000 jobs.
* Therefore, the total number of workers employed in the tourism sector is 11,000 representing 40% of the total labour force.
* When compared to statistics which indicate that globally tourism accounts for 8.3% of the total work force, Antigua & Barbuda can clearly be considered one of the, if not the most tourism dependent countries in the world.

Tourism Human Resource Audit

- A tourism human resource audit should be conducted to give true and reliable data relating to the tourism work force.
- Such data must of necessity address the issues of:
  * male/female ratio.
  * age-group.
  * percentages employed in various sectors, for e.g. accommodation, F&B, yachting, adventure, etc.
  * education.
- It is important to note that the paucity of reliable data is a regional problem and unfortunately the experience of many economic sector areas, the tourist industry being no exception.

* As recently as February 2006, CTO in recognition of this situation include the improvement of data collection as one of its Key Focus Areas.

Assessing Training and Education Needs

* In a 1998 study conducted by the CTO within its member countries, the focus was on assessing training and education needs for the tourist industry in the new millennium.
* The study was designed to provide data about the nature and level of skills deficiencies in the industry so as to inform Caribbean Governments and regional training agencies where their training priorities should lie and how their training $$ should be spent.
* It was intended that the study would provide a launching pad for tourism training in this millennium as well as to represent a benchmark for future studies.
* The information provided on HRD in the Caribbean region as a whole (through this study), is quite applicable to the Antigua & Barbuda situation.

Highlights of the Study

- Industry Profile:
  * Majority of the responding organizations were from the Accommodation sector, with F&B and Transportation sectors running a far second and third behind, respectively.
  * Events and Conferences and Attractions provided least number of respondents. Reflection of the level of development of these two sectors in the Region.
  * ¼ less than 5 yrs. Old/¼ over 20 yrs. Old
  * Majority of the work force permanent full-time staff with more males than females (56% to 44%). Over 70% under 40 yrs.
- Recruitment and Retention of Staff:
  * Local and regional tourism training institutions are not a preferred source of employees.
  * Most organizations recruit their staff from secondary/

primary schools and from university, depending on the level of staff.

  * Many also hire from their competitors or from among relatives and friends.
  * Generally, managerial and professional vacancies are difficult to fill.
  * Also difficult to recruit skilled/semiskilled persons in the accommodation, F&B and adventure sectors.
  * Unskilled positions generally easier to fill.

- Industry Training and Development.
  * Only 1/3 of the establishments in the survey had a full-time trainer on staff.
  * Training done primarily in customer relations and technical skills.
  * Of 1/3 of the respondents providing information on training budget, 2/3 spent less than US$5,000 for a year.
  * On the job-training is the preferred training strategy for all levels of staff.
  * External trainers and local tourism training institutions used but to a much lesser extent.
  * Local and regional tourism training institutions are not perceived by the industry as important or effective in satisfying its training needs.

Training Needs Identified

- General and technical training deficiencies identified at different staff levels.
- General training needs:
  * Interpersonal skills deficiencies found at all staff level.
  * Marketing and management deficiencies at managerial level.
  * Computer literacy and foreign language deficiencies (also found).
- Technical training needs: these were linked to deficiencies within the various tourism sectors; accommodation, food & beverage, transportation, travel trade, adventure and tourism services.

Accommodation

Technical Skills:

* Culinary.
* Maintenance.
* Housekeeping.
* F & B Service e.g. Bartending, Waiting.
* Front Desk.
* Tour Guiding.
* Customer Service.
* Other, e.g. Safety & Security, Tourism Awareness, Computer.

Food & Beverage

Technical Skills:

* Culinary.
* Food & Beverage Services e.g. Bartending, Waiting.
* Customer Service.
* Other e.g. Inventory Control, Maintenance, Cashing, Sanitation.

Transportation

Technical Skills:

* Ticketing.
* Customer Service.
* Tour Guiding.
* Maintenance.
* Other e.g. Customer Procedures.

Travel Trade

Technical Skills.

* Ticketing.
* Tour Guiding.
* Other e.g. Customer Service, Maintenance, Computer, Marketing.

Adventure

Technical Skills.

* Tour Guiding.

* Watersports e.g. Boating, Sailing, Scuba Diving, Fishing.
* Maintenance.
* Culinary.
* Other e.g. Customer Service, Golf, Housekeeping, First Aid, Piloting, Food & Beverage Service.

Tourism Services

Technical Skills:

* Statistical Analysis.
* Property Management.
* Environmental Protection and Conservation.
* Public Relations.

Attractions

Technical Skills:

* Tour Guiding.
* Customer Service.
* Other e.g. Ticketing, Heritage Conservation/Preservation, Museum Management, wildlife Management, Environmental Protection, Marine Biology, Heritage Studies.

Meeting Technical Training Needs

The Antigua and Barbuda Hospitality Training Institute.

Antigua & Barbuda Hospitality Training Institute.

* Mission To provide training and education with a commitment to excellence; to equip persons to work in the Tourism and Hospitality Industry with a high degree of professionalism.

One Year Certificate Programme

* Food and Beverage Service.
* Training at Skills level.
* Basic Cookery.
* Knowledge & Skill in basic Cookery techniques.
* Housekeeping.
* Training at skills level.

2 Year Diploma Programme

- Culinary Arts.
    * In depth practical and supervisory level training.

- Reception and Sales.
  * Broad base training in Front Office Operations.
- Hospitality Management.
  * Knowledge and skill to embark on supervisory or junior management level.

Accreditation

- 2 Year Diploma Programmes.
  * Hospitality Management.
  * Culinary Arts.
- University of the West Indies.
- Monroe College.

In-House Training Courses

* Butchery Techniques.
* Caribbean Cuisine.
* Art and Science of Service.

Collaboration with Tourist Operators

- Federation of Tour Operators.
  * Food Hygiene & Safety Seminar.
- Antigua Hotels and Tourist Association.
  * Internship for students.
  * Membership on Board & Sub committees.
  * Partnership with Trans Caribbean Marketing & US meat Export Federation.

Regional Collaboration through Caribbean Tourism Organization

* Core Curriculum.
* Certified Hospitality Educator.
* Dynamic Supervisory Management Programme.
* Quality Assurance and Articulation.
* Human Resources Conference.
* Promotional material on careers in Tourism.

Sources of Funding

* Consolidated funds of Antigua & Barbuda Government.

* European Commission.
* Organization of American States.
* First Caribbean International Bank.

Annual Government Funding Allocation

* ABHTI Estimates 2006 $1.8 Mil 21%.
* ASC (Antigua State College) $5.7 Mil 65%.
* ABICE $1.2 Mil 14%.
* ABIIT unknown-
* Total $8.7 Mil 100% Revenue (2005) ABHTI $122,000 ASC $60,000.

Conclusion

* Tourism is a high-touch, high-tech, high-involvement industry where it is the people who make the difference.
* The ability for the industry to succeed and the future performance of the industry and related activities will depend largely on the skills, qualities and knowledge of its employees. Indeed the challenges facing the industry can only be met successfully by a welleducated, well-trained, bright, energetic, multi-lingual and entrepreneurial work force.
* A high-quality tourism work force can only be achieved through high standards of tourism education and training which in turn will impact our destination's ability (the ability of our twin-island state) to compete successfully in this global competitive industry.

Special Symposium on APU's Tourism Human Resource Development Project

A Special Symposium on APU's Tourism Human Resource Development Project titled, "Creating the Future of Regional Tourism-Fostering Talent for the Next Generation" was held at Beppu B-con Plaza on Friday, March 10. The Special Symposium was held for people who will have major roles in the future of the tourism and service industry including the accommodation sector.

APU's "Tourism Human Resource Development Project" was commissioned by the Ministry of Economy, Trade and Industry as part of its "AY2005 Power Supply Regional Service Human Resource

Development Business." Mr. TOYODA Masakazu, Director-General of the Commerce and Information Policy Bureau of the Ministry of Economy, Trade and Industry Mr. TOYOTA Masakazu commenced the first-half of the Symposium with a keynote address on "Promoting the Hospitality Industry." Afterwards, the President of the All Japan Ryokan Association, Mr. Kohara Kenji gave a presentation on "Creating a Tourism-Orientation Nation."

A panel discussion on the theme of "Creating the Future of Tourism in Kyushu-Regions and Business/Developing Human Resources" took place in the second-half of the Symposium. The participants listened attentively to the animated exchange of ideas.

Human Resources in Tourism: Still Waiting for Change

People, we are frequently told, are a critical dimension within the successful delivery of tourism services.

"The story of successful tourism enterprises is one that is largely about people—how they are recruited, how they are managed, how they are trained and educated, how they are valued and rewarded, and how they are supported through a process of continuous learning and career development" points to recognition of this philosophy in the mission statements of hotel companies within which a far higher proportion of respondents include reference to human resources than is the case within manufacturing companies.

This contemporary manta or reflection of the "'soft' rhetoric of people as an organisations's greatest asset" (Bolton & Houlihan, 2007) may have had equal veracity at various points during the development of tourism over the past century, but the practical implications of the claim, in terms of the role that people play, will have been interpreted in different ways at varying points over this timeframe.

In particular, there is an apparent paradox in the dramatic evolution of the global tourism sector over the past half century and, within it, the manner and conditions in which people deliver tourism services which have remained timeless in many respects but also subject to significant change.

During this time, debate about labour intensity, the number and cost of people required to work in many areas of tourism, has sat alongside discussion of the skills necessary to deliver quality tourism services, remuneration and working conditions and the role that technology plays in both supporting and changing this delivery.

Inevitably, the nature of such analysis has shifted over time. In particular, the profile of many workers, but by no means all of those in tourism's work force, and the role that they play in the labour markets of developed countries, has been subject to change. At the same time, tourism work must be set alongside major economic and labour market restructuring in post-industrial societies so that direct comparison between tourism and traditional heavy manufacturing work in shipyards, mines and steel works, which formed an important element of the early industrial sociology in the emerging service sectors, is less relevant.

Rather, tourism work now sits alongside and is compared to other activities within the dominant service economy of developed countries, and the analytical paradigm for such comparison should consider employment opportunities in the sector in a rather different light. Whether such comparison leads to a positive assessment of work in tourism is a matter that we shall consider in this paper.

In the light of external change, in developed countries, certain aspects of human resource management in tourism demonstrate evolution over time, by responding across the breadth of the contextual environment within which tourism is located, notably in sociocultural, marketrelated and technological terms. Such change is clearly evident within some of the large tourism companies in transport, entertainment and accommodation.

At the same time, the headlines of change do not reflect reality across the totality of the tourism sector. There is a real contrast between major multinational tourism companies and smaller operators within some sub-sectors of tourism (particularly accommodation and restaurants) which contain areas of work where many things have not changed over the past 20 years—productivity remains stubbornly low, working conditions are poor and remuneration levels are well below national averages in many countries.

In some areas of tourism, businesses have been unable to cope with the pressures of external change-induced competition so that, for example, work opportunities in traditional travel agents have declined in many countries.

By contrast to the developed world, in poorer countries, the picture is rather more homogeneous whereby much work in low labour cost economies, including that of the tourism sector, has an appearance of timelessness so that change, if any, has been at the margins of the overall employment experience.

This paper seeks to make a partial assessment of the impact of external change on the human resource environment within tourism over the past 20 years, with particular focus on work and employment themes within the sector. In addressing a topic as broad as this, there is a real danger of uncritical generalisation within a highly heterogeneous sector such as tourism.

There is real and on-going debate with regard to definitional issues in the tourism sector and this has presented some challenges in the context of this paper. Discussion here seeks to embrace an inclusive interpretation of tourism with illustrations of human resource practices across various sub-sectors. This challenge is illustrated by highlighting features such as the diversity within tourism with its various sub-sectors (accommodation, food service, transport, facilitation, heritage); the size of operations; the location of these operations; business arrangements that are in place to deliver services within tourism; and the economic context within which operations do their business.

Published empirical and conceptual analysis of human resource issues in tourism has focused disproportionately on the hospitality sub-sector and, inevitably, evidence here is substantially drawn from hotels and restaurants to the possible neglect of major areas of employment such as transport.

This is a challenge faced by others in considering human resource themes in tourism in this way. Our assessment is further complicated as a result of ambiguity in understandings of what the term, human resources and its management, encompasses. This ambiguity includes the consequences of changes that have taken place at a functional level as the traditionally accepted concept of personnel management has given way to a broader functional application in human resource management, operating as part of a company's wider business and strategic environment.

Human resource themes are also applicable at both the levels of the firm and in a macronational or regional context. This paper adopts conscious selectivity in focusing on human resources in the specific context of the work place and considers whether and how the employment environment has altered over the past 20 years.

Attempting a retrospect, with regards to a theme such as human resources in tourism, presents a challenge in determining an appropriate benchmark against which to measure possible change. Notionally, a 20-year yardstick is used, taking us back to the mid-1980s. At the same time, it is important not to ignore the insights from earlier times and to consider these in a contemporary context. Conceptually, the most useful and comprehensive framework against which to judge change is that provided by Wood's (1992, 1997) consideration of work in the hotels and catering sub-sector of tourism.

While Wood's discussion purposefully does not address the breadth of what is taken to be tourism here, it provides a valuable insight into research and analysis across the largest of tourism's subsectors, but one that is both the best studied and most problematic. Wood's assessment of the evidence discussed in his book, much of it drawn from the 1970s, 1980s and early 1990s, is that Hospitality work is largely exploitative, degrading, poorly paid, unpleasant, insecure and taken as a last resort or because it can be tolerated in the light of wider social and economic commitments and constraints. Our concern here is to consider whether the context of and practice in contemporary tourism is such as to allow work in the sector to have moved significantly beyond the bleakness of this assessment and, if it has, to consider the extent to which wider contextual change has imposed itself on the management of human resource within tourism.

Therefore, this paper is concerned with assessing the nature and extent of contextual change on the management of human resources across the international tourism sector. This is a very broad aspiration, given the scope and scale of tourism as an economic activity, consisting of widely differing sub-sectors and located across virtually all communities, countries and cultures. The themes and contexts addressed here, therefore, must necessarily be selective, and include dimensions that appear to have broad salience across major tourism destinations, both established and more recently emerging.

The paper commences with a brief look back to the nature of work in tourism as depicted in early research into the sector, substantially the sources which led Wood to his bleak assessment. The paper then focuses on a number of themes which allow us to evaluate the extent of change and its impact—undertaking an assessment of the practice of the management of human resources in contemporary tourism; followed by consideration of the consequences of global and social forces on perceptions of work and careers; the impact of ICT on work and employment in tourism; changing interpretations of skills within tourism; and, finally, the increasingly diverse nature of the tourism work force in developed countries.

The paper concludes with an assessment of whether change, within these selected areas, outweighs the dead hand of the status quo that may appear to pervade tourism employment in other respects.

Where we have Come From

Recorded and formal accounts of what was and is involved with work in tourism, beyond passing fragmentary evidence, are relatively recent. One of the first in-depth pictures of aspects of tourism work comes from the 1930s and the writing of George Orwell (1933). His description of the work of the plongeur within the working hierarchy of Paris hotels is as perceptive as it is moving and, in many ways, provides a benchmark against which much subsequent sociological discussion of working conditions in the tourism and, particularly, the hospitality industry can be assessed.

Orwell's approach is to describe his own experiences of working in Paris hotels and his relationship with colleagues and superiors from the perspective of the foreigner and the 'down and out'. Orwell's objective is to expose the extremes of social deprivation during the depression of the 1930s and, as such, is one of extreme pessimism. He considers the work of the plongeur in its social context.

When one comes to think of it, is strange that thousands of people in a great, modern city should spend their waking hours swabbing dishes in hot dens underground.

The question I am raising is why this life goes on—what purpose it serves, and who wants it to continue, and why I am not taking a more rebellious attitude. I am trying to consider the social significance of the plongeur's life. I think I should start by saying that the plongeur is one of the slaves of the modern worldy he is no freer than if he were bought and sold. His work is servile and without art; he is paid just enough to keep him alive; his only holiday is the sack.

Orwell was looking at society through eyes that would have sat comfortably alongside that of other social commentators of the time, such as Seebohm Rowntree, a major contributor to understanding of poverty in Britain during the first half of the twentieth century. Rowntree prepared three assessments of social conditions in York and these progressively analysed the causes of poverty at the respective times, gathering increasing optimism as greater levels of state engagement with work, health and related social matters impacted upon British society and the work place.

Rowntree and Orwell shared a faith in the capacity of the state to improve the lives of the poor and were part of a movement that spawned detailed analysis of social conditions through initiatives such as the Mass Observation project. This included the domain of work.

Political change since the early 1980s has, perhaps, weakened the basis of such faith, notably through the impact of "Thatcherism" in thc UK and elsewhere.

Therefore, contemporary commentators question the basis for optimism in assessing the conditions of work to which may service workers, including those in tourism, are exposed. For example, Orwell's disenfranchised and marginalised world of the plongeur has resonance in more contemporary studies.

Toynbee (2003), walking in the footsteps of Orwell, describes life in low-wage Britain, including her experiences in sectors of hospitality, and this world is not dramatically different from that of 1930s Paris within which Orwell talks about work as a "sort of delirium" within which "we were going as though we had only five minutes to lively. It was now that the tempo of the shift moved from hard and fast work to a controlled frenzy of washing up. Conversation came to an end. We were, I suppose, cheaper than industrial dishwashing machines but we imitated them quite well.

The tough reality that is presented in early descriptions, building from the influence of Orwell's analysis and, subsequently, reflected in Toynbee, can also be seen in other more recent studies of the industry (primarily but not exclusively, hospitality), many of which focus on problematic aspects of tourism work in a comparative social context. There is, therefore, little evidence, notwithstanding exceptional best practice examples by some organisations from across the industry, that working conditions in tourism have improved significantly from the time of Wood's pessimistic assessment.

Returning to Orwell, however, also brings us to his depiction of the craft and professionalism of hospitality work, set so starkly alongside the grim "below stairs" experience out of which the waiter seamlessly moves.

> It is an instructive sight to see a waiter going into a hotel dining-roomy. As he passes through the door a sudden change comes over him. The set of his shoulders alters; all the dirt and hurry and irritation have dropped in an instant. He glides across the carpet with a solemn priestlike air. And you cannot help thinking, as you see him bow and smile, with the benign smile of the trained waiter, that the customer (is) put to shame by having such an aristocrat serve him.

There is another side of the coin which perhaps depicts tourism work in a rather more positive light and one which highlights what Riley et al. describe as "the obvious contrast of glamour on the one hand and low menial status on the other". One example of the glamour, that is equally precise and from the same period as Orwell, is represented by the accounts written, between 1937 and 1942, in five books by Ludwig Bemelmans.

However, in contrast to Orwell, Bemelmans is the supreme optimist and describes hotel work from the point of view of someone climbing to a senior position in a luxury New York hotel.

In a similar vein, Le Sueur's (1998) account of managing a hotel in Tibet presents an upbeat and very positive perspective on work at this level within the industry. The airline sector was also, historically, held up as the glamorous side of work in tourism, particularly in the 1950s and 1960s, and was widely depicted as one of the "blue ribbon" sectors for employment within personal services.

During the 30-year period up to airline deregulation in the United States (1979) and Europe (early 1990s), it is fair to say that employment in the airline sector, especially with major national flag carriers, had many of the security of tenure attributes of public sector work and its attendant benefits combined with high levels of trade union participation while, at the same time, offering perceived glamour and a "fun" image. Calder describes this in terms of "A job in aviation—glamorous, secure, well-paid employment".

This perspective of airline work has been critically assessed by, among others, Bolton and Boyd (2003), Tyler and Taylor (1998) and Williams (2003) and further debunked as a result of high profile disclosures relating to work in some new model low-cost airlines as well as post-2001 changes within the aviation industry.

However, vestiges of status and glamour remain current in the airlines of many developing countries. Other areas of tourism work, while not well covered in the research literature, also point to clear ambiguities with respect to the working environment of tour guides and tour operator representatives.

Riley's application of internal labour market models to tourism provides a useful analytical framework in seeking to understand and explain the lack of significant change with respect to working conditions and remuneration in many areas of tourism work.

Riley and Szivas describe tourism as a sector "where easily acquired, transferable skills coexist and engender weak internal labour markets in organisations that economically are bound to a rate of throughput." Riley (1996) points to the features of employment in these conditions in terms of recruitment, training and professional status and, unsurprisingly, notes that many areas of tourism work typify weak internal labour market characteristics.

Alongside this assessment sits trends within most developed countries and within economic regions such as the European Union which point to erosion of elements of labour market strength and a general weakening of work place conditions. This has been driven by both economic and labour relations changes, notably in countries such as Spain and the United Kingdom but also, to a lesser extent, in bastions of strong labour markets such as France and Germany.

As we shall see, access to low cost sources of migrant labour in many European countries has further acted to weaken labour market conditions within businesses in the tourism sector, despite the introduction of national minimum wage levels in countries such as Ireland and the UK.

An assessment of progress or otherwise, with respect to the overall working conditions and remuneration levels of tourism employees, does not provide clearcut answers.

There has been progress in some countries and within many, particularly, larger, organisations where case examples of high quality working lives and opportunity can be found to match that within most other sectors of the economy. However, much tourism work remains menial and under-valued and the plethora of smaller organisations also point to working environments where practices remain Dickensian and show little change from Wood's let alone Orwell's depiction.

Reflections on the Role of Human Resources in Tourism

The underlying premise of Failte Ireland's ground breaking strategic plan for human resource development in Irish tourism is predicated upon the argument that "good HRM practices will be adopted because they deliver bottom line profitability". This primarily economic justification for investment in HRD has underpinned much of the history of this field, whether in the guise of personnel management, strategic human resource management, high commitment management or the management of human capital, among other iterations.

This, in turn, is manifested in a range of good practices, adopted by companies recognised for their leadership in the management of people within the tourism sector. Failte Ireland (2005a, 2005b) identify a number of good practice themes, based on a study of excellence in the tourism sector in Ireland and other countries.

Bolton and Houlihan (2007), in their powerful plea to reintroduce a human dimension to our consideration of HRM, note that these dimensions are uni-dimensional in their focus on employer benefits so that they ignore any notion of reciprocity. They effectively encapsulate this oneway street in their assessment of the HRM contract in terms of its humanity.

Bolton and Houlihan's case is, on the face of it, simple. Arguments in favour of work place flexibility among other forms of accommodation and change in the work place are generally, business and employer driven. Notwithstanding blandishments that advocate recognition of employee lifestyle requirements and work-life balance, some of which is enshrined in legislation addressing matters such as paternity leave, the overwhelming evidence is that reciprocity with regard to flexibility and accommodation in the work place is relatively rare, both for remunerated employees and among volunteer workers in tourism and heritage organisations.

Bolton and Houlihan point to imbalance in the expectations of contemporary industrial relations within tourism. As a weak labour market sector, tourism in most developed countries has never been highly unionised and what strength trade unions may have offered in seeking greater reciprocity in the human resource contract has been eroded further in recent years.

High profile disputes in international tourism companies have taken place in recent years, primarily in larger organisations located in transport related sub-sectors. Examples of these include disputes in Irish Ferries, Gate Gourmet.

Unions have succeeded in achieving partial amelioration of employer plans, but in no sense can these be taken as indicative of change in a general labour market process which is designed to weaken the position of employees within the sector.

Indeed, in the wider context of services, especially in smaller businesses, Korczynski argues that if trade unions "are to have meaning for frontline workers, their strategies must be informed by the daily work experiences of these workers" and that strategies that are derived from such experiences are likely to appear contrary to traditional union practice.

He notes the failure of trade unions to adapt to the needs of the contemporary service economy but, in the context of most businesses in tourism, this does not really represent change from past experience within which trade unions were of but marginal relevance within the sector. There are specific contexts within which trade unions can operate effectively in tourism.

"Traditional" airlines are one example as are hotels in Dublin, Ireland where Piso (2003) reports structural factors in the local labour market as being supportive of union participation. Perhaps the main barrier to unionisation in tourism's private sector is the attitude of management. Royle (2000), in considering work in the McDonalds fast food chain across a number of European countries, identifies the strategies employed by the company to ensure that unions cannot operate effectively.

Within tourism businesses, a process of organisational delayering and the reduction in specialist human resource staff means that many human resource responsibilities have substantially been devolved to front line managers. Brewster and Larsen (1992) suggest that there are a number of reasons why many human resource activities have been devolved to line managers, and these are cost reduction, to provide a more comprehensive approach to HR Management, and to place the responsibility with the people who are most responsible for it.

Renwick's (2003) study established that line managers are now responsible for a larger number of employees than ever before, which in turn means that there are more issues in this area for them to manage. Storey (1992, 1995, 2001) suggests that if the work force is so critical to organisational success, the responsibility for human resource activities rests with all line managers and should not be left to HR specialists.

While larger organisations have undoubtedly invested in providing front-line managers with the new HR skills necessary for the responsibilities identified, there is little evidence that the majority of smaller tourism businesses have done much to meet this need. As a result, it is arguable that the quality of human resource management has deteriorated.

Approaches to human resource management that are suitable for a complex sector such as tourism remain contentious. The evidence is that larger organisations have become more professional in their application of key HR principles within the work place, but that such professionalism frequently remains absent in smaller businesses. The notion of reciprocity, which we introduced with regard to work place flexibility, can also be largely absent when organisations implement wider HR policies and practices.

People management may be recognised as a concern for all those in positions of responsibility in organisations, but there is little evidence that those charged with this responsibility have a full comprehension of what this strategic role means in practice.

This failure or neglect is not just one that is of concern at the level of the tourism firm but reflects a charge that can equally be directed at tourism development policies and practices at a community, regional or national level.

Liu and Wall are rightly critical of this neglect when they state that "tourism's human resource issues are poorly conceptualised and the many studies of tourism development approaches, both theoretical and practical, provide no consolidation of useful recommendations to situate the human dimension as an integral part of a comprehensive planning framework for tourism".

There is little evidence that this recent criticism has any less validity today than it might have done in the mid-1980s, and this is a real indictment of the large number of master plans and similar documents for tourism that have been funded by international agencies during this time.

A Global Industry, A Global Work force

The tourism sector offers many and varied opportunities for working lives across its diverse sub-sectors and at different levels throughout the world. The industry's heterogeneity, geographical spread and stochastic demand cycle provides both opportunity and challenge in terms of mapping these against the aspirations and expectations of those attracted into the tourism industry, either as new entrants to the labour force or in the context of change opportunities within their working lives.

In most developed countries, traditional models of one sector working lives, built on the notion of a logical and progressive career "ladder" represents a reality which will face fewer and fewer entrants to the jobs market in the future. For some people, this is not a concern or a fear but provides the basis for challenge and opportunity, the ability to take control of aspects of their lives and to respond to changes within the external environment in a positive manner. Unlike their grandparents, today's school leavers and college graduates are more likely to think of their working lives in terms of finite segments rather than sustained and permanent careers, viewing the future in terms of what have been called "boundaryless careers" or "fragmented futures". Sennett, in recognising this phenomenon from a somewhat different perspective, notes that "flexible capitalism has blocked the straight roadway of career, inverting employees suddenly from one kind of work into another".

The trend data in many countries also point clearly to people being more mobile in their working lives and spending less time in the same job. For example, with respect to the UK, Macauley highlights evidence that "in 1996, half of all employees had been working for the same firm for 5 years or less. This had fallen to 4 years by 2001". The same source, points to the decreasing proportion of both full-and part-time employees who had been in their current job for at least 12 months during the same timeframe.

Similarly, the same UK labour market has seen a significant increase in the proportion of people in nonpermanent jobs. McOrmond (2004) reports on changes between 1993 and 2003 which point to increasing temporary engagement by, in particular, those aged below 24 years and those aged over 50 years.

Notably, the intermediate group, both male and female, saw a decrease in temporary employment over the same time period. Given the importance of younger workers to the tourism sector, this trend is evidence of this process of fragmentation and its likely impact within the industry and has stimulated response through, for example, recruitment from new labour markets.

Notwithstanding the trend indicated here, temporary employment in the UK, by wider European standards, remains quite low at about 7% of the total work force compared to a figure of 32% in Spain, 20% in Portugal and almost 18% in Finland. The temporary employment of female workers is consistently higher than then of males throughout the European Union. The structure of tourism is particularly conducive to supporting vocational mobility, particularly because of stochastic demand within the sector. However, the working environment in many sectors of tourism is such that labour turnover is higher than in other sectors of the economy.

Weir (2003) reports labour turnover in the UK and notes that the hotel and restaurant industries display the highest job separation rates of major sectors. High labour turnover is a reflection of the work environment within tourism and also of economic prosperity and opportunity combined with changing demographic structures and increased educational opportunity in developed countries. In the Irish Republic, for example, a centralised recruitment service for craft-level courses in tourism has seen demand move from a situation of very significant under-supply of training places in the late 1980s to one today where many courses are significantly under subscribed and some have been withdrawn.

Bauman's (2005, 2006) concept of liquidity is equally effective in explaining movement from one dimension of life to another and between relationships, whether in personal or working terms. Liquidity also points to blurring in the distinctions between working and nonworking lives, or as Hochschild puts it "family life had become like 'work' and work had become more like 'home'".

Adler (2004) reinforces this notion in his discussion of how the initiation of new work place practices, based on interdependence, can spread over into the home and change domestic behaviour in terms of a weakening of traditional gender roles. Fluid movement between working life segments allow individuals frequent mobility between different sectors of the economy, periods of study within models of lifelong learning and episodes that consist of travel or volunteering sabbaticals.

Vocational mobility is greatly facilitated by recognition of the underpinning "generic" skills set which much education and working experience provides today and which permits ease of both formal (qualifications driven) and informal (experience driven) transition, particularly within the tourism sector's weak labour market conditions.

Fragmentation or fluidity may be a relatively new phenomenon in the context of many sectors of the economy, but the reality of such employment models, generally employer rather than employee driven, is well established in many areas of tourism. Writing more than a decade ago, Riley infers that, in moving towards a future of "rising insecurity of job tenure, more unsocial hours working, more uneven workflow, a greater sense of immediacy in tasks", production industries are, essentially, playing what might be called "catch down" with a range of low skills service industries, including tourism.

Fragmentation or fluidity have long been features of work in these sectors, as noted by Orwell (1933) and are driven by, among other things, employer management of stochastic demand and growing responsiveness to customer demand or whims. What is new, however, is that work place mobility and job change are increasingly employee driven, with workers unwilling to make long-term commitments to one organization or work place. Unlike the disapproval that fragmentation or liquidity in working lives may have attracted in the past, today such mobility is less likely to be seen in terms of a lack of commitment or disloyalty to an employer nor does it necessarily create a sense of fear and insecurity for those moving between various working phases.

Perceptions of working lives held by younger people today are focused more on short-term wealth accumulation or debt reduction and much less on job status, security or permanence of employment than was the case with previous generations. Therefore, within the timescale allotted to work in a particular company or sector, commitment may be strong despite the transitory nature of the employment relationship.

Alongside the flexibility which characterises working relationships within the contemporary global work force, vestiges of the past remain within the labour market.

Major cities undergoing post-industrial transformation can face the paradox of high residual, long-term unemployment, mainly within the former work force of heavy industries such as automobile manufacturing alongside a large number of unfilled vacancies in contemporary tourism businesses, most of which can only be filled from student or migrant worker labour pools.

Sennett (2006) talks about the "spectre of uselessness" which haunts post-industrial society, in his terms the result of automation and technology substitution in the industrial work place but equally relevant where communities have witnessed growth in service, notably tourism, work and parts of the work force have not been enabled to buy into this new model of employment. At the heart of the causes of this uselessness is Bauman's notion that "the impetuous growth of new knowledge and no less rapid ageing of the old combine to produce human ignorance on a massive scale, and continuously replenish, perhaps even beef up, its supplies".

At its simplest, leading businesses have already recognised the changing nature of the employment relationship and have responded by a reconfiguration of operations and service delivery at certain levels within the traditional quality spectrum. As a leader within this process, McDonalds early on accepted that they would offer, at best, transitory job opportunities for many school and college students as well as others in the work force.

Therefore, they ensured that processes can be learnt very quickly by able people who are productive within a short period of time. Both parties know very well that there will not be a long-term commitment to the working relationship but that, while it lasts, both sides seek to maximise respective benefits.

For McDonalds and similar operators, this involves streamlining and simplifying processes and relying on the energy and enthusiasm of their workers for the delivery of their services.

McDonalds have recently taken acknowledgement of the transitory nature of employer–worker relationships a step further with their announcement of the McPassport, providing opportunity for their employees working anywhere within the European Union to transfer to positions in McDonalds' shops across boundaries elsewhere in the EU, for short or longer periods of time, thus facilitating lifestyle and educational opportunity.

Other tourism businesses have recognised the value of this approach. In major cities in the UK and elsewhere perhaps half of all tourism workers are notionally full-time students. As a result, the tourism industry is configured to depend upon this source of labour and education providers have also had to adjust their delivery models accordingly. For businesses, there has been some modification of both product and technical skills demands with a greater focus on "generic skills" of communication, personality (aesthetic and emotional labour) as well as greater use of technology. Traditional training, as offered through tourism colleges in the form of formal courses and qualifications, plays a lesser role in meeting industry needs within this new model of tourism employment.

The decline in relevance of and demand for technical courses in tourism also increases the marginalisation of those with low qualifications in contemporary society (the traditional recruitment pool for such courses) who, as a result, may be further economically and socially excluded. In their place, the flexible student labour market offers employers many perceived advantages which traditional training routes do not.

Likewise, many tourism businesses in rural areas have turned to short-term labour pools of students and others from abroad, in Ireland/UK to learn English (from countries such as Spain or Germany) or for their year out (from New Zealand or Australia) as ready made, articulate and, in some cases, lower cost alternatives to local labour.

"Lifestyle"—attractive employment in Donegal, West Cork or Kerry in Ireland can be offered seasonally to workers from elsewhere in Europe at lower cost and difficulty than would be involved in drawing on local labour markets. Training required and offered is minimal and there is hassle-free disengagement at the end of the tourist season.

An extension of this employment culture is reflected in the increasing use of other flexible labour strategies within tourism. Shackleton (1998) points to the contribution of targeted part-time labour in the development of 'superservice' in food retailing.

Likewise, agency staff, in some areas of tourism employment, are of increasing importance, particularly in urban locations. Hotel housekeeping and banqueting are the main work areas where agencies provide a "just in time" model for businesses which allows for rapid response to variable demand and eliminates surplus staffing on an employer's books. This also creates an environment where longer-term employment relationships and structured longitudinal training models have little relevance. These expedient models of employment are most prevalent within the systematised, middle quality rankings and "fast" delivery sectors of the tourism sector. The concept of a career within this sector for all but a minority in positions of managerial responsibility is of limited and decreasing value.

The role of education and training in the context of transitory working lives, both within the external college environment and in industry itself, is to support mobility, mid-life entry and re-entry to the sector and development in relation to new technologies and products. This represents a fast-moving, ever-changing and challenging model of lifelong learning which, in the future, will play an important role in support of the "popular" sector of the tourism industry.

"Fragmented" and transitory employment relationships and practices may still leave problems for those "high end" businesses which remain locked within traditional skills paradigms and which employ craft personnel in the conventional mode. For them, the concept of the traditional, longitudinal career within a chosen craft area has relevance and career management in this sense requires active participation by employees themselves, their employers but also by those responsible for maintaining, managing and enhancing quality within tourism. At the same time, paying for and marketing the outcomes of such skills necessitates premium pricing and careful management of the price–value relationship.

The working lives projected for today's young people bear little relationship to the linear career models aspired by their grandparents and will be characterised by change, short-term goals and on-going renewal.

Those planning for human resource development in tourism may need to more responsive to the challenges and opportunities presented by fragmented learning and working lives and recognise, as Adler and Adler (2004) do, the diversity of motivations and interests that workers typically bring into their employment relationships with tourism sector employers. Change, with regard to this theme, has moved employee aspirations for reciprocity in the utilisation of flexibility up the agenda so that notions of work place flexibility, as introduced by Atkinson (1984) and others, can no longer be seen solely in terms of approaches that are designed to benefit organisational needs.

The response to global trends in tourism, by educational and training providers, has been mixed. Baum (2000) points to the institutional and cultural barriers to change within most educational systems, factors that mitigate against the adoption of common tourism programmes and qualifications across national boundaries, notwithstanding the intentions of initiatives such as the Bologna agreement in Europe. The range of national case studies that address educational and training themes in tourism and the wider economy also points to the intransigence of diversity.

At the same time, there has been a growth in programmes in tourism education offered to a worldwide audience online and demand for education in this field through overseas study in Australia, Hong Kong, the UK, the USA and elsewhere remains high.

However, such provision is largely structured upon demand from students from developing countries seeking to acquire skills and knowledge as imparted by academic and professional experts in the developed world.

This is a questionable model of knowledge transfer and one that Botterill and Baum (2006) describe as neo-colonial in impact. It is similar to the underpinning assumptions behind the growth of tourism education in many developing countries over the past 20 years, assumptions that see European and North American models delivery put uncritically in place in the colleges and universities of recipient countries.

The Impact of ICT on Work and Employment in Tourism

There is little questioning of the impact of technological development on all aspects of working and living in developed countries and, to an increasing extent, within the developing world as well. The impact of such change on the work place and beyond is well documented.

These assessments highlight the importance of changes in the work place linked to a wide range of issues, including perceptions of time and work intensity within the work place; organisational fragmentation; flexibility and enabling the recognition of work-life balance issues in the work place; the polarisation of skills and the decline in demand for less skilled workers; disparities in remuneration linked to use/non-use of ICT in the work place; outsourced working; home and teleworking; social inclusion, ICT and the work place; ICT and knowledge management; and technology substitution among a much wider range of concerns. These changes in the work place mirror wider adoption and use of technology within society and, in many respects, feed off familiarity with and expectations of technology that stem from everyday life. A comprehensive assessment of the impact of ICT and wider technology on the work place and working lives in tourism and beyond has the potential to be a subject for separate analysis in its own right. Here, we touch on a number of key themes and issues drawn from this discussion.

What is true, with regard to ICT in a general sense, is equally valid as an assessment of change within services and tourism and, in particular, within the context of work and employment and the changing role that people play as a result of such change. It is not an understatement to argue that ICT and wider technological change have revolutionised aspects of tourism operations (particularly distribution) while leaving others virtually untouched (food preparation and service in many smaller operations).

In terms of employment in tourism and the past 20 years, technology has had a direct effect on both the elimination of work areas and on the creation of others. Some destinations, dependent on airline and other transport stop-overs for their tourism business, have been by-passed by advances in transport technology so that the work associated with this industry may no longer exist. For example, Gander in Newfoundland, Canada, a major refuelling stop for trans-Atlantic flights until the early 1980s now no longer serves this purpose and work associated with the sector has ceased to exist.

Similarly, changes in technology mean that the work of hotel telephonists has faded and, in many cases, disappeared with the advent of automated telephones in bedrooms and guest mobile phones. The technology challenge, particularly the consumer option to purchase and manage the booking of tourism products direct with suppliers such as airlines and hotels via the Internet, has reduced the need for and changed the role of travel agents, check-in staff and others involved in work in the sector in developed countries.

Such change is dependent on the availability and quality of the technology and, in many developing countries, the role of the travel intermediary remains important in the absence of Internet or, at least, Broadband connectivity. A final example of changing or diminishing role is that of the tour guide whose work can, in part, be superseded by flexible, electronic alternatives at tourism sites, allowing choice of language and giving visitors a selection of perspectives on events and the site environment.

However, ICT in particular has also created new forms of work in tourism, notably through the application of ICT and its use in distribution and management of key functions such as yield. The advent of specialist Internet travel companies such as Expedia is clear evidence of this change, but the growth of specialist electronic distribution is complemented by website communications, marketing and booking options within virtually all "traditional" tourism companies so that the boundaries between them and e-companies has narrowed greatly. These developments have created demand for technology specialists in the tourism sector and also for new marketing and management skills in a more general sense, allowing companies to maximise the benefits they derive from ebusiness.

ICT has also changed the role of management information within the sector, allowing far greater depth and access to key information about guests and their behaviour. At the same time, it has revolutionised the management of pricing and yield so that human intervention is far less frequent than it would have been in the past.

Technology has also changed the nature of work and skills required for many employees, not least in tourism. Many areas of work have been moved from relatively skilled levels to the routine or lesser skilled. A good example of such change is in the area of hotel front office where enhanced reservations and guest management systems have reduced the training and technical skills requirements of such work by up to 90% in terms of the time required to acquire full competency. As we shall see, the technical demands of such work have been more than compensated for by the wider bundling of skills requirements within such work.

Moving Beyond Technical Skills

Tourism work has, historically, been calibrated in terms of its technical skills demands. This is most evident in the approach adopted by the International Labour Organization (1979) in their Taylorian breakdown of hospitality work into individual, measurable micro-tasks that, in turn, can be re-built into a training curriculum and assessment instrument.

On the basis of this, tourism and related service work has traditionally and widely been characterised as low skills although this stereotype is challenged in the context of hospitality by a number of authors on the basis that this represents both a technical and western-centric perception of work and skills.

In developed countries, the merging of family and working life has particular pertinence here in that many of the technical and interpersonal skills demanded of employees in tourism have close parallels with those learnt during socialisation in the home. Baum's (2006a) notion of social distance between the experience and behaviour of the tourist and employee is also of relevance here in that, in developed countries, there is considerable role crossover between the two in terms of transfer of experiences between the contexts. In less developed countries, such crossover is less likely.

Grugulis, Warhurst, and Keep (2006) talk about the evolution of what we understand to be a skill over time. In terms of tourism work, perhaps the first manifestation of change from a dominantly technical focus can be found in Hochschild's (1983) seminal study, which was one of the first to take our understanding of such work beyond the technical and professional domain, focusing on "the relational rather than the task-based aspect of work".

Hochschild's work inspired recognition of what Westwood (2004) notes are commonly referred to as 'soft skills' and, in doing so, highlights less tangible dimensions in the bundling of skills and work in tourism. Hochschild argues that service employees are required to manage their emotions for the benefit of customers and are, in part, paid to do this. Likewise, Seymour (2000) considers the contribution that this notion of emotional labour makes to work in fast food and traditional areas of service work and concludes that both areas demand considerable emotional elements in addition to overt technical skills.

Bryman defines emotional labour as relating to Employment situations in which workers as part of their work roles need to convey emotions and preferably to appear as though those emotions are deeply heldy (emotions) that are supposed to make the recipient of the emotional labour feel good about the worker and the organization for which he or she works.

Sandiford and Seymour (2002) take this definition a step further in talking about the management of emotions for financial reward. This link between human emotion and commercialisation has not been without detractors such as Wouters (1989) and Newton, Handy, and Fineman (1995). The expectations of emotional labour add significantly to the skills demands of work in tourism.

There are few areas of front-line or boundary spanning work in tourism that do not have a very evident and, in some cases, all important emotional dimension.

In many respects, as Bryman notes with respect to Disney, employees are expected to give the appearance of enjoying their work as much as visitors are enjoying their time in the theme park. Maintaining this emotional facade in working conditions that are, often, anything but conducive to such behaviour takes its toll and requires skills and the outcome of extensive training in order to be maintained.

Blythman (2005) discusses the problems that such demands present in the context of supermarket work. After several hours at a time, any urge to be cheery or pleasant was overtaken by an all pervasive, mindnumbing blankness. I began to feel spaced out, as though dulled by drugs. Any energy I might feel at the start of a shift soon ebbed away. Even if you wanted to try to be pleasant with people, after only so long it was impossible to keep it up.

The demands that emotional engagement in the work place entails have not traditionally been recognised within skills hierarchies and have either been neglected or put to one side as of lower value and status than "real" productive activities.

Bolton (2004) argues a strong case for the recognition of the skills dimensions within emotion work. She argues that emotional inputs are inherently skilled elements within the work routines, control processes and socially constructed demands that typify much service work. On this basis, Bolton argues that "emotion work is indeed skilled work which contains recognisable elements of discretionary content, task variety and employee control". Ritzer (2005) extends this notion of emotional involvement in his discussion of "simulated people". Obvious examples are Ronald McDonald and the characters to be found in Disney theme parks but Ritzer notes that "Far more important, however, is the fact that most of the people we encounter in the new means of consumption are simulations, even if they are not wearing costumes".

Ritzer argues that employers prescribe how workers look, what they say and how they behave in a more general sense with the result that "these positions can be filled by a wide range of individuals. There is little or no room for creativity or individuality".

Work with a strong emotional labour component is, however, not exclusively about theatre. Williams (2003) highlights the safety and regulatory context which trumps any considerations of service and emotional engagement with passengers in the work of airline attendants.

Safetyrelated skills may be considered to be technical in nature and this illustrates that, while some areas of tourism work may focus almost exclusively on soft or ephemeral skills, the roles of government regulation and passenger concern are such that emotional engagement must always take second place to the hard skills demands of safety in the work place.

To the requirements of emotional labour in tourism can be added the skills demands of what Warhurst, Nickson, Witz, and Cullen (2000) describe as aesthetic labour, the skills required to look, sound and behave in a manner that is compatible with the requirements of the job and with the expectations of your customers.

In many cases, aesthetic labour involves staff demonstrating the ability to respond to fashion and trend imperatives in the consumer marketplace in a way that can be socially exclusive of many groups and cultures within society. Aesthetic labour is about appearance but can also be underpinned by cultural cache, the ability of front-line staff to understand and engage culturally with their customers on terms dictated by the latter.

Thus, service staff in some tourism contexts (luxury hotels, premium airline cabins, fitness centres, oneto-one personal training or other sports tuition) need to be able to make informed conversation with their guests or clients about politics, music, sport and almost any other imaginable topic, often from an international perspective. This requirement presupposes a certain level of prior education and cultural exposure as well as a commitment to remain up-to-date in these areas, what Nickson and Warhurst describe as the "gentrification of skill demand".

This implies a very significant change in the profiling of tourism skills in that work which has traditionally provided opportunity for those at the economic margins of developed country societies is, in part, now demanding a skills set that lies within the competencies of those with good general education and a more "middle class" cultural profile. This skills set is, therefore, beyond the reach of traditional recruitment pools for many tourism jobs.

Warhurst etal's interpretation of the commodified aesthetics of labour clearly builds upon Tyler and Taylor's discussion of aesthetics and gender in the work place (in the context of flight attendants), which looks specifically at "those particular aspects of women's work which takes place outside formal, contractual relations of exchange, yet upon which formal, contractual relations of commodity exchange depend". Tyler and Taylor's interpretation of aesthetics in the work place draws on "women's attributed nature, femininity and sexuality the commodification of women's Otherness" (166). Thus, aesthetic skills can be seen as both an innate dimension of gender and as an area of skill which processes socialisation, education and training can develop and hone.

Westwood (2004) notes that in ascribing a 'soft skills' descriptor to labour with an emotional and/or aesthetic dimension, there is an implicit assumption that such skills are somehow less important than their 'hard' counterparts.

This is a view disputed in Bolton's (2004) argument that emotional work has a clear high skills dimension. Of importance in wider human resource terms is Westwood's comment that such skills, whatever their level of demand, "are a very long way from the kinds of skills that the UK's education system is used to supplying" which persists in a focus on "the processing and supply of more academic skills".

This indictment is applicable to many other countries and has particular bite in the context of tourism, pointing to a significant mismatch between education and training and the requirements of the contemporary industry.

Managing Diversity in the Work place

Diversity in the tourism work place is not a new phenomenon, but full recognition of its impact and managerial implications in developed countries is relatively recent, driven by demographic, labour market and legislative change. Wood adopts an encompassing definition of diversity management when he talks of "a set of evolving philosophies and practices concerned with the utilisation of a variety of human characteristics, orientations and dispositions in satisfaction of ethical precepts and the pursuit of business goals".

In the context of this paper, our main concern is with the consequences of diversity in the tourism work place that have arisen through mobility in the form of labour migration, but we will also acknowledge the significance of other forms of diversity to contemporary HRM within the sector.

Indeed, as Adib and Guerrier (2003) rightly point out, it is rarely possible to consider the impact of any dimension within the diversity agenda in isolation in that, for example, ethnicity and disability are frequently closely associated with social class and economic status including labour market participation.

Governments in the developed world increasingly recognise the apparent benefits of labour migration to a country's economy. Home Office research shows that in the UK over a single year, migrants (including asylum seeks and refugees) contributed £2.5 billion to the UK economy.

Migrant workers can be beneficial to the economy in a multitude of ways: in particular, they are able to fill gaps in the domestic labour market and alleviate skills shortages as well as increasing the levels of employment which, in turn, helps to raise gross domestic product. Their age profile is such that they use less in the way of services but contribute to tax and national insurance payments which, in turn, help to finance future pensions.

The importance of labour migration to the work force of the contemporary tourism industry is well documented. Tourism businesses have long relied on a culturally diverse work force. Baum (2006a) traces examples of vocational mobility in the sector in Europe back to the 13th century and discusses the important role that, primarily, southern Europeans played in developing the culture and character of tourism operations in industrialised Europe in the 19th and much of the 20th centuries.

However, contemporary labour migration, within tourism in Europe, has received limited attention from researchers. Widespread labour shortages and other labour market changes resulting from the impacts of a combination of, among others, demographic, globalization and economic factors in Europe are leading tourism companies to hire new employees from a wide range of less developed and transition economy countries.

Traditionally concentrated in core, urban centres, multiculturalism within the tourism labour market is now a phenomenon that has reached geographically peripheral areas and has implications for the marketing of destinations such as Ireland which have depended significantly on images of people and place in their destination branding. The numerical impact of migrant labour on the delivery of tourism services in these locations is particularly noticeable.

As an example, it is estimated that there are over 250,000 non-Irish nationals employed in the economy of the Irish Republic or some 13% of the entire work force.

This figure reaches 17% in the Irish tourism industry and is up to 25% of the work force in key areas of hospitality work. This growth was stimulated further in 2004 following the accession of 10 new

Member States to the European Union. It is estimated that new arrivals to Ireland from within the Union reached 50,000 in 2004, primarily from Poland. In addition, some 9000 work permits were issued to non-European Economic Area nationals.

The changing nature of labour markets in the tourism sectors of developed countries, as a result of increasing migration, raises issues that have been subject to analysis across a range of the social sciences. Conceptually, this discussion can be located within debate about different forms of mobility in contemporary society and their specific impact in the tourism context. The nature of mobility discussed here and its impact are less common in their analysis in that they are a form of migration (labour) that exists solely because of the presence of another form of mobility, that of tourism.

The issue under the microscope here also responds to Rosello's (2001) notion of the immigrant as guest in her consideration of hospitality and immigration in postcolonial France. If migrants are, themselves, guests in the communities in which they work, interpretative representations of the destination in that context may be provided for guests (visitors) by guests (workers). This context has the potential to place strain on understanding of working roles within the tourism sector and the nature of hospitality provided by those employed as front-line staff.

It is arguable that the widespread recruitment and use of migrant labour in the tourism industry of developed countries has acted to the detriment of real change within the sector's work place. The argument that the tourism sector cannot recruit to unfilled vacancies and, therefore, turns to external labour sources is predicated upon the assumption that the labour economics of the industry remain appropriate and need not change.

There are exceptions, as evidenced in good practice examples across the sector, but much of the industry operates on the basis of a labour economics model that depends upon high turnover, low pay, poor conditions and minimal investment in training. Accessing low cost but untrained migrant labour is likely to act as a dead hand with respect to change within the work place economics of the sector. As a consequence, many tourism businesses do not perceive the need to change.

They are not required to consider strategies designed to enhance labour productivity, notably through real investment in training and development, in order to reduce the numbers they need to employ at higher rates of pay because low cost employees remain readily available. This analysis accords with Riley and Szivas' comment that "by not recruiting fully trained workers, employers forego productivity in favour of lower labour costs". It is also consistent with Riley's assertion, based on conceptual rather than empirical evidence, but valuable here nonetheless, that "where unskilled labour is imported to fill a shortage, the effect is to deflate existing pay levels".

Notwithstanding the advent of minimum wage legislation in the buoyant tourism economies of countries such as Ireland and the UK, there is little doubt that the availability of migrant labour does allow tourism businesses to employ more untrained workers at lower cost than might have been the case had this source of employee not been available, thus imposing deflationary pressures on individual but possibly not total remuneration costs.

Our discussion thus far, in the context of diversity, has focused on culturally induced dimensions. The management of people in the contemporary tourism sector in many countries is increasingly either legally or morally bound to recognise diversity in terms of a far wider interpretation.

These manifestations of diversity are not wholly new in tourism and there is evidence of their recognition, to a limited extent, in early analysis of the sector. However, highlighting such diversity in today's tourism work place is both functionally and ethically important. Dimensions that merit acknowledgement in this context include:

- Gender and the evident and continuing institutionalised disparity that exists in the status and pay of men and women in the services work place. Services work in most societies is highly gendered and this universal reality across national boundaries and continental divides is clearly evident in the range of contexts that are addressed by Sinclair (1997) and her contributing colleagues. Women, as Toynbee (2003) clearly illustrates, often undertake the least desirable and lowest status work in hospitality and other evidence from elsewhere in the services sector suggests that gender has an underpinning influence on rewards, achievement and status in the work place. Likewise the culturally induced absence of working women in the services sectors of some countries is tempered by evidence of gradual change in, for example, Iran and Saudi Arabia. Some areas of gendered work in services can be seen to represent exploitation and degradation and, therefore, combating sex services, particularly in relation to children, has become a major concern of governments and NGOs in some countries. Some areas of services work have, historically, been a predominantly male preserve. Mills (1998, 173–4) notes, with respect to airline pilots that "In the first two decades of commercial flying the characteristics of heroism and experience came to form a unique type of organisational masculinity—the pilot. Indeed, British Airways' earliest corporate image was that of the experienced, heroic and supremely confident pilot." While gender balance on the flight deck has improved, Mills notes that it was the late 1980s before British Airways appointed their first female pilot. Progress towards gender balance, in this area of high status services work, has been varied across different airlines but female pilots are commonplace today in many countries. Ali Khan (2004) even reports the appointment of the first female airline pilot in Saudi Arabia. However, this area of work remains masculine in its operating culture so that the experiences of female pilots can be challenging and degrading at times.

- Sexual orientation is a theme that has been addressed in services in terms of consumer markets. The experience of gay employees in the sector is not widely recorded except in anecdotal form. This may be because, as Wood notes, "gays and lesbians are not always visible, indeed adopting invisibility as a strategy is one way in which homosexuals cope with organisational life and avoid the disapprobation of those who possess animus against homosexuals".
- Ability and disability is an area of increasing interest in services. The services industry is frequently portrayed as an industry for the young, beautiful and super-fit and this projection is used to create the image of vibrancy, energy and fun. The services

sector can be described as one that offers opportunity to members of a society across much of its ability and disability range. It is a sector that can accommodate the expectations and abilities of those with exceptional talent (in culture, entertainment, sports, technology, entrepreneurship as examples) as well as those in most communities who face challenges of a different sort in terms of physical or intellectual ability.

- Age in the sense that services work is frequently perceived to be an area for the young and historic data in developed countries certainly bears this out. However, changing demographics in wealthier countries means that traditional sources of labour are no longer so readily available, creating the potential of opportunity for more mature workers, returners to work and those retired from first careers. As we have already seen, this solution is, in part, countered by the availability of low cost and young workers from overseas.
- Social inclusion reflects the capacity of services, as a sector for employment, to provide opportunity to potential workers from across a wide social and economic spectrum. This capacity is not always delivered in what is a growing labour market contradiction within the sector, that of widespread employment vacancies in services existing alongside endemic and long-term unemployment within communities in both cities and in rural areas. A partial explanation can be drawn from the aesthetic demands of the industry in that some sectors of services impose implicit or overt entry barriers based on appearance, cultural cache and education upon those seeking work and many of those from socially excluded communities do not meet such criteria.
- Motivation and choice, in terms of why people choose to work and also factors that underpin voluntary, unpaid work in services.

Uncritical claims for the virtue and value of diversity in the work place must be put forward with some degree of caution. The aspiration of effective diversity management in the tourism work place can easily be blinded by what Wood calls "the worthiness of the concept" which belies the rather more pessimistic consensus of the research literature.

Furthermore, as we have argued with respect to the employment of migrant labour in the tourism sector's of developed economies, their impact, while making sound short-term business sense, also has the effect of deflating remuneration, permit the continuation of variable working conditions and allowing employers to fudge investment in skills development. If this is true with respect to one form of diversity in the work place, may be necessary to question whether some of the other forms of diversity touched on here are also adopted with similar objectives.

Conclusions

We started this paper with a fairly damning assessment of work and working lives in tourism, arguing that, in many respects, Wood's bleak (1997) assessment of the industry remains substantially unchanged in many countries, both developed and less developed.

We have considered themes wherein wider contextual change can be identified that has a direct impact upon people and their management in the tourism sector and we have considered the consequences of such changes. The evidence points, unsurprisingly, to conclusions in the form of a curate's egg and, indeed, contradictions in terms of practice across the industry. For example, we have evidence of the gentrification of tourism skills from Nickson and Warhurst (2007) while, at the same time, ready access to low cost migrant labour, both legal and illegal, permits many tourism businesses to sidestep this trend and to ignore issues of productivity, skills development and general work place enhancement. As in other areas of work, it is clear that polarisation is taking place within tourism work, but the criteria of distinction relates to the branding and image of the work rather than to its technical or professional status. "Cool" work is equated with style, fashion and consumer branding (bars, night clubs, boutique hotels, creative venues) while "uncool" includes the work of drudgery in the sector (cleaning, popular service) and also some glamour work from the past, airline cabin crew, particularly with some newer, lowcost airlines. Another example of contradiction is that vocational and educational opportunities for most young people in developed countries are such that many areas of tourism work are much less obvious and attractive longterm career options than they might have been 20 years ago. At the same time, growth in tourism in developing countries means that the sector has become an important source of employment for those previously dependent on subsistence living so that what is, ostensibly, the same work in a technical sense is constructed in very different ways across social, cultural and economic contexts.

It is true that, at an organisational level, human resource practices in tourism have changed in many developed countries and in most larger operations. This change has been driven by a combination of the effects of commercial, legislative, ethical and external environmental pressures. At the same time, tourism remains a sector within which, worldwide, very poor employment practices persist, incorporating both minimal compliance with the law and transgression beyond legally accepted behaviour. Some of the changes over the past 20 years that are considered here, notably the mass mobility of economic and political migrants from the world's poorer countries, have allowed tourism work and employment to remain firmly located at the margins of many societies in terms of benefits and status and has acted counter to attempts to reform and modernise the sector with regard to its employment practices.

In the final analysis, the conditions of work in tourism are attributable to the outcomes of market force pressures, temporised in part and in places by government and wider societal interventions. In parallel to our bleak assessment of the work environment, it is important to recognise that insatiable and growing demand for low cost tourism services, across the globe, means that consumers must also take responsibility for pressurising operators into undesirable, marginal or even illegal employment practices. It is self-evident that downward pressures on the overall cost of tourism (low cost airlines, aggressive tour operators, electronic distribution, deregulation) encourages the use of low cost labour and, to an extent, may also deflate expectations of service and product quality. Growth projections for tourism, over the next quarter of a century, are such that it appears unlikely that we will see fundamental change in this environment in the foreseeable future.

Human Resource Module of the Tourism Satellite Account, Update to 2006

The aim of the Human Resource Module (HRM) is to provide timely and reliable statistics on the human resource dimension of tourism. It serves as a useful planning and forecasting tool for policy makers in the tourism, employment and training areas. Various tourism-affiliated agencies, academics, and decisionmakers in tourism will also be able to use it for research and analysis, planning and development. Travel Services accounted for 47 thousand jobs in 2006, up 1.3%, following a 5.9% gain in 2005. This industry group accounted for only 2.6% of all jobs in tourism. The average hourly compensation for jobs in this industry group was above average ($21.56 per hour versus $17.95), as were the hours worked (1,805 hours per year versus 1,559). Travel counsellor was the predominant occupation, accounting for 42% of the industry's employee jobs.

Jobs, Hours and Earnings in Tourism Industries

A total of 2.8 billion hours was worked in tourism industries in 2006, accounting for 9.7% of the 29.1 billion hours worked in the economy overall. This reflected an average 1,559 hours of work per year, somewhat less than the economy-wide average of 1,738 hours. The lower hours of work reflected the higher proportion of part-time jobs found in tourism. It is interesting to note that the average annual hours worked increased slightly in 2006 in tourism industries, but were unchanged for the economy overall. In Retail Trade, a sector characterized by a high proportion of part-time jobs, like tourism, the average annual hours of work per job fell from 1,584 hours in 2005 to 1,566 hours in 2006.

Profile of Employees in Tourism Industries

The HRM includes details on three characteristics of employees namely, gender, age group and immigrant status. The following highlights some of the HRM results according to these demographics.

Women held 920 thousand employee jobs in tourism industries in 2006, an increase of 22,000 from 2005. These gains were mostly full-time and accounted for nearly half the job gains in the sector. Among women, the number of employee jobs held by those aged 45 and over increased the most in 2006 (+3.5%). Among men, on the other hand, jobs held by those aged 25-34 increased the most (+3.9%). The number of jobs held by women and men aged 35 to 44 hardly changed. Women were notably under-represented in Other Transportation, holding only 26% of the employee jobs.

Conversely, 68% of jobs in Travel Services were held by women. Women were more likely to be working part-time than men. They also earned less. Women working in tourism industries earned $19,100 in

2006, compared to $30,500 for men. There was significant variation in women's wages and salaries, with jobs in Air Transportation paying the most ($42,269) on average, and jobs in Food and Beverage Services paying the least ($14,632).

Youth aged 15 to 24 years held 658 thousand employee jobs in the tourism industries in 2006. These young workers were more likely to be working in part-time jobs than other tourism workers, accounting for two-thirds of all the part-time work in the sector. Their wages were also considerably lower.

For example, the average hourly wage among workers aged 15-24 was $8.82 in 2006, just over half the average across tourism industries. Over 1997 to 2006, the number of jobs held by younger (15 to 24 years of age) and older (45 + years of age) employees in tourism has grown significantly, averaging 2.8% and 4.8% per year, respectively. Over the same period the number of jobs held by 25 to 44 year olds has declined.

Immigrants (persons born outside Canada) held 344 thousand jobs in tourism industries in 2006, or 20% of employee jobs. They were more likely to be employed in Travel Services and less likely to be employed in Recreation and Entertainment compared to non-immigrants. Immigrants were also more likely to be older: 18% were between 15 to 24 years old, compared to 44% for non-immigrants. Over 40% of immigrant workers belong in the 45+ age group.

Immigrants working in tourism industries were more likely to be men (53% versus 43%) and more likely to be in full-time jobs (72% versus 58%) than their non-immigrant counterparts. These results have been quite stable over 1997 to 2006. On average, immigrants worked longer hours than their non-immigrant counterparts, 1,755 hours per year versus 1,485 in 2006. This was the case for both men and women and for full-time and part-time jobs, across the period covered by the HRM. Immigrants also earned higher annual wages and salaries on average ($28,769 versus $23,112 in 2006), although this reflects the fact that the immigrant labour force in tourism industries is older and that older workers earn more than younger workers 6: Human resources for travel and tourism Learning outcomes.

By completing this unit candidates will develop knowledge and understanding of human resources procedures and issues relevant to travel and tourism organisations. They will also develop an understanding of the recruitment process and the skills required in an interview situation. Candidates will produce evidence to meet the unit assessment objectives in order to show that they understand:

- the responsibilities of the human resources department in a travel and tourism organisation.
- how travel and tourism organisations manage their human resources.
- the recruitment process.

Candidates will also demonstrate their practical skills in interview techniques.

Assessment Objectives Knowledge, Understanding and Skills

Describe the responsibilities of the human resources department in a travel and tourism organisation Human resources department responsibilities:

- human resources planning.
- recruitment and selection.
- training and development, e.g induction, mentoring and coaching.
- internal and external training.
- dismissal, redundancy, promotion, demotion, transfer.
- support and advice, e.g staff and line managers.
- policies and procedures, e.g grievance, disciplinary, equal opportunities, maternity, paternity, sickness.
- contracts, terms and conditions, holidays and hours of work.
- adherence to legislation, e.g race, religion, gender, gender identity, sexual orientation, disability or age (equality and diversity).
- staff welfare.
- ethical issues.

Explain how travel and tourism organisations manage their human resources Organisational structures:

- flat, tall Management styles.
- formal, informal Motivation of staff.
- motivation theories.
- job enlargement, enrichment, rotation.
- pay, bonuses, benefits.
- appraisals.

Leadership:

- styles (democratic, autocratic, laissez-faire).
- importance of clear targets.
- communication channels.

Explain how travel and tourism organisations manage their human resources;

- line management Teamwork.
- team roles.
- targets.
- importance of effective communication.

Chart the Recruitment Process

The need for staff:

- staff turnover.
- organisational growth.
- internal change.

Examples of recruitment:

- internal.
- external.
- use of agency.
- headhunting.
- advertising.

Stages of the recruitment process:

- job analysis (production of job description and person specification).
- attracting candidates (timing, different methods and their benefits).
- short listing (from CVs and application forms).
- selection interview (planning, the panel, good techniques).
- testing (psychometric and aptitude).
- appointing (contracts, terms and conditions).
- evaluation of process.
- equal opportunities issues.
- induction.

Costs:

- of poor recruitment.
- poor performance.
- impacts on team.
- advertising, staff time.

Demonstrate interviewer and interviewee techniques Interviewer:

- planning.
- questioning techniques.
- format and style of interview.
- use of interview record sheets.
- awareness of legislation regarding equality and diversity.

Interviewee:

- production of curriculum vitae.
- planning and preparation for interview.
- knowledge of organisation and job role.
- awareness of dress code.
- non-verbal communication.
- dealing with questions.
- asking appropriate questions.

Assessment

This unit is centre assessed and externally moderated. In order to achieve this unit candidates must produce a portfolio of evidence showing that they have met all of the assessment objectives. Portfolios of work must be produced independently. They will need to be made available, together with witness statements and any other supporting documentation, to the OCR Visiting Moderator when required.

Centres must confirm to OCR that the evidence produced by candidates is authentic. An OCR Centre Authentication Form is provided in the Centre Handbook and includes a declaration for assessors to sign. It is a requirement of the QCA Common Criteria for all Qualifications that proof of authentication is received.

Guidance on Assessment and Evidence Requirements

This unit aims to develop candidate's knowledge and understanding of the role of the human resources department and its importance within the organisation. The unit also aims to develop the skills required to perform effectively in an interview situation.

This unit has links with Unit 4: Customer service and selling skills in travel and tourism, Unit 8:

Planning and managing a travel and tourism event, Unit 9: Living and working overseas, Unit 11:

Career planning for travel and tourism, Unit 12: Developing skills through work experience in travel and tourism, Unit 13: Working as an overseas resort representative, and Unit 27: Working as airline cabin crew.

Links with a selection of travel and tourism organisations are encouraged for the delivery of this unit. Centres may wish to establish these. Alternatively, candidates may be able to research organisations, either individually or in small groups, share information and make comparisons. Information may also be provided through a case study, visits, talks, work experience or alternative. Ideally, organisations from different sectors of the industry and different types of organisation will be used to highlight different procedures and practices.

It is envisaged that such links with organisations will highlight the fact that the role of the human resources department varies from organisation to organisation and that management techniques and recruitment practices vary enormously. Classroom discussion of the different practices should be encouraged. However, it is recommended that underpinning knowledge of all areas is provided prior to organisational visits. This will enable candidates to make comparisons and comment on good practice. There is a wide selection of printed and video material available on all aspects of human resource management. When developing candidates' understanding of management techniques, tutors should draw upon candidates' experience of being 'managed' at work experience, within a work place and even within the classroom. Where candidates have worked in teams, they should be encouraged to consider whether the teams worked well and if so why. Tutors may wish to use the Belbin questionnaire to demonstrate the different team roles and the fact that a range of roles within a team is important.

It is envisaged that this unit will be used to develop candidates' awareness of the recruitment practices and the necessary preparation needed to gain employment within a travel and tourism organisation. Candidates should chart the stages of the entire recruitment process, with explanatory notes of each stage. Again, contact with organisations will highlight differences and possible 'short-cuts' taken by organisations. Candidates should be encouraged to discuss these and comment on good practice. An understanding of the recruitment process can be used to encourage candidates to consider the need for their own applications to be professional and the costs involved in recruiting one person.

When preparing for Assessment Objective 4, candidates should be encouraged to produce curriculum vitae and complete job application forms to a professional standard. They could collect and evaluate job descriptions and person specifications. The paperwork used to shortlist candidates should be made available to candidates. Candidates should develop an awareness of their own body language. Self-reflection on skills gained and those requiring further development should be encouraged. It is anticipated that the practical activities used to develop candidates' interview techniques both as an interviewer and interviewee will help their preparation for their own interview situations, on completion of the course. Candidates can work in pairs or small groups for the assessment of Assessment Objective 4, with each candidate taking a turn as the interviewee and interviewer or interview panel member. Tutors are encouraged to video these interviews and candidates should be encouraged to self-evaluate. This could be cross-referenced with Unit 11: Career planning for travel and tourism.

Candidates may provide portfolio evidence for all of the assessment objectives in this unit using a range of presentation techniques. This may include assessor testimony/witness statements logbooks, diaries, the use of video, audio and presentation software, posters/charts, written work. Where video and/or audio evidence is provided this must be supported by assessor testimony/witness statements. Where candidates demonstrate competence, centres should record skills demonstrated on appropriate recording documentation

6

Empirical Studies of Tourism Demand

International Tourism Demand for Turkey: A Dynamic Panel Data Approach

Tourism has grown significantly since the creation of the commercial airline industry and the advent of the jet aeroplane in the 1950's. By 1992, it had become the largest industry and largest employer in the world. According to the World Travel & Tourism Council (WTTC), travel and tourism is the biggest industry in the world on virtually any economic measure, including gross output, value added, capital investment, employment, and tax contributions.

In 2003, the industry's gross output was estimated to be in excess of US$4.5 billion of economic activity, more than 10 percent of the total gross national product spending. The travel and tourism industry is one of the world's largest employers, with nearly 195 million jobs, or 7.6 percent of all employees. Furthermore, the World Tourism Travel Council (WTTC, 2005) expects that the scale of the world tourism industry, which made up approximately 10.4% of the world's GDP in 2004, will increase to 10.9% in 2014. When all components of the tourism industry are taken into account, i.e., investment, tourism consumption, government spending and exports, the industry grew 5.9% in 2004 alone, reaching US$5.5 trillion.

Furthermore, it is expected to contribute 3.6 % to Gross Domestic Product (GDP) in 2007 and 231.2 million jobs in 2007, 8.3% of total employment by WTTC. The 76.1 million T&T Industry jobs account for 2.7% of total employment in 2007 and are forecast to total 86.6 million or 2.8% of the total by 2017.

This growth led to the development of a major new industry: tourism. In turn, international tourism became the concern of a number of world governments because it not only provided new employment opportunities, but it also produced a means of earning foreign exchange. For these reasons, thoroughly examining all aspects of tourism development and economic growth is tremendously significant for governments. Despite its importance for the world economy, applied economists have paid little attention to tourism as Papatheodorou (1999) and Balaguer et al., (2002) argue in their papers.

The current papers on this issue are Balaguer et al., (2002) for Spain, Dritsakis (2004) for Greece, Gunduz and Hatemi-J (2005) and Aslan (2008) for Turkey, Oh (2005) for Korea and Kim et al., (2006) for Taiwan. The possible causal relationship is analysed between tourism and economic growth in a bivariate context by these papers; nevertheless, not all of them find evidence of the longrun causality from tourism to economic growth. Therefore, economic growth strongly contribute to tourism growth is a question not well answered at this moment in time. The purpose of this paper is to empirically examine the whether tourism growth causes the economic growth or not in Turkey by using dynamic panel data models based on the Generalized Method of Moment estimation (GMM). The main contributions of the present research can be found in the following: the estimated model, the applied methodology and the variables included in the model.

The rest of paper is organized as follows. The section 2 describes the importance of the tourism sector in economy. Section 3 describes the data, methodology and results from this empirical analysis. Section 4 presents the concluding discussion and further comments.

The Importance of the Tourism Sector in Turkey

In regards to the total tourist arrivals to Turkey, it seems that the number of foreign visitors has accelerated rapidly in the last two decades. In 1990, Turkey attracted 4.8 million foreign tourists, which generated an income of $3.4 billion but reached $18.2 billion in 2005 with 20.3 million visitors.

In addition, when taking into consideration top destinations for international tourism according to international tourism receipts and international tourist arrivals, Turkey has assured its position in recent years due to its cultural and natural attractions as the fourth most important destination in the Mediterranean region and the sixth in Europe after the tourism giants France, Spain, Italy, the UK and When comparing with 2004, the top ten destination rankings in 2005 remained unchanged. For international tourist arrivals and tourism receipt, the major change has been that Turkey entered the ranking in the ninth position in arrivals and eighth in receipt, as a result of its 21% and %14 increases in 2005.

Moreover according to the WTTC forecasts, real Turkish visitor exports growth will be 7.5% over the ten years (2001-2010), which is the highest rate in comparison to the EU countries. However, in contrast with the important role of the tourist industry in the Turkish economy, little attention has been paid to its quantitative analysis. Existing empirical research of the international tourism demand in Turkey is based on traditional econometric techniques without examining the stability situation of the estimated regression equations; see for example, Uysal and Crompton (1984), Var et al., (1998) and Akis (1998).

Uysal and Crompton (1984) have found the income variable to be statistically significant and the income elasticity to be generally above unity. In addition these finding for Turkey, Var et al. (1998) illustrated that the elasticity for all of the variables significantly vary from negative values to highly elastic measure. In another study, Akis (1998) concluded that there has been positive relationship between tourist arrivals and national income of tourist generating countries and a negative relationship between tourist arrivals and relative prices by using double-logarithmic functional form of the regression model.

Sample and Model Specification

In this paper, it is aimed to apply dynamic approach to the Turkey case by using panel data estimation. Since static regression models can suffer from a number of problems, including structural instability and spurious regression, in order to avoid these problems, dynamic analysis has started to be explored in the tourism field especially co-integration analysis such as the works by Sieddighi and Shearing (1997); Divisekera, (2003); Dritsakis (2004); Halicioglu (2004); Narayan (2004); Croes and Vanegas (2005); Han, et al., (2006); Munoz, (2006); Song and Witt (2003, 2006); and Toh, et al., (2006); Munoz and Martin (2007).

However, panel data estimations are relatively rare in the empirical literature, especially involving dynamics. The panel data approach is used to estimate the demand function of tourism in Turkey with respect to its nine major clients, Germany, Russia, United Kingdom, Holland, France, Austria, Iran, Bulgaria and Ukraine, for a period of 10 years (1995-2004). There are two main advantages in using this type of data. First, the use of annual data avoids the seasonality problems, which are dominant in this sector. Second, the utilization of a pooled timeseries or cross-sectional data set enables us to have more degrees of freedom than with time-series or cross-sectional data, and one can control for omitted variable bias and reduce the problem of multi colinearity, hence improving the accuracy of parameter estimates. Accordingly, the estimated demand function for tourism in Turkey involves the following variables;

Supply Dynamics

Supply conditions from the point of view of the hosting country are important factors in attracting more tourism inflows. It is introduced two main supply measures. The first is accommodation capacity (S) measured by the number of foundation available each year to host the tourists who visit Turkey. The data are collected from TURKSTAT, Tourism Statistics. The second is a more general supply measure related to infrastructures (airports, railways, roads, hospitals, and telecommunications). The ratio of public investment to GDP (PI) is used as a proxy to capture the welfare effects emanated from public infrastructure networks. The data for the public investment ratio in Turkey is collected from State Planning Organization, Public Investment Expenditures. Finally, two dummy variables (D99 and D01) are included to capture the influence of possible effects on tourism of the Marmara Earthquake in Turkey which takes a value of 1 in 1999 and 0 otherwise and September 11th events, which takes value of 1 in 2001 and 0 otherwise.

The empirical literature suggests that the most commonly specifications used for estimating the demand function of tourism are linear and log linear functions. Witt and Witt (1995) concluded that 75% of the analysed models used a double log functional form. The preference given to the double log specification is due to more satisfactory estimation results obtained and easy interpretation of the estimated coefficients through the demand elasticity. In this paper, the dynamic structure of tourists' preferences is considered because knowledge about the destination spreads as people talk about their holiday, thus decreasing the uncertainty for potential visitors to that country. Because of this reason, if people are satisfied with a destination they may be more likely to come back and tell others about their favorable experiences related to the destination. That's why the parameter for the lagged dependent variable may be considered as a measure of habit formation and interdependent preferences.

Empirical Results and Policy Implication

In order to insert dynamics into the demand function of tourism in Turkey, it is introduced a lagged dependent variable as an explanatory factor to capture persistence effects of the tourists behaviour. However with this dynamic specification, it is faced that the correlation between the lagged variable and error term. Therefore the estimations with fixed effect (OLS) or random effects (GLS) would not be appropriate since the obtained estimates would be biased. One way suggested by Doornik et al., (2002) to solve this problem is to estimate dynamic panel data models based on the Generalized Method of Moment estimation (GMM).

In this methodology, it is assumed that there is no second-order autocorrelation in the errors; therefore a test for the previous hypotheses is needed. It is also conducted a test for autocorrelation and J statistic for the validity of instruments as derived by Hansen (1982). Failure to reject the null hypothesis in both tests gives support to model and the Wald test denotes the joint significance of the independent variables.

The value of the adjustment coefficient (72%) gives evidence of a rather low adjustment process between the actual variation of the demand for tourism and the desired long-run level. This means that the number of tourists visiting Turkey each year differs substantially from the previous years giving evidence of some kind of inertia or rigidity in the tourism inflows. As for the tourism demand studies, general conclusions indicate that income elasticity has commonly been found to be greater than one, confirming the luxury nature of tourism travel. However, contrary to expectations, income in nine major clients is positively related to the demand for tourism in Turkey with the elasticity less than one.

The estimated coefficient for the income variable suggests that the demand for tourism in Turkey is not dependent on the economic situation in nine major clients. This means that tourism in Turkey is considered by nine major clients as not a luxury. The own-price elasticity is normally negative, although magnitudes vary considerably among studies. Generally elasticity estimates show negative values ranging from 0 to-1. Consistent with demand theory, relative prices are negatively related to tourism demand. This means that %1 decrease in relative prices, demand for tourism rise around %0.2 However, contrary to expectations, the ratio of public investment to GDP (PI) which is used as a proxy to capture the welfare effects emanated from public infrastructure networks is negatively and Marmara Earthquake is positively related to the demand for tourism in Turkey. A possible explanation could be that public investment gains speed in summer. Therefore these actions make life difficult for tourists. On the other hand, a possible explanation of positive effect of Marmara Earthquake could be caused by important price dumping in Turkey.

Based on the above empirical studies that have carried out the calculation of elasticities in both the short-and long-run demonstrate that the values of both income and price elasticities in the long-run are greater than their short-run corresponding items, suggesting that tourists are more sensitive to income/price changes over the long-run.

Conclusion

The model was used to measure the performance of tourist arrivals from nine generating countries to Turkey between 1995 and 2004, and it was estimated by using the GMM-DIFF estimator proposed by Arellano and Bond (1991) for the case of dynamic panel data models. The dynamic model used in this study provides short and long-run elasticity for the variables of interest. This is an additional advantage over most studies of tourism demand, which are based on static models and only estimate long-run elasticity. This is a substantial improvement, since these models are only valid for short-term predictions. One of the main conclusions of the study is the significant value of the lagged dependent variable (0.28), which may be interpreted as a minor word-of-mouth effect on the consumer decision in favour of the destination.

The value of the adjustment coefficient (72%) gives evidence of a rather low adjustment process between the actual variation of the demand for tourism and the desired long-run level. This means that the number of tourists visiting Turkey each year differs substantially from the previous years giving evidence of some kind of inertia or rigidity in the tourism inflows. The estimated values of the income elasticity suggest that the economic conditions of tourists who visit Turkey are not very important factor in determining tourism demand in Turkey. The estimated values of the income elasticity are not in line with the results of previous studies. Therefore tourism to Turkey is not a luxury good.

Moreover tourism to Turkey is not very sensitive to prices. According to the selected model, the estimated values for the own-price short-and long-run elasticities are –0.23 and -0.32, respectively. In order to capture the welfare effects emanated from public infrastructure, the ratio of public investment to GDP (PI) is used as a proxy. And finally, just as in other studies, it has been found that external and internal shocks (e.g., September 11th events and the Marmara Earthquake) may have an impact on tourism demand by using dummy variables. Contrary to expectations, public infrastructure networks are negatively Marmara Earthquake is positively related to the demand for tourism in Turkey and it is found that September 11th events affect negatively Turkey tourism.

International Tourism Demand: the Italian Tourist Flows to Ireland

Tourism is one of the world's major industries and in recent times its social and economic benefits have grown significantly and consistently. As tourism industry is highly competitive, destinations are more concerned about variables that influences tourism movements and moreover, in order to take advantage of tourism effects most destinations have implemented appropriate strategic and operational marketing activities and increased marketing expenditure.

Although, West European countries and North America have dominated previous research, with more than one hundred empirical studies among these only few attempts have been done to evaluate the marketing expenditure impact and moreover very scarce attention has been paid on identifying the determinants of international demand in the Irish market. The purpose of this study is to redress this situation in the Irish context analyzing both the importance of different determinants in explaining variations in tourism demand and the effect of Bord Failte's marketing expenditure. This empirical study is a country-to-country regression model as it examines the outbound tourism demand from Italy to Ireland. Italy is the fifth most important market for Ireland and its growth is surprising if compared to other European origin countries. In this respect, the purposes of this study are to (a) identify major explanatory variables of Italian tourist arrivals to Ireland through a regression model; and (b) investigate the effect, on Italian market, of marketing variable by incorporating Bord Fáilte's marketing expenditure.

Model Specification and Estimation Procedure

Based on a review of literature in this study the authors selected income, relative prices, marketing expenditure and dummy variable (in order to evaluate terrorism effect) as the important determinants of Italian tourism demand to Ireland. Preliminary estimation indicated that the double-logarithm forms fitted the data better than did linear forms in terms of expected signs and statistical significance. Indeed, this functional form has had good empirical performance in most of the previous studies. Secondary data were used and the model was estimated using annual time series from 1989 to 2000.

This period and frequency were chosen because they provided the most consistent data set available to the authors at the time of writing. The *dependent variable* was measured as the number of total arrivals from Italy to Ireland divided by the Italian population in the same year. Data were supplied by Bord Failte and they are estimated based on (1) information from the Central Statistical Office's Country of Residence Survey-which is the best estimation and is based on count at frontiers- and (2) Bord Failte's Survey of Overseas travellers.

The choice of the *explanatory variables* was based on a meticulous analysis of previous studies findings but it was also influenced and limited by data and time constrains. *Income.* According to the economic theory, income is one of the most important variables in tourism demand and for this reason it was considered in this study. The Italian GDP was considered as the most representative variable for Italian income; it was included in the model in per capita form and at 1995-price. ISTAT supplied the Italian GDP and population data.

***Relative prices*:** For the countries in consideration it was decided to include only the price of tourism in the form of cost of living in the destination country and in the substitute country. Moreover, as

Italians tend to travel more in Italy than anywhere else, this study assumed that domestic tourism was the best and the only real substitute product in modeling Italian tourism demand. An exchange-rate-adjusted-consumer-price-index was created dividing the Irish Consumer Price Index for the Italian Consumer Price Index and multiplying for the Exchange Rate between Italian lira and the Irish pound. Central Statistical Office of Ireland and ISTAT supplied data used herein. Both of CPIs were considered at 1995-price. The exchange rates used here were obtained from the Italian Office for Exchange (Ufficio Italiano Cambi).

***Marketing expenditure*:** Marketing expenditure from the destination country to the origin country was the most important explanatory variable included in the model. Consistent with the previous literature that included marketing activity, it was considered the amount spent in market the destination by the National Tourism Organisations (NTOs) that is in this case Bord Failte who furnished the data used herein. In particular, data from 1989 to 1993 are our estimated based on European marketing expenditure while from 1994 the data are effective marketing expenditure in Italy.

A general-to-specific process was carried out and the equations were regressed using Ordinary Least Square and attention was paid to the: (a) estimated coefficients both at significance level (statistic) and sign coherency to the theory; (b) Adjusted R2; (c) F statistic to test the joint significance of all coefficients; (d) SSR, the sum of squared residuals. Initial results and a market analysis of the two countries under investigation showed that the static model could be an appropriate specification for modeling Italian tourists flows to Ireland. The results of this estimate showed that the Static model was the most consistent with economic theory and it was parsimonious and encompassed all the other models considered in the analysis.

Results and Discussion

Two explanatory variables, relative prices and marketing expenditure, were statistically significant at the 5% level of significance and the signs were found as expected from the tourism demand theory. Using diagnostic tests for autocorrelation, heteroscedasticity, functional form and structural instability rigorous statistical analysis was performed.

The model fits the data reasonably well, was correctly specified and showed structural stability. There was no evidence of autocorrelation and heteroscedasticity although a suspicious of multicollinearity can arise, as in all previous studies, but it was unlikely that multicollinearity was serious. The suspect of the endogenicity of the marketing expenditure to the dependent variable was not confirmed by the Wu-Hausman test.

Results indicate that income and the dummy variable for the ceasefire in 1994 may not be as important for Italians as expected. The estimated coefficient of the relative price is highly statistically significant and its sign is negative as expected.

Italian tourism demand to Ireland is highly price elastic, as the absolute value of the price elasticity exceeds unity and this means that an increase of prices of 1% will result in a decrease of almost 5.2% in arrivals. The variable of marketing expenditure has the expected positive sign and it is highly statistically significant.

The results of the current study provide strong evidence of a link between the marketing variable and international tourism. However, NTOs are more interested in the amount of additional tourist expenditure than in the increase of arrivals.

Consequently, the relationship between estimated marketing elasticity and its impact in terms of possible additional Italian expenditure during Italian holidays in Ireland was calculated showing an average increase in receipt of 1,222,000 (Irish Pound) when an increase of 1% of marketing expenditure was hypothesised.

Moreover, the ratio between increased tourism receipt and the increase in marketing expenditure necessary to generate the increase in receipts is 276:1. This result is in line with the results of Crouch, Schultz and Valerio (1992) and represents the highest benefit/cost ratio calculated to date.

Conclusion

The aim of this paper was to identify the determinants of Italian tourism demand to Ireland and to estimate the impact of Bord Failte's marketing expenditure on the number of tourist arrivals. Results from the regression analysis indicate income and marketing expenditures as key determinants.

The results of the model are consistent with findings of previous studies demonstrating the link between both economic and non-economic factors and tourism demand. Although, it is important to emphasise that caution should be used in interpreting these results overall, they provide some encouraging evidence on the cause-effect relationship between Irish marketing expenditure in Italy and Italian arrivals to Ireland.

Modelling and Forecasting Malaysia's Tourism Demand

Within the global tourism market, Malaysia can be considered as a relatively new tourist destination. Serious and integrated efforts to develop this industry were only started in the middle of the 1980s immediately after the world economic recession.

The government has been playing a very important role to stimulate the growth and development of the tourism industry. In 1987 the government had established the Ministry of Culture, Arts and Tourism and later upgraded it to the Ministry of Tourism in 2004 to manage, monitor, synchronize and ensure all tourism development activities and programs are in line with the National Tourism Master Plan.

At the same time, various attractive incentives and assistance were given to private operators to encourage them to be directly involved in the tourism industry. The government was also allocated substantial amount of fund to this industry besides providing sufficient basic infrastructure.

To further promote tourism, the government also involved in marketing by launching several Visit Malaysia Years. Malaysia is also fortunate for having abundant stock of natural tourism products.

Given the scenario above, the growth of Malaysian tourism was fantastic in the last two decades. In 1985, the total tourist arrivals were 3.11 million and increased to about 16.43 million in 2004. In terms of growth, within the last 20 years tourist arrivals to Malaysia had increased at an average of 14.9 per cent annually. According to WTO (2005), Malaysia was ranked as the thirteen world's top tourist destinations. Within ASEAN region Malaysia was the leading country in receiving inbound tourists by controlling about 32.37 percent of total arrivals in 2004 (WTO, 2006). In the same year the market share of Malaysia in the Asia and Pacific region was 15.7 per cent which was the third most visited destination after China and Hong Kong.

Increase in total tourist arrivals would also bring in more tourist receipts. From 1985 to 2005, tourist receipts had increased at an annual average of 16.4 per cent or from RM1.543 billion to RM31.954 billion. In 2006, tourism was the second largest contributor of foreign exchange earnings to the country after the manufacturing sector.

The major markets for Malaysian tourism are mostly from the ASEAN region, followed by the Far East, Australia and the UK markets. For example in 2006, out of 17.547 million arrivals, the four major ASEAN countries namely Singapore, Thailand, Indonesia and Brunei had contributed to more than 77 per cent, followed by China, Japan, Australia, United Kingdom, India and the United States of America which contributed slightly above 10 per cent. In order to diversify the economy, the government is trying hard to further stimulate the growth of the tourism industry.

For this purpose, all stakeholders in tourism must be able to anticipate changes that might occur to tourist arrivals and respond to them accordingly. Prediction of the changing pattern in tourist arrivals can be done by knowing the factors that influence their arrival to this country.

The objectives of this paper are to model and investigate the most important factors that affect the inbound tourists to Malaysia and to forecast their arrivals in the next ten years using the most recent cointegration technique known as the Autoregressive Distributed Lagged (ARDL).

Tourism Demand Analysis: Variables and Data

Tourism Demand Analysis: Studies on tourism demand and forecasting have been carried out since the 1960s. However, most of the studies were based on the Ordinary Least Square (OLS) approach. Some of the studies used multiple regression using the Cochrane Orcutt (CO), Almost Ideal Demand Function (AIDS), Generalized Least Square (GLS) etc. In the middle of the 1990s, emerged new approach. Most authors in the field of tourism demand have shifted to other methodologies, and most of them were using the dynamic approaches. One of the approach or method is a cointegration which is the most preferable. The details of other methodologies beside the importance of selected variables in tourism demand studies. The discussion is as follows:

Dependent Variables: Tourist arrivals have been used as a dependent variable in most studies on tourism demand. It has been supported by Witt and Witt (1995), Crouch et al. (1992), and Li (2004). Summary, that about 59 per cent of tourism demand model had used this variable. Other possible variables are tourist expenditure (32%), average length of stay (6%) and number of nights (3%).

Independent Variables: A survey of 100 empirical studies on tourism modeling by Lim (2004) found that income and price were the most commonly used explanatory variable. The importance of income (81%) and tourism price (65%) in tourism demand model. This is followed by travelling cost (53%), exchange rate (39%), dummy (29), time trend (18%), lagged dependent variables (16%) and population (13%), tourism price at substitute destinations (12%), marketing/ advertisement (10%) and travelling cost to substitute destinations (3%).

Data: This study will also use some of the variables, and details are as follows:

Dependent variable: Tourist arrivals will be used as a proxy for the tourism demand. Annual data are used for the period from 1970-2004. Data on tourist arrivals were collected from the Malaysia Tourism Statistical Report.

Independent variables: The independent variables in this study are tourism price, travelling cost, income, tourism price at the alternative tourism destinations, exchange rates, lag dependent (repeat tourists) and the dummy variables. Details are as follows:

i) Tourism price refers to the price of all goods and services consumed by tourists at the destination. Since most countries do not have the price index for goods and services consumed by tourists, the next best alternative is the general Consumer Price Index (CPI) of that particular country. The calculation of tourism price is based on the consumer price index (CPI) of the visited country divided by the CPI of the origin country. In this study, the calculated ratio shows the cost of living in Malaysia relative to the origin country. It is expected that tourism price and arrivals will have a negative relationship.

ii) Transportation or travelling cost can be measured by air fares between the visited destination and the origin country; ferry fares and/or petrol costs for surface travel; and price of crude oil. In this study, the price of crude oil will be used. It is expected that the higher price of oil will reduce the arrivals.

iii) Tourism prices at the alternative tourism destinations are a substitute price. The calculation is similar to the estimating of tourism price, where the visiting destination now refers to the alternative tourism destination. In this study the alternative tourism destinations are Singapore, Thailand and Indonesia. Thus, tourism price at the alternative tourism destination will be the cost of living for tourists in Singapore, Thailand or Indonesia relative to the origin country. The important of substitute price has been proven in tourism study.

iv) The income variable refers to the real per capita income (RPI) or per capita gross domestic product. Income is the most popular variable included in the tourism demand function. Normally, the higher income will increase the total arrivals.

v) The exchange rate is the ratio of currency between the destination country and the origin country. The change in exchange rate will affect the currency value of the origin country. Any change in exchange rate will lead to an appreciation or depreciation of tourist currency. Any appreciation in tourist currency may encourage more people to travel.

vi) Lag dependent or repeat tourists variable is usually used on the international tourism demand as a proxy for informal promotion (word-of-mouth effect), since the knowledge about the destination will be spread as people talk about their holidays, and thereby reducing the uncertainty for potential visitors. Hence, it will encourage more tourists to come to that destination. In the dynamic model of tourism demand analysis, the lagged dependent variable (the previous year's number of tourist arrivals) must be included. If the impact of past tourism is neglected, the effect of the relevant variables considered will tend to be overestimated (as the estimated coefficients will involve direct and indirect effects). Several authors point out that tourism demand analysis will suffer from this neglect of the dynamic structure. Studies that include lagged dependent variables to explain tourism include those by Narayan (2004), Moòoz (2007) and Toh, Habibullah and Goh (2006).

vii) In this study the dummy variables have also been included. There are three dummies, which are the Asian economic crisis in 1997-98 (D97), the Gulf War in 1991 (D91), and the outbreak of SARS in 2003 (D03).

Most of the above data have been collected form World Development Indicator 2005.

The Long-run and Short-run Elasticities

Empirical estimation of the variables in the model indicate that most of them are statistically significant and consistent with the demand theory except for the exchange rates and Thailand as an alternative destination variable. In tourism, exchange rates may not play an important role especially with regard to the Malaysian Ringgit which is quite stable against other currencies.

Among the most important significant variables are tourism price, travelling cost, income and alternative destinations. For the tourism price almost all the countries show this variable is significant except for Japan and Australia. The sign of the variable is consistent with the economic theory except for Indonesia, Japan, the United Kingdom and Australia. For Japan, the United Kingdom and Australia the positive sign may indicate tourists from these countries are from rich countries and they are not really affected by the increasing of tourism cost in Malaysia. Furthermore, the tourism price in Malaysia is among the cheapest within the region.

Travelling costs from the origin countries to Malaysia are found to be significant for Singapore, Thailand, Brunei, China and Hong Kong while other countries are not significant. Most of these countries are a long-haul market. The insignificance of this variable can be because to their arrival is not direct from their countries but that they visit Malaysia from nearby countries.

Tourists from Thailand, Brunei, China, Hong Kong and the United States consider Singapore as a substitute destination for Malaysia. Tourists from Indonesia, Japan, United Kingdom and Australia, on the other hand, consider Malaysia and Singapore as complementary destinations. Similarly, tourists from all countries put Indonesia as a substitute destination for Malaysia except for Hong Kong and the United Kingdom which consider Malaysia and Indonesia as complementary destinations. In this study, Singapore is the most significant an alternative tourism destination for Malaysia compare to Indonesia and Thailand.

As for income, it is significant in all countries except Indonesia and the most developed countries. Some countries consider Malaysia as an inferior destination due to its negative sign. In general, the majority of tourists from these countries visit Malaysia mainly to visit friends and relatives. For example, in 2003 about 47.2% tourist from Singapore visited their friends and relatives in Malaysia. The magnitudes of the variables in the long run in general are acceptable and comparable to similar studies except for tourism price which can be considered as slightly high which implies tourist arrivals are quite sensitive to changes in prices of tourism services in this country.

The short-run relationships between tourist arrivals and its determinants have also been estimated. Following the general-to-specific approach Song and Witt (2003), only significant or close to significant variables will be included in the short run including the lagged dependent (repeat tourists) variable and the dummies.

In the short-run repeat tourists in all countries are statistically significant affected the tourism demand for Malaysia except for Singapore, China and the USA. Hong Kong and Australia however, show a negative sign, meaning that promotion (word-of-mouth effect) by repeat tourists is not effective. In order to make repeat tourists as an effective promotion agent, good tourism facilities and services must be provided at a very reasonable price. Their satisfaction while visiting Malaysia is very important because this experience will be shared with their friends and relatives, and indirectly will encourage or promote them to visit Malaysia in the future. This was supported by a survey conducted by MTPB which found that most tourists got information on Malaysia and visited the country through the encouragement of their friends and relatives.

The Gulf War (D91), Asian economic crisis 1997-98 (D97) and the outbreak of SARS in 2003 (D03) are expected to affect Malaysia tourism demand negatively. Dummy Asian economic crisis 1997-98 (D97) is significant in Singapore, Thailand, Hong Kong and Japan, which means that the Asian economic crisis did significantly decrease the volume of tourist arrivals to Malaysia. The outbreak of SARS (D03) which is significant in Singapore, Indonesia, Brunei, the United Kingdom, indicates that tourists from these countries were really concerned with the issue of safety. The Gulf War was only included in the USA market and it is significant.

Tourism Demand Modelling and Forecasting with PROC VARMAX

Overview

Tourism demand modelling and forecasting are very important for tourism-related business decision making. This example illustrates modelling tourism demand using the VARMAX procedure.

Analysis

Tourism demand can be measured in terms of:

* number of tourist visits from an origin country to a destination country.
* tourist expenditure by visitors from the origin country in the destination country.
* tourist nights spent by visitors in the destination country.

Generally, the explanatory variables for tourism demand include origin country income, destination country tourism prices, substitute destination country tourism prices, tastes, etc. Empirical studies usually use living costs for tourists in the destination as the tourism price. Various demand models can be used to estimate and forecast tourism demand. This example considers modelling tourism demand in a vector autoregressive (VAR) framework. The goal is to forecast the number of holidays in Spain taken by United Kingdom (U.K.) residents using annual tourism data from 1966 to 1994 obtained from Song and Witt (2000). The variables in the data set are described in the following table:

SAS Variable Name	Description
VSP	The number of holidays in Spain taken by U.K. residents
PDI	U.K. real personal disposable income
PUK	The implicit deflater of U.K. consumer expenditure
EXSP	Exchange rate index of Spanish pesetas against the US dollar
EXUK	Exchange rate index of U.K. pound against the U.S. dollar
POP	U.K. population
CPISP	The consumer price index in Spain

The log of the number of per capita holiday visits to Spain by U.K. residents is plotted, the following code:

```
data tourism;
    set sashelp. tourism;
    lpvsp = log(vsp);
    lppdi = log(pdi);
    lrcsp = log( (cpisp/exsp)/(puk/exuk) );
    label lpvsp='log(per capita holiday visits to Spain)'
          lppdi='log(per capita disposable income)'
          lrcsp='log(living costs in Spain relative to
                 UK living costs adjusted by the exchange rate)';
run;
proc gplot data = tourism;
    plot lpvsp*year/cframe = ligr vaxis = axis1 haxis = axis2;
    title 'Log of Per Capita Holiday Visits to Spain';
    symbol c = blue i = join v = star;
    axis1 label = (angle=90 'log(per capita visits to Spain)');
    axis2 label = ('Year');
run;
quit;
```

Figure 1: Log of Per Capita Holiday Visits to Spain

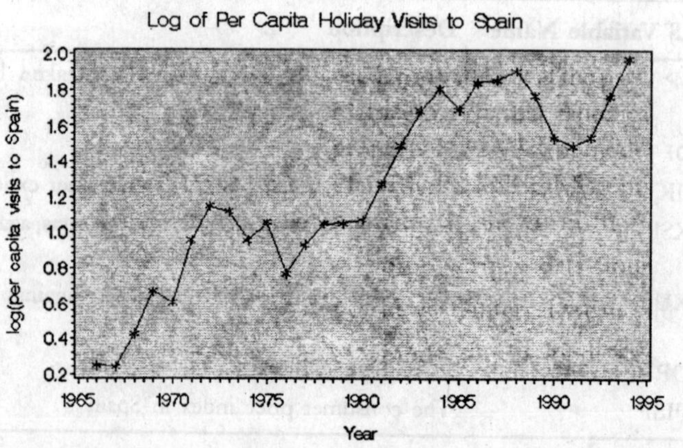

The VAR model of order one can be expressed as follows:

$$Y_t = C + \Phi Y_{t-1} + \epsilon_t$$

where Y_t is a k by 1 observation vector, is a k by 1 white noise vector, C is a k by 1 vector of parameters, and is a k by k matrix of first order autoregressive parameters.

In the tourism model, the vector Y_t is ($LPVSP_t$, $LPPDI_t$, $LRCSP_t$), where *LPVSP* denotes a log of the number of holidays in Spain taken by U.K. residents, *LPPDI* denotes a log of U.K. real personal disposable income, and *LRCSP* denotes a log of living costs in Spain relative to the U.K. adjusted by the exchange rate. *LRCSP* is obtained by the relation

$$LRCSP = \ln([(cpisp/exsp)/(puk/exuk)])$$

where *cpisp* is the consumer price index in Spain, *exsp* is the exchange rate index of Spanish pesetas against the U.S. dollar, *puk* is the implicit deflater of U.K. consumer expenditure, and *exuk* is the exchange rate index of the U.K. pound against the U.S. dollar.

The tourism model can be written as;

$$LPVSP_t = c_1 + \phi_{11}LPVSP_{t-1} + \phi_{12}LPPDI_{t-1} + \phi_{13}LRCSP_{t-1} + \epsilon_{1t}$$
$$LPPDI_t = c_2 + \phi_{21}LPVSP_{t-1} + \phi_{22}LPPDI_{t-1} + \phi_{23}LRCSP_{t-1} + \epsilon_{2t}$$
$$LRCSP_t = c_3 + \phi_{31}LPVSP_{t-1} + \phi_{32}LPPDI_{t-1} + \phi_{33}LRCSP_{t-1} + \epsilon_{3t}$$

You can use the VARMAX procedure to fit this VAR(1) model. First, state the variable names in the MODEL statement. Then use the P= option in the MODEL statement to specify the order of the VAR processes.

To determine the appropriate order of the VAR processes to be used, you can look at the partial autoregressive matrices, partial correlation matrices, or partial canonical matrices. These matrices have the cutoff property for a VAR(p) model at lag = p. Using the PRINT=(PARCOEF PCORR PCANCORR) option enables you to print out the necessary matrices, as shown in the following code:

```
proc varmax data=tourism;
id year interval=year;
model lpvsp lppdi lrcsp/p=1 print=(parcoef pcorr pcancorr)
lagmax=6;
run;
```

The VARMAX Procedure

Schematic Representation of Partial Autoregression

Variable/Lag	*1*	*2*	*3*	*4*	*5*	*6*
lpvsp	...	...	...	...	...	...
lppdi	.+.	...	...	...	...	...
lrcsp	..+	...	...	..-	...	...

+ is > 2*std error, - is < -2*std error, . is between

Figure 2: Partial Autoregressive Coefficients

Figure 2 shows that the model can be obtained by an AR order p=1 since partial autoregression matrices are insignificant after lag 1 with respect to two standard errors.

Schematic Representation of Partial Cross Correlations

Variable/Lag	*1*	*2*	*3*	*4*	*5*	*6*
lpvsp	+..	...	...	...	...	...
lppdi	.+.	...	...	...	...	...
lrcsp	..+	...	...	..-	...	...

+ is > 2*std error, - is < -2*std error, . is between

Figure 3: Partial Correlations

The partial cross-correlation matrices in Figure 3 are insignificant after lag 1 with respect to two standard errors. This indicates that an AR order of p=1 can be an appropriate choice.

Partial Canonical Correlations

Lag	*Correlation 1*	*Correlation 2*	*Correlation 3*	*DF*	*Chi-Square*	*Pr > ChiSq*
1	0.91597	0.79703	0.49657	9	48.18	<.0001
2	0.36954	0.22093	0.12404	9	5.42	0.7962
3	0.37745	0.28020	0.02363	9	5.76	0.7637
4	0.60568	0.25861	0.03195	9	10.87	0.2848
5	0.57268	0.28654	0.07127	9	9.96	0.3535
6	0.51369	0.16498	0.04311	9	6.74	0.6644

Figure 4: Partial Canonical Correlations

Figure 4 shows that the partial canonical correlations between y_t and y_{t-p} are {0.91597, 0.79709}, {0.36957, 0.22090}, {0.37744, 0.28023} for lags p=1 to 3. After lag p=1, the partial canonical correlations are insignificant with respect to the 0.05 significance level, indicating than an AR order of p=1 would be an appropriate choice. Since the results show that the partial autoregressive matrices, partial cross correlation matrices, and partial canonical correlation matrices are all insignificant after lag 1 with respect to two standard errors, a VAR(1) model is appropriate. The parameter estimates of the VAR(1) model are shown in Figure 5.

Model Parameter Estimates

Equation	*Parameter*	*Estimate*	*Standard Error*	*t Value*	*Pr > |t|*	*Variable*
lpvsp	**CONST1**	-8.78015	3.61890	-2.43	0.0231	1
	AR1_1_1	0.66753	0.11795	5.66	0.0001	lpvsp(t-1)
	AR1_1_2	0.73131	0.29788	2.46	0.0217	lppdi(t-1)
	AR1_1_3	-0.76821	0.22902	-3.35	0.0026	lrcsp(t-1)
lppdi	**CONST2**	1.32903	0.63340	2.10	0.0466	1
	AR1_2_1	0.05094	0.02064	2.47	0.0211	lpvsp(t-1)
	AR1_2_2	0.89084	0.05214	17.09	0.0001	lppdi(t-1)
	AR1_2_3	-0.02118	0.04008	-0.53	0.6020	lrcsp(t-1)
lrcsp	**CONST3**	1.44949	2.99679	0.48	0.6330	1
	AR1_3_1	0.08103	0.09768	0.83	0.4149	lpvsp(t-1)
	AR1_3_2	-0.12599	0.24667	-0.51	0.6142	lppdi(t-1)
	AR1_3_3	0.61769	0.18965	3.26	0.0033	lrcsp(t-1)

Figure 5: Parameter Estimates of the VAR(1) Model

Figure 6 plots the residuals obtained from the equation for *LPVSP*.

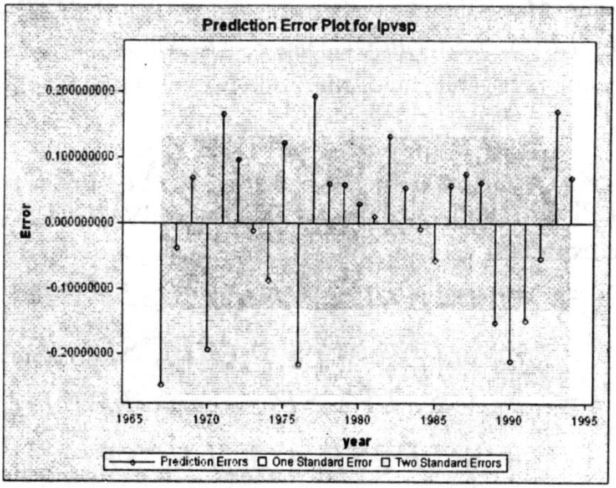

Figure 6: Residual Plot of the VAR(1) Model

The preceding residual plot shows that prediction errors from the VAR(1) model are all within two standard errors. This also provides some support for choosing the first order VAR model.

You can also use the CAUSAL statement in the VARMAX procedure to perform a Granger-Causality test on the variables of interest. The GROUP1=(VARIABLES) GROUP2=(VARIABLES) option enables you to specify the variables to be tested. The null hypothesis of the Granger-Causality test is that GROUP1 is influenced by itself, and not by GROUP2. If the test of hypothesis fails to reject the null, the variables in the GROUP1 may be considered as independent variables. The Granger-Causality test results are shown in Figure 7.

```
proc varmax data=tourism;
id year interval=year;
model lpvsp lppdi lrcsp/p=1;
/* Test for Causality */
causal group1=(lrcsp) group2=(lpvsp lppdi);
run;
```

The VARMAX Procedure

Granger-Causality Wald Test;

Test	DF	Chi-Square	Pr > ChiSq
1	2	0.99	0.6105

Figure 7: Granger-Causality Test Results

The Granger-Causality test statistics shows that *LRCSP* is not influenced by *LPVSP* and *LPPDI*. Hence, *LRCSP* should be treated as an exogenous variable, and the following VARX(1) model is appropriate.

$$Y_t = C + \Phi Y_{t-1} + B_0 X_t + B_1 X_{t-1} + \epsilon_t$$

where Y_t=(*LPVSP*$_t$, *LPPDI*$_t$), and X_t=*LRCSP*$_t$. The VARX(1,1) model can then be expressed as

$$\begin{aligned} LPVSP_t &= c_1 + \phi_{11} LPVSP_{t-1} + \phi_{12} LPPDI_{t-1} + \\ &+ \beta_{01} LRCSP_t + \beta_{11} LRCSP_{t-1} + \epsilon_{1t} \\ LPPDI_t &= c_2 + \phi_{21} LPVSP_{t-1} + \phi_{22} LPPDI_{t-1} + \\ &+ \beta_{02} LRCSP_t + \beta_{12} LRCSPt - 1 + \epsilon_{2t} \end{aligned}$$

You can use the MODEL statement in the VARMAX procedure to estimate the VARX(1,1) model. You first specify the dependent variables, then the equality sign, and then the independent variables. You then use the P= option to specify the order of the VAR processes and the XLAG= option to specify the lag order of the exogenous variables. The VARMAX parameter estimates are shown in Figure 8.

```
/* Fit the VARX(1,1) model */
   proc varmax data=tourism;
   id year interval=year;
   model lpvsp lppdi = lrcsp/p=1 xlag=1;
   run;
```

The parameter estimates results show that and are not significant at the 10% significance level, hence, these two parameters can be restricted to be zero. The following residual plot in Figure 9 shows that prediction errors from the VARX(1,1) model are all within two standard errors.

The VARMAX Procedure

Equation	*Parameter*	*Estimate*	*Standard Error*	*t Value*	*Pr > |t|*	*Variable*
lpvsp	**CONST1**	-8.24987	3.54014	-2.33	0.0289	1
	XL0_1_1	-0.36584	0.23997	-1.52	0.1410	lrcsp(t)
	XL1_1_1	-0.54224	0.26773	-2.03	0.0546	lrcsp(t-1)
	AR1_1_1	0.69718	0.11646	5.99	0.0001	lpvsp(t-1)
	AR1_1_2	0.68522	0.29156	2.35	0.0277	lppdi(t-1)
lppdi	**CONST2**	1.20369	0.59326	2.03	0.0542	1
	XL0_2_1	0.08647	0.04021	2.15	0.0423	lrcsp(t)
	XL1_2_1	-0.07460	0.04487	-1.66	0.1100	lrcsp(t-1)
	AR1_2_1	0.04394	0.01952	2.25	0.0342	lpvsp(t-1)
	AR1_2_2	0.90174	0.04886	18.46	0.0001	lppdi(t-1)

Figure 8: Parameter Estimates of the VARX(1,1) Model

The parameter estimates results show that β_{01} and β_{12} are not significant at the 10% significance level, hence, these two parameters can be restricted to be zero. The following residual plot in Figure 9 shows that prediction errors from the VARX(1,1) model are all within two standard errors.

Figure 9: Residual Diagnostic for the VARX(1,1) Model

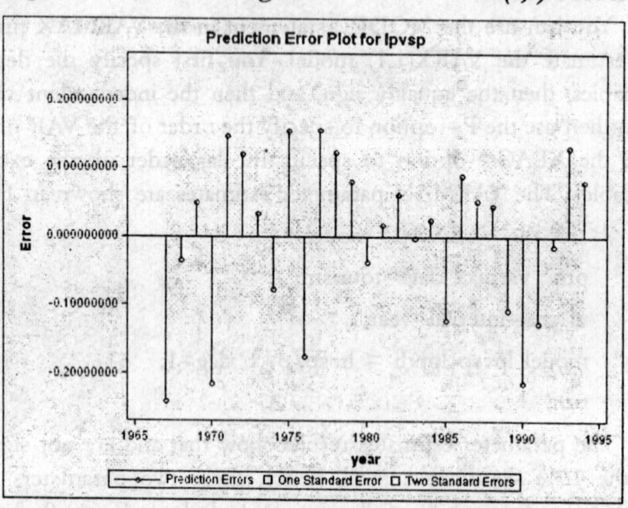

You can use the RESTRICT statement in the VARMAX procedure to restrict parameters in the model.

To perform forecasts based on the model estimated, you can use the OUTPUT statement. You need to specify the number of observations to be forecasted with the LEAD= option.

The restricted VARX(1,1) model parameter estimates are shown in Figure 10.

```
/* Fit the VARX(1,1) model with parameter restriction */
proc varmax data=tourism;
   id year interval=year;
   model lpvsp lppdi = lrcsp/p=1 xlag=1;
   restrict XL(0,1,1) = 0 XL(1,2,1)=0;
   output out=forecasts lead=6;
run;
```

The output also shows the six-year-ahead forecasts on a log of the number of holidays in Spain taken by U.K. residents (*LPVSP*) and a log of the U.K. real personal disposable income (*LPPSI*) and their corresponding 95% confidence intervals.

The VARMAX Procedure

Model Parameter Estimates

Equation	Parameter	Estimate	Standard Error	t Value	Pr > |t|	Variable
lpvsp	CONST1	-8.25141	3.51106	-2.35	0.0277	1
	XL0_1_1	0.00000	0.00000			lrcsp(t)
	XL1_1_1	-0.70675	0.22039	-3.21	0.0039	lrcsp(t-1)
	AR1_1_1	0.68178	0.11456	5.95	0.0001	lpvsp(t-1)
	AR1_1_2	0.68825	0.28903	2.38	0.0259	lppdi(t-1)
lppdi	CONST2	1.73555	0.51150	3.39	0.0025	1
	XL0_2_1	0.05806	0.03310	1.75	0.0928	lrcsp(t)
	XL1_2_1	0.00000	0.00000			lrcsp(t-1)
	AR1_2_1	0.05946	0.01731	3.44	0.0023	lpvsp(t-1)
	AR1_2_2	0.85819	0.04218	20.34	0.0001	lppdi(t-1)

Figure 10: Restricted Parameter Estimates

These results suggest that on average, U.K. residents are expected to spend about seven days in Spain in 1995. Note that the numbers in the Forecast column in Figure 11 are in logarithm form.

Forecasts

Variable	Obs	Time	Forecast	Standard Error	95% Confidence	Limits
lpvsp	30	1995	2.01513	0.13531	1.74993	2.28033
	31	1996	2.06105	0.18052	1.70723	2.41487
	32	1997	2.10908	0.21402	1.68960	2.52855
	33	1998	2.15711	0.23793	1.69077	2.62345
	34	1999	2.20441	0.25504	1.70455	2.70427
	35	2000	2.25080	0.26781	1.72590	2.77569
lppdi	30	1995	12.91046	0.02370	12.86401	12.95692
	31	1996	12.93041	0.03369	12.86438	12.99643
	32	1997	12.95011	0.04117	12.86941	13.03080
	33	1998	12.96979	0.04751	12.87666	13.06291
	34	1999	12.98948	0.05337	12.88487	13.09410
	35	2000	13.00917	0.05898	12.89358	13.12477

Figure 11: Six-Year Forecast

Figure 12 plots the forecasts on a log of the number of holidays in Spain taken by U.K. residents and their 95% confidence intervals. The plot shows that future holiday visits to Spain by U.K. residents are expected to increase over the next several years.

Figure 12: Forecasted Log Number of Holidays in Spain

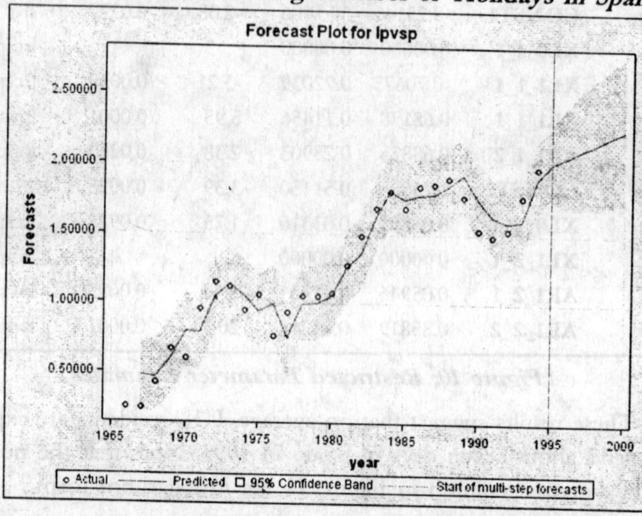

A Panel Data Analysis of Demand for Tourism in Africa

Tourism is one of the most flourishing and emerging industry in the world with the international receipt growing by over 10 percent over the last ten years, while international tourism expenditure amounted to over US$525billion in 2003 (WTO, 2004). Despite its potential of creating many employment opportunities and foreign exchange in any economy, it is also a means of enhancing each country destination's infrastructural facilities as well as promoting cooperation and understanding among people all over the world.

Tourism has become a means by which many countries, especially the developing countries, improve their income base and at the same show case their traditional heritage. Tourism in African continent has been seen as a means of enhancing economic growth and development as well as launching the image of the continent to the outside world.

According to Christie and Crompton (2001), the contribution of tourism industry in the gross domestic products (GDP) and exports in many African countries has been improving overtime. As identified by WTO (2004) report, there has been significant growth in the level of international tourist arrivals in Africa. The World Travel and Tourism Council (WTTC) also put the value of US$39.6billion as the amounted that was generated in 2003 from economic activities in the travel and tourism industry in sub-Saharan Africa. The report also shows that about 2.5% of the GDP in the region is accounted for by tourism industry that has generated about 5.5% of all employment in the region.

However, in spite of Africa's potential in tourism, the continent's tourism endowments have been underdevelop and underutilized. WTO (2004) report indicates that Africa has attracted less than 5% of international tourist arrivals in 2004, and had received less than 3% of international tourism receipt. Africa in 2001 received about 27.7 million international tourist arrivals and got an international tourism receipts of US$11.7 billion, which implies that 3.7 arrivals per 100 of population that is compared poorly with the world average of 11 and the 44 per 100 in Europe. Furthermore, despite African potentials in tourism industry, there are limited empirical studies on issues concerning the hypothetical subject matter in the continent.

This is the reason why Christie and Crompton (2001) opined that the lack of appropriate empirical studies on tourism in Africa is what contributed to the inadequate policy guidance to the industry. It is against this background of shortage in empirical studies of tourism in Africa that we intend to contribute to the frontier of knowledge in tourism literature in Africa by including both endogenous and exogenous variables in explaining the factors that determine the demand for tourism in Africa through dynamic generalized method of moment (GMM) of panel data analysis between the period of 1995 to 2004 (an update of Naude and Saayman (2004) data paints).

Tourism in Africa

Tourism is one of the major global economic activities. Tourism is said to be an important ingredient for economic development through its impact on employment generation, enhancement of infrastructure provision, generation of income taxes, exports and by acceleration global peace. According to Sinclair (1998), the contribution of tourism to development is well documented and tourism is now among the fastest growing industries in the world. Competition among destinations has intensified to attract more and more tourists.

Tourism growth has been impressive in recent years and this shown in the number of tourism arrivals in all countries that increased from 25.3 million in 1950 to 69.3 million in 1960 and later to 165.8 million in 1970. Despite the drag in the growth rate of tourist arrivals since 1970, world tourist arrival multiplied by a sector of about 27 between 1950 and 2000. Thus, from 25.3 million in 1950, international tourist arrivals (now arrivals) reached 763.2 million in 2004, with an average annual growth rate of 6.4 percent.

In terms of global tourism receipts, the world witnessed an increase in tourism receipt from US$2.1 billion in 1950 to US$17.9 billion in 1970 and later rise to US$106.5 billion in 1980. Due to more and more arrivals in the world and with their accompany expenditure, international tourism receipts move from US$2.1 billion in 1980 to US$479.2 billion in twenty years after. This increasing trend continues till 2004, where the total global tourism receipts amounted to US$622.7 billion.

Thus, tourism is one of the most flourishing sectors in the world given that it global receipt have grown by 12 percent over the last ten years. This has led to the case where many countries are setting targets in attempts to gain the additional income, foreign currency, employment and tax revenue that the sector can provide.

It is as a result of this that many African countries have started tapping the potentialities that is embedded in tourism and hospitalities. According to Kester (2003), tourism has the potential to contribute significantly to economic growth and development in Africa. Naude and Saayman (2004) opined that Africa's cultural and natural resource endowment are such that it ought to be benefiting largely from tourism, while Christie and Crompton (2001) believe that African has an "exceptional" tourism potentials and that the it is increasingly contributing to the continent's gross domestic products (GDP) and exports.

International tourist arrivals to Africa destinations increase from just 500,000 in 1950 to over 15 million in 1990. This increase in arrivals continues, as it got to 28.2 million in 2000 and later rise to 33.2 million in 2004.

This really shows that Africa tourist arrivals have been growing overtime. According to WTO (2003) figures, Africa tourism has grown significantly since 1990. In terms of the continent receipts on global tourism, that African receipts on international tourism rise from US$100 million in 1950 to US$3.4 billion in 1980, which later increased to US$6.4 billion in 1990. By 2000, African tourism receipts have risen to US$10.6 billion and got to US$18.3 billion in 2004. These incremental trends in African arrivals and receipts literarily depict that Africa is performance in term of tourism, but when we look at its share in the global tourism, we could sea that through it share in international tourist arrivals increased from 1.98 percent in 1950 to 4.25 in 2001, which is about 130 percent increment. This latter fall in 2002 to 4.21 percent and picked up by 2004 to 4.4 percent of the global tourist arrivals.. In terms of the growth rate, the continent witnessed a negative growth in 1960 of about 42 of its arrivals. This later change to a positive growth rate of about 81 percent in 1980 (the peak), afterwards, there the growth rate has been increasing at a decreasing rate up to 2004 when she witnessed a negative growth rate in arrivals of 6 percent.

The case of the growth rate of Africa's tourist arrivals is not that different with her receipts, as she experienced a negative growth rate of her receipt in 1960 (39 percent) and by 1990, it has reduced to –27percent and later to –0.7 percent in 2004.

Regionally, there are different in performance of these regions in the continent. According to WTO figure (2003), there has been considerable improvement in tourism in Africa, especially in 1990, especially that of southern Africa that has grown by about 300% between 1990 and 2002.

However, North Africa still remains the most attractive regional destination, capturing 1.5% of the total international tourism market share. Worth of noticing is that as the tourist arrivals in Africa increased in 2001 that of the world tourism decreased during the period. The report of WTO (2003c) indicates that there had been increasing trend in tourism in Africa despite the SARS virus that affected the Asia counties and the war in Iraq. Central Africa remains the least tourist arrivals destinations in the continent followed by the West African destinations. This might be due to the inadequate infrastructural facilities that are available for tourism in these destinations.

Literature Review

In general, the tourism literatures on the modelling of tourism demand focuses either on analyzing the impact of different determinants and/or on the accurate forecasting of the future tourism demand.

This study lies within the group focusing on the underlying determinants. The comprehensive reviews of the empirical literature on tourism demand by Crouch (1994a, 1994b, 1995), Witt and Witt (1995), Lim (1997, 1999) and Li et al (2005) Suggest a substantial agreement regarding both the tourism demand measures and the variables that are important in explaining international tourism flows. A lot of these existing empirical works have used tourist arrivals/departures and tourism receipts/expenditures as dependent variables. The number of overnight the tourists stays in their destination countries and the average length of stay has also been studied, but much less frequently.

As for the explanatory variables, empirical models of tourism demand borrow heavily from the consumer theory, which predicts that the level of consumption depends on the consumer's income, the price of the good/service in question, the prices of related goods (substitutes and complements), and other demand shifters. As a result, income and prices are the most commonly used variables in terms of the major factors influencing tourism demand.

Given that the leisure tourism is generally regarded a luxury good, the income remaining after expenditures on necessities, or the so-called discretionary income would be the preterred income variable. However, discretionary income is a subjective variable and is not precisely measurable. Therefore, most researchers have relied on the nominal or real (per capital) personal, disposable, or national income, as well as GDP as measure for income in origin countries.

Apart from being sensitive to their own income, tourists are also sensitive to prices. The tourism includes two price elements: the cost of travel to the destination and the cost of living in the tourist destination. Also, the literature shows that the most often employed variables aimed at measuring the cost of living at the tourist destination relative to the origin country (and possibly to alternative destinations) have been relative consumer price indices. However, their deficiency comes from the fact that the expenditure patterns of a tourist might be quite specific and therefore different from that of the average household in a certain country. As a result, some studies have used specific price indices such as hotel, drink and tobacco, shopping, meals, and entertainment and other variables. However, we should understand that the work of Martin and Witt (1987) has shown that such tourism-specific indices do not perform any better than the overall price indices.

Studies often use exchange rate in tourism demand model in addition to/or combined with the relative price variables. There is some group of authors that argued that tourists respond to exchange rate movements much more than to changes in relative inflation rates when they make decisions on the travel destination. However, Martin and Witt (1987) argued that the exchange rate alone is not an acceptable proxy for tourism costs. Most empirical works on tourism demand models have used the exchange rate adjusted for relative prices (i.e. real exchange rate) to capture the substitution between domestic vacations and international travel. In this way, the impacts of (relative) inflation and exchange rate movements are measured through a single variable.

There has been less attention on transportation costs in the literature due to the fact that there is lack of adequate measure of effective transportation costs. In countries where the most of the tourists arrive by car, the proxy are usually oil or gasoline prices while in the case of far-off destinations, airline fares represent the preferable alternative. In the latter case, according to Mervar and Payne (2007), data problems arise due to the pricing practices of airlines that often include "special" have that are difficult to collect and use for àn empirical analysis. Furthermore, multicollinearity between the transportation cost and income variables presents an often cited reason for omitting the transportation cost variable from tourism studies.

Furthermore, the dynamics of tourism demand has been incorporated in a lot of studies to account for lagged effects of supply constraints in the form of shortages in hotel accommodation, passenger transportation capacity and trained staff, which cannot be adjusted rapidly. Sometimes, a time trend is included to capture qualitative factors in the tourist destination or changes in tourist faster for foreign travel. Also, during variables are employed in order to capture the impact of wars, political crises or natural disasters, as well as seasonal variations.

Given the above, tourism demand model is usually estimated as a function of income of tourists origin country, transportation costs between dimension and origin, exchange rates, relative prices, dummy variables and the deterministic trends. Despite the fact that in the literature, annual data is often used, there has been increasing use of quarterly data in recent literature, which is in line with the increasing interest in the seasonality of global tourism flows.

In terms of the estimation techniques, the log-linear regressions are the most frequently employed functional forms as the estimated coefficients can be interpreted as elasticities. However, while traditional econometric technique dominated studies up to the mid-1990s, the use of cointegration, vector autoregressive model, almost ideal demand systems, and time-varying parameter models have since become familiar approaches. Thus, given the fact that the trend parallels the overall trend in applied econometric studies since it has been shown that most time series data are not stationary and, therefore, the use of traditional econometric techniques may serious affect the credibility of the results. However, some studies have tried to forecast the demand for tourism for a particular period of time suing various for casting methods. Martin and Witt (1989) compared the accuracy of several quantitative methods in forecasting tourism demand in an international context; Johnson and Ashworth (1990) had survey articles on the determinants of tourism demand; Witt and Witt (1995) reviewed about sixty five empirical studies on the tourism demand; while Sinclair and Stables (1997) made a synthesis of several tourism analyses, discussing and particularly the use of different kinds of models, with explicit consideration of the single-equation and system of equations approaches, and their respective advantages and disadvantage.

Thus, studies on the determinants of tourism demand are subjected to specific problems. The reasons to the problems according to Mello et al. (1999) are twofold: the special nature of the demand for tourism, which can be attributed to the complexity of the motivational structure underlying the decision-making process, and the scarcity of relevant data that are fundamental in econometric modelling. The quantitative studies of tourism demand require the framework of a formal mathematical model that can provide estimates of the sensitivity of demand to changes in the variables on which it depends. The econometric modelling also supplies a good basis for accurate forecasting that is of considerable value for policy purposes and an important element in public and private investment decisions.

However, tourism demand modelling is not easy due to the complexity of the decision-making process, the multiplicity and heterogeneity of the products and services specified, the fact that transportation plays a role in the consumption of tourism, the intertemporal dependence of current demand on its past and future values, and the nonseparability between leisure consumption and labour supply and/or between tourism demand and the demand for other goods and services. These difficulties in the specification of a comprehensive and reliable model of demand for tourism arecompounded by the existence of unquantifiable factors influencing demand, as well as by the inaccuracy or unavailability of data for those that are, in principle, measurable.

Thus, the conceptual and practical problems underlying the empirical studies in this area accounted for the simplifying assumptions that investigators make in their attempts to specify econometric models for explaining the behaviour of tourism demand.

So long as the assumptions do not distort the estimated results, they perform an important role in facilitating the provision of information which can be useful for policy formation and decision making. When the assumptions are inadequate and questionable, they give rise to models that may embody misspecification bias, leading to accurate and unreliable estimation results that cannot be used for any sound inference and forecasting or policy purposes.

The major examples of this latter type of models can be found in the single equation approach within a static context. These adhoc models lack the theoretical basis within which the reasonable testable hypothesis of consumer theory can be included and often neglect the possible interdependency among competing destinations Mello et al. (1999). Also, they usually ignore the dynamic nature of demand for tourism, disregarding the possibility that the sensitivity of tourism demand of its determinants may differ between different time periods.

Modelling procedures constrained by these theoretical faults lead to empirical inadequacies, such as the omission of relevant variables and incorrect functional form that result in misspecified models and biased estimates.

Thus, given the above, we have discovered that in the literature of empirical studies of tourism, there are two main types. The first consists of those that prefer modern time series and cointegration techniques in the attempt of modelling and forecasting the dependant variable, between one or several pairs of countries, Kulenderan and Witt (2001), Seddighi and Theocharous (2002), Song et al. (2003 and Dritsakis (2004)). The second type includes those studies that estimate the determinants of international tourism demand using classical multivariate regressions, Witt and Witt (1995), and Lim (1997)).

Therefore, in this study we explore these two types of models, vis a vis, single equation and system of equation using annual panel data. The use of these two models will really afford us to make comparative analysis on the outcome of the two results so as to really know the model that suit the explanation of the demand for tourism.

This two stage least square only presents two different outcome, from fixed effect and none cross-sectional effect angle. We could see that we the system of equations, the result has drastically changed to that of OLS above. Here, all the outcomes show that the autonomous variable, constant, has negative effect on Africa's tourist arrivals. This means that if the regressors in the model are put into consideration and there is no encouragement,. Provision of infrastructure and political stability in the continent. Then the continent will not be attractive for tourists and there will be reduction in the number of arrivals.

Both outcomes of the two stage least square also show that the previous tourists number have statistically significant influence on the present tourist arrivals. Their degree of responsiveness is elastic, meaning that the prospective tourists are very significant to previous treatment and hospitality given to previous tourists. The two results show that tourists are very sensitive to prices in Africa, though the degree of responsiveness is inelastic. Exchange rate for both outcomes in the two stage least square is negatively related to tourist arrivals. This means that as the destination countries currencies get appreciated there will be loss of welfare to the tourists and this is in form of giving more of their domestic currencies to destinations currencies, and this will make their travels and adventures more expensive.

Their degree of responsiveness to exchange rate appreciation is elastic and statistically significant at the non cross-sectional effect level. The measure of infrastructure in both outcomes of two stage least square (Teline) has statistically significant direct effect on tourist arrivals. This means that as more and more infrastructural facilities are provided in the continent, tourists are eager to come and explore the opportunities and endowments that are embedded in Africa. The coefficient of the variable that stands for elasticities indicate that the variable is inelastic at both outcomes. Here, the political instabilities in different parts of the continent have adverse effects on tourist arrivals. This shows that tourists are sensitive to what is happening in the polity before embarking on their trips. World income has an inverse relationship with arrivals under fixed effect, while direct effect in the none cross-sectional case. This reason for this is that since the fixed effect captures the individual destination effect and there are crises in same of these destinations in Africa, then even if the tourists have more income to spend on tourism, they will not prefer coming to the crises ridden destinations.

The result of the dynamic panel data techniques used in this study. The dynamic result gives four different outcomes of the technique vis a vis, fixed effect, random effect, difference and the orthogonal deviation. The dynamic results show that in all the four outcome of the model, consumer price index, a measure of relative price in the destinations is inversely related to the number of arrivals. The significant of this variable in all the outcomes except that of difference model, indicate that prices are important factors that tourists consider in their choice of destinations in Africa and the degree of responsiveness of tourist to changes in prices in inelastic in the models of the dynamic panel analysis. Exchange rate in all these models is also inversely related to tourist arrivals, indicating that appreciation of destinations currencies often discourage prospective tourists form coming to Africa. It is important to note that this variable is significant at 5 per cent level for all the models and it is highly inelastic. Crime rate in the continent also has an inverse effect with the tourist arrivals, that is, as the incidence of crime increases in the destinations, there will be reduction in the inflow of tourists to those destinations.

Source: Author's calculation The lagged value of tourist arrivals which is the number of previous tourist arrivals, the number of available telephone lines and world income all have direct effects on the number of tourist arrivals. The number of telephone lines for the four outcomes are statistically significant indication that it is an important factor that influences tourists' choice of destinations. The same can be said to the previous number of tourist arrivals in the continent, as all the outcomes show that this variable is relevant determinant of tourist demand and interesting thing here is that the autonomous variable indicates that if countries of destinations do not make efforts to develop tourism through improvement in infrastructure, crime rate and the political situation, there will be reduction in the number of tourist arrivals in

Africa. These results contradict with those of the OLS results. Therefore, the results of this study have shown that the dynamic panel data analysis is a better technique in explaining the factors that influence tourism demand in Africa, since it is always used to correct for endogeneity problems, the issue of heteroscedasticity and dynamics of the variables.

Conclusion

We have tried in this study to econometrically determine factors that influence the demand for tourism in Africa. Analysis has been done on the structure, pattern and trend of African tourism overtime.

In selecting the variables for this study, we considered both the endogenous and exogenous variables. That is, we have selected the economic variables as well as the sociopolitical variables that influence the tourists' choice of destinations. In this study, we specified the single equation model and that of system of equations. The single equation model makes of OLS estimators with fixed and random effects, while the system of equation makes use of the two stage least square and the dynamic panel data technique. We find out from the analyses of this study that political instability, crime rate, exchange rate appreciation and consumer price index serve as signal to prospective tourists to the continent. However, the previous tourist arrivals, number of telephone lines, a measure of infrastructure, and world income, positively influence or determine tourist arrivals to Africa. Another interesting thing we found out in the study is that the results of system of equations are better than that of single equation model and this result was confirmed by Naude and Saayman (2004), Eilat and Einav (2003)

7

Tourism in an International Context

Tourism in Context

Tourism is a powerful driver of community prosperity. Tourism exports (ie; foreign revenue earned in Australia) are larger than coal exports, wool exports and most other categories. It makes both a direct (tourism industry jobs and income etc.) and an indirect (retail, hospitality, goods and services etc.) contribution to the Australian economy.

The tourism industry represents the quintessential expression of the small business ethic of Australia, with a large number of small and medium-sized operators, including many that are family run businesses. Tourism is a labour intensive activity overall, employing proportionally more people per dollar of GDP than most other industries.

Chief beneficiary industries are transport, accommodation, cafes and restaurants, manufacturing, retail and property and business services. After the airlines, large hotel chains, big tour companies and major man-made attractions, most tourism business is small, and reliant on local support for its viability. This is especially true in the CoPP.

An Australian snapshot: Tourism in Australia continues to trend upwards generally year on year at about 1%, despite periodic unforeseen spikes in the market occasioned by such factors as SARS or 9/11.

Between 2000-2001, tourism contributed around $59 billion to Australia's GDP, which equates with 9% of GDP. Between 2004-05 tourism accounted for $18.3 billion in exports.

According to most recent available data, tourism in 2000-01 directly employed 549,000 people (6% of total employment). Indirect employment for the same 2000-01 period accounted for about 351,000 people, some 4.4% of the work force. When combined, in 2000-01 tourism accounted for the employment of around 900,000 people, or 10.4% of the Australian work force.

A Victorian Snapshot:

According to the latest research, in 2003-2004, the combined direct and indirect contribution of tourism to Victoria's Gross State Product (GSP) is estimated to be 5.3% or $10.9 billion (a 49% increase from $7.3 billion in 1997-1998).

Overall, The tourism industry contributes more to the Victorian economy than many traditional industries including agriculture, forestry & fishing; mining; electricity, gas & water supply; Government administration and defence; and Cultural and recreational services.

Victorian Employment in the Tourism Industry

In 2003-2004 tourism accounted for 159,000 jobs or 6.6% of all people employed in Victoria (a 19% increase from 134,000 in 1997-1998).

Visitation to Victoria

Sixty-four percent of overnight visitors to Victoria were sourced from the intrastate market, followed by 28% from the interstate market and 7% from overseas. 37% of domestic visitor nights to Victoria were sourced from the intrastate market, followed by 36% from the international market and 26% from interstate.

Domestic Overnight Visitation

Victoria received 17.3 million domestic overnight visitors for the year ending June 2006 and 53.0 million domestic visitor nights. The average length of stay for the year ending June 2006 was 3.1 nights.

Domestic Daytrip Visitation

There were 31.8 million domestic daytrip visitors to Victoria for the year ending June 2006.

Domestic Visitor Expenditure

Domestic overnight expenditure in Victoria in 2005 is estimated to be $7.6 billion, with visitors spending on average $148 per night and $454 per visit. Domestic daytrip visitors spent $2.9 billion in Victoria in 2005, spending on average $92 per daytrip. Domestic overnight visitors to Victoria spent most of their money on food and drink (26% of total expenditure) and accommodation (20%).

Domestic Forecast

Over the period 2006 to 2015, domestic visitor nights to Victoria are expected to grow by an average annual rate of 0.5%, to reach 52.9 million nights in 2015. Holiday/Leisure travel to Victoria is forecast to grow at an annual average rate of 0.5% over the period 2006 to 2015 to reach 25.5 million nights.

A Melbourne Snapshot: In the year ended September 2005, Melbourne had almost 17.3 million visitors from all sources. Of those, nearly 5.9 million were domestic overnight visitors.

Total Travel to Melbourne in the YE Sep 2006

Looking at travel to Melbourne overall, there were nearly 40.7 million visitor nights. Of these, International overnight visitors to Melbourne numbered 1.3 million and they stayed 22.7 million nights or 55.9% of all visitor nights.

New Zealand is Melbourne's biggest international source market of visitors, with UK second, while China in third place, is the second biggest contributor of visitor nights in Melbourne. A significant proportion of the Chinese visitation is attributable to learning English.

A visit for 'Holiday/pleasure' continues to be the main purpose of visit for international overnight visitors to Melbourne, and 'Education' remained the biggest 'purpose of visit' contributor to international visitor nights in Melbourne. Because of people who come for education, and backpackers who use Melbourne as a work base, the average stay in Melbourne by international visitors is quite high at 18.1 nights (contributed mainly by education and backpackers). This makes sense of the notion that 'Rented house/apartment/unit/flat' remains the most popular accommodation type for international visitor nights in Melbourne.

Domestic visitors (from interstate and intrastate) made up 44.1% of Melbourne's visitation, while another 58% were on a domestic day trip.

Together, these visitors spent an estimated $7.1 billion in Melbourne, and almost certainly, a good proportion of that spending took place within the boundaries of the City of Port Phillip.

Domestic Overnight Travel

In the year ended September 06 Domestic visitors staying overnight in Melbourne numbered 6.6 million, and contributed 19.6 million nights, an increase on the previous year of 11.9%

The biggest source of interstate overnight travel to Melbourne is still NSW. The main purpose of a visit is 'Visiting friends or relatives', and the average stay in Melbourne by domestic overnight visitors is now 3.0 nights.

The most popular accommodation type remains a 'Friends or relatives property' and when here, eating out at restaurants' continues to be the most popular activity for domestic overnight visitors.

The Local Snapshot

CoPP is a significant beneficiary of visitation to Melbourne. Beyond anecdotal experience, understanding exactly what the share is, difficult to quantify other than to take a simple division of the Melbourne figures for visitation, and then apply those to CoPP.

It could be argued that on any given day or evening, many people dining in our restaurants and cafes, or gathering in our pubs and bars to listen to live music, laugh at a stand up comedian or meet friends are a mixture of local and inner Melbourne people. Added to this, the breadth of budget accommodation options within CoPP, means that additional visitors from elsewhere, including overseas might be numbered in the crowd, or staff behind the bar.

In addition, on weekends our local population swells considerably as leisure time pursuits are taken up within our city boundaries.

Measuring the impact of this visitation and the indirect economic impacts of tourism are difficult. Visitors do not recognise lines on a map, and in any given day, a single visitor from interstate, staying 2 nights and spending $500 may spend part of their time and money in several LGA's. Presently, best estimates suggest that most people staying more than one night in Melbourne will likely visit the City of Port Phillip as part of their itinerary.

Accounting Systems for Tourism in an International Context

Within the globalized economic and business environment, the assessment of accounting systems has become a crucial process for researchers. Accounting throughout history industry has undergone a drastic change. As a branch of economics, accounting provides information about a firm and its transactions to facilitate resource allocation decisions by users of that information. Via an extended literature review, researchers have attempted to approach theoretically accounting's catalytic contribution to the tourism business environment. However, a review of the hospitality literature revealed a paucity of academic research to assess the connection between accounting for tourism and its applications within the last five years. In this context the purpose of this paper is to provide the importance of accounting systems for tourism enterprises in an international context.

The next section presents the literature review. In this section, we analyse the concepts of "accounting", "tourism business" and "accounting systems for tourism". Then the research is specified in the applications of accounting systems in international hotel business. The results indicate that accounting is a catalytic element which offers additional value to the modern hotel business. Finally, the concluding remarks are discussed and some possible future research directions are highlighted.

Literature Review

General: This section presents the results of a literature review in order to illustrate the relevant theoretical models of accounting systems for tourism in an international context.

Conceptual Framework of "Accounting"

Accounting interest and approaches have expanded in recent years. Accounting history is worth studying since it puts contemporary accounting into perspective and may easily give us an account of all the information collected in the past which could provide solutions to the problems of the present. It is worth teaching as part of the overall cultural formation of future accountants, in particular to stress that "presently acceptable practices of accounting have not been immutable over the decades and centuries of environmental change".

Accounting historians have long been conscious that a full understanding of accounting's past needs to embrace international dimensions. The key role of accounting is to provide information for economic decision making (SAC 2, 1990) in support of the current political paradigm of economic growth and development.

Solomons (1991) describes accounting as being like a telephone – a neutral medium that promotes the exchange of information between the enterprise and the user; and while it is not an actor in the exchange, it is important that accounting measures be representationally faithful.

Miller and Napier (1993) argue that like any social phenomenon, accounting presents a "historically and geographically localised result", but that does not imply that accounting should be viewed in isolation at a particular point of space or time. Just as international accounting aims to situate local accounting practices of today within a comparative framework across space, so country-based histories of accounting attempt the same process across time.

In their prospectus for accounting history into the twenty-first century, Carnegie and Napier (1996) proposed the notion of "comparative international accounting history" (CIAH). This research field is not entirely unexplored. However, its expansion can assist in generating "a focus on examining and explaining cross-national differences in accounting development".

Accounting history literature witnessed a vast growth during the recent years. This growth has manifested itself not just in the number of publications but in the topics examined, research approaches adopted, and range of theoretical perspectives applied to the study of accounting through its history. Accounting concepts, techniques and institutions have been diffused through both space and time. Based on an admittedly limited population of English language papers appearing from 1996 to 1999 in the specialist accounting history journals, Carnegie and Potter (2000) concluded that their analysis indicates "the existence of a relatively insular international accounting history research community dominated by a small number of institutions and authors".

Carnegie and Potter contended that accounting history authors seldom engage in cross-border collaborative research and display a limited tendency to venture beyond core themes and the modern period. A subsequent study of the sex distribution of authors in the same journals revealed, unsurprisingly, that authorship and editorial board membership in accounting history is male-dominated. Furthermore, Edwards (2004) broader review of the accounting history literature identified concerns about areas of fading interest, publication media and the dissemination of research findings.

Fleischman and Radcliffe's (2005) celebration of the advance of accounting history during "the roaring nineties" is challenged by fears of its quiet demise in the United States. It takes accounting to be a translucent medium which presents factual data to the world about an enterprise's financial transactions and economic events. A good accounting is deemed to be one that represents the entity in a way that users recognize as commonsensical.

Theoretical Background of "Tourism Industry"

Tourism industry is of great importance for the world economy today. It is one of the largest single employers and in many countries it is the largest services exporting sector, making an outstanding contribution to the balance of payments.

Tourism industry has many of the characteristics of a competitive market:

* there are few barriers to enter;
* it is a truly global market with few unnatural barriers to trade;
* there is a large number of firms and
* prices are set on the basis of market expectations.

A lot of researchers have tried to define the concept of tourism. According to Monique Dacharry (1964), tourism owes to be delimited in its historical prospect. Years later, Kaspar (1976) defines tourism as the total of relations and events that arise from the travel and the eve of individuals, when the place of stay is neither the initial and permanent residence nor the usual place of work. In this context tourism, according to United Nations (1994) and Frechtling (1999) is the activities associated with travel away from a person's usual environment and most countries of the world are interested in the impact of tourism on their economies.

Nowadays, tourism organizations are becoming truly international and the issues they face equally universal. In "the age of service competition" that is depicted by international hospitality and tourism, the customer reigns supreme.

Such is the power of customers that the term "service management" is increasingly used to emphasise management imperatives in this age of service competition and market forces. Therefore, to sustain competitiveness hospitality and tourism providers must continue to meet if not exceed customer expectations that are themselves dynamic.

A properly planned, developed and controlled tourism industry will positively affect the society and the economy. Enrichment of the tourism industry with national characteristics is vital for a healthy development of tourism. Tourism has outperformed most other sectors and contributed significantly to the economic and employment growth. Generally speaking travel and tourism encompassing transport, accommodation, catering, recreation and developing economies worldwide.

Accounting Systems for Tourism

Consideration will also be made of the literature that reviews the impact of accounting systems for tourism, directly. It should be noted that there is little objective research on this specific impact. At first, Harris and Brown (1998) presented an overview of development in accounting management with particular emphasis on the contribution of applied work for the tourism industry. One year later, Graham and Harris (1999) presented a paper that illustrated the development and implementation management accounting techniques in the Europe, Middle East and Africa division of an international hotel chain.

In this context Mia and Patiarb (2001) stressed the use of management accounting system in hotels. More recently, Mongiello and Harris (2006) described the design of managerial accounting systems in multinational hotel companies. Moreover, Anderson and Guilding (2006) emphasized the potential of competitor-focused practice to hotel business. Finally Burgess (2007) emphasized the major importance of outsourcing accounting functions, particularly in the hotel sector.

Applications of Accounting Systems in International Hotel Business

There are many proponents who now define the industry as competing on global terms. Tse and West (1992) provide persuasive reasoning when they indicate that a firm competes on global terms when its competitive position in one country is significantly influenced by its position in other countries.

Internationalization has become a key research theme in the study of the hospitality industry and its constituents. Like its domestic counterpart, the international hotel industry competes via the placement of its units in significant and appropriate locations.

Recall that accounting entails several broad processes:

* *Measurement* is the process of identifying and quantifying economic activities. These measurements provide insights into the profitability of a firm's operations and the strength of its financial position.
* *Disclosure* is the process by which accounting measurements communicated to their intended users.
* *Auditing* is the process by which specialized accounting professionals attest to the reliability of the measurement and communication process.

The accounting procedure is considered to be the security belt of the business for avoiding either the involuntary or the intentional release of information as well as the avoidance of loss of income from misuse or from any errors in operation.

In this context, accounting plays a vital role in the verification of incomings and expenditure per field of operation in the hotel business. By the term 'fields of operation' of a hotel we mean those sections of the hotel in which the production procedure of the tourist goods and services occur with the purpose of achieving profit. The main fields of utilization within a modern hotel unit are:

* the bedrooms.
* the bar.
* the buffet.
* the restaurant.

A lot of researchers argue that all these fields of operation are the most essential centres of earnings and cost and accounting plays a vital role in them.

Furthermore, accounting includes those actions related to the funding of the hotel unit, that is, with the capital which is necessary for its smooth running. The risk of losing capitals and also credit risk appear to be the determining factors from its viability.

Within the framework of limiting the risk of correct constitution of financial affairs, the following actions are in effect:

* Controls of the procedures, whereby a check is held to ensure whether the investments are always in accordance with the approved investment policy.

* Controls of the evaluations, whereby the cost of the investments with the running values is mainly compared as well as a check of the "deposits" and the "loans".
* Controls of the availabilities, the bank deposits and loans, during which their frequent update and the confirmation of other ones is necessary.

Furthermore, accounting systems contribute to the provision of information for performance measurement. From the above mentioned, it is clear that accounting enables the hotel management to examine whether the right strategy of financial management is followed. Furthermore an appropriate accounting system is able to satisfy hotel managers' information needs aiming to support management decision-making. Simultaneously, accounting is essential in the correct valuation of mergers and acquisitions. Unfortunately, hotel companies do not fully utilize accounting information to assess the value of merger and acquisition, which is increasing to improve international competitiveness. This neglect of accounting information in merger and acquisitions leads to inappropriate evaluation of its value in markets.

Conclusion

The last few decades have been characterized by unparalleled change. Researchers have not paid much attention to accounting systems in tourism, despite its importance for the world economy. However, events may persuade many developing countries to reconsider their industralization policy: in this new world, tourism can provide a very important alternative for economic development and growth. The concept of tourism business was brought to the surface at the dawn of the 20th century. Simultaneously, accounting is established as an essential mean for the exact management of any business economic resources.

A possible limitation of the results is the short time interval covered. Furthermore with few exceptions such as Kreul (1993) and Burgess (1996) little work has been undertaken in an international context. There is also need for articles to which connect quality and environment with accounting systems for tourism.

Thus a suggestion for future research would be to examine the possible applications of accounting systems in tourism for a longer period. Another promising research initiative would be to further explore how an accounting system might be best operationalised to a tourism industry.

From the above it is clear that accounting adds up value, offering at the same time a systematic scientific approach on the improvement of the effectiveness of the tourism business. As the saying goes, "the future is bright, but the road ahead is tortuous". Realization of the major significance of accounting in tourism will set accounting as a priceless support in the hotel business management effort.

Geneva Seminar on International Sustainable Development Policy and Tourism

A Seminar on International Sustainable Development Policy and Tourism was held on Monday 25 November 2002, at the Palais des Nations in Geneva. It brought together much of the findings of UNRISD research in the area of tourism conducted in the late 1990s and early 2000s. The Seminar was organized by Institute jointly with the Geneva-based organization Europe-China Management Improvement Foundation (ECMI), presided by Professor Paolo Urio, former Dean of the Faculty of Economic and Social Sciences of the University of Geneva.

The 30 participants represented mostly the West-Central Qingshai province of China, with one representative from Hainan. They included senior representatives of the local government, heads of city and provincial tourism bureaus, university professors and academics, environmental specialists and lawyers as well as professional trainers.

The panel consisted of Krishna Ghimire, UNRISD Research Coordinator, who made a presentation on "Sustainable Development and Tourism: What Is New?"; Nicolas Bovay, UNRISD Information Officer, who presented a paper titled "Tourism, Ethics and Human Rights"; Behzod Mingboev, UNRISD Research Assistant, who spoke about "The Development of Tourism in Countries in Transition: The Case of the ex-Soviet-Union", and Li Zhaodong, correspondent in Geneva for the *Guangming Daily*, one of China's largest daily newspapers.

Krishna Ghimire, who moderated the seminar, made a presentation highlighting the linkages between sustainable development and tourism planning. He first presented a comparative analysis of tourism issues in Europe and developing countries which indicated many similarities in the evolution of lifestyles and rapid expansion in movements of people.

However, he said that many negative impacts of tourism were especially felt in the developing world. He then went on to discuss the context in which the 2002 World Summit on Sustainable Development in Johannesburg was organized and where, for the first time ever, tourism issues were included on the agenda in a major UN summit. Regrettably, however, the Summit merely called for increased investments in the tourism sector. In conclusion, Mr. Ghimire said that investment in small-scale community tourism projects should receive priority if tourism were to be used as a tool for poverty eradication. Tourism should be developed in an integrated manner with other sectors of livelihood provisioning so that local communities are not made helplessly dependent on tourism. In order to reduce vulnerability related to international tourism, developing countries should also explore the possibility of promoting national and regional tourism. He summed up by stating that the recent World Trade Organization's scheme to liberalize the service sector in tourism was especially unwelcome for developing countries as their tourism earnings are heavily derived from the service sector.

Nicolas Bovay pointed at the fact that tourism had an uneasy relationship with human rights and ecology. He recalled that human categories most at risk were children, indigenous peoples, women and local communities, and said that tourism, and particularly sex tourism, had led to violations of a number of existing international human rights standards and norms, including labour conventions and the concept of decent work.

He said that although present efforts to combat paedophilia in the context of tourism at the international and domestic levels were commendable, much more remained to be done in legal and policy terms. He also said that the development of tourism had led to ongoing violations of economic, social and cultural rights of the local communities in which it was taking place as well as the destruction of the local ecosystem and their peoples' ancestral ways of life. He went on to say that sustainable tourism would only succeed if it involves tourism workers that have a stake in it, and that means that they should be much more democratically involved at work. Workers needed livable salaries and better training in the environment if the industry was to have a beneficial impact on their local communities. He concluded by stating that if tourism wanted to survive as an industry it should not harm the local cultures and landmarks which are exactly what attract tourists in the very first place.

Behzod Mingboev stated that although all the countries of the former USSR were trying to develop their tourism industries, many factors limited their success. He recalled that many of the countries concerned lacked political stability and security and were economically and socially volatile. He also pointed at the fact that local touristic infrastructures, when they existed, were often well below international standards. In the case of Belarus there had even been a sharp decrease in the number of visitors due to the consequences of the 1986 Chernobyl disaster. Other forms of pollution, including the dumping of nuclear and industrial waste had taken a heavy toll on the environment. On a more positive tone, Mr. Mingboev said that the citizens of the newly independent states were now free to travel abroad and that the experiences and ideas that they gained abroad were proving useful to the nascence of a political culture in the post-Soviet geographical space.

Li Zhaodong made a presentation on the development of the tourism industry in Europe and particularly in Switzerland and its historical relevance to developing nations. In his presentation on the new phenomenon of outbound Chinese tourists he said that the new situation presented formidable opportunities for learning from past experiences of developed nations.

The presentations were followed by a lively debate. Professor Paolo Urio made the concluding remarks in which he stressed the importance for China of developing a tourism industry that would be sustainable and would be accessible to the emerging domestic touristic market. He concluded by saying that developing countries should privilege endogenous development and place more value on the development of their own local potentialities to diminish dependency on foreign interests.

Tourism And Environmental Issues

Environmental Implications of the Tourism Industry

Energy Consumption: Preliminary figures from a draft Sustainable Tourism Roundtable Report indicate that the tourism industry uses 72.1

Gwhours of energy per year. This amount is only a very small percentage of total U.S. energy consumption approximately 0.3% in 1997.

Water Consumption

The preliminary figures from the above-mentioned report indicate that the tourism industry in the aggregate uses 93.9 billion gallons of water per year. This amount is 4.0% of total U.S. commercial consumption (including the chemical, pulp and paper, primary metals, and the textiles industries). Tourism-related water use in the lodging industry accounts for approximately 46.2 billion gallons of water per year. In 1995, total freshwater withdrawals in the United States for offstream uses (e.g., withdrawal of surface and ground-water for public supply; domestic use; agriculture, including irrigation and livestock watering; industry, including mining; and thermoelectric power uses) was 340 billion gallons per day. By contrast, tourism related hotel water use accounted for under.04% of the total.

Pollution and Waste Outputs

Water Quality: The tourism industry impacts water quality through construction and maintenance of tourist infrastructure, recreational boating, and certain activities of the cruise industry. Tourist infrastructure increases the pressure on existing sewage treatment plants and can lead to overflows during peak tourist times. A more gradual impact is the leaching of nutrients from septic systems of tourists' waterfront homes, accelerating eutrophication of adjacent water bodies, and depleting dissolved oxygen supplies. The construction of tourist facilities and infrastructure also increases the amount of impervious surfaces, which in turn increases the amount of polluted runoff reaching water bodies.

The most significant problem from the standpoint of human health associated with recreational boating and water quality is the discharge of sewage into water bodies with limited flushing, where the discharge occurs near the location of shellfish beds. Diseases that can be potentially transmitted through human contact with fecal discharge and/or ingestion of contaminated shellfish include typhoid fever, dysentery, infectious hepatitis, and nonspecific gastroenteritis.

Spills and discharges of oil and toxic chemicals are other impacts that recreational boats and the cruise industry can have, although such impacts are not necessarily significant. In 1997, recreational vessels were responsible for 535 reported oil spills, comprising 6.2% of the total spill incidents in U.S. waters. The cruise industry was responsible for an even smaller percentage, at 1.6% of total spills in U.S. waters.

Air Quality

Most tourism-related air pollution comes from automobiles. Automobiles emit by far the most carbon monoxide of all transportation modes. In 1997, they emitted 26 million short tons of carbon monoxide, compared with 1.7 million short tons from recreational marine vehicles, and 1 million from aircraft. Specific information on tour bus emissions was not available, but all heavy-duty diesel vehicles (most tour buses fall into this category) emitted 1.4 million short tons in 1997.

Habitat/Ecosystem Alteration and Fragmentation

Ecosystems and natural habitat can be damaged by tourist infrastructure, tourist activities, recreational boating, and the cruise industry. Recreational boats and cruise vessels can damage aquatic vegetation by cutting it with their propellers or otherwise damaging it when running aground. Wetlands have been destroyed in order to build tourist-related infrastructure, such as airports, roads, and marinas. For example, in Jamaica over 700 acres of wetlands have been destroyed since the 1960s for tourism development.

When snorkelling and hiking, tourists can damage ecosystems by littering, and trampling coral and vegetation. This type of damage is cumulative in nature. One or two tourists may not cause visible harm, but hundreds over time can do substantial damage.

Impacts on Wildlife

Wildlife can be adversely affected by the construction and maintenance of tourist infrastructure, and by tourist activities. Impacts from tourist infrastructure can be direct, such as when development in lower elevations of mountain resorts restricts the migratory range of certain wildlife, or indirect, such as when marine turtles are disoriented by automobile headlights and resort illumination. The two primary ways in which tourist activities disturb wildlife are by altering their eating habits and feeding patterns, and by altering their habitat. Feeding patterns are altered directly by tourists feeding animals, and indirectly by littering, which encourages wildlife to scrounge for food. Wildlife habitat is altered by tourists' trampling and by the use of off-road vehicles (ORVs).

Aesthetic and Cultural Impacts

Tourism can diminish the aesthetic appeal of a destination through the construction of buildings that clash with the surrounding environment, creating "architectural" or "visual" pollution. The high-rise hotels along the coastal zone of Atlantic City and Miami are examples, as are several high-rise hotels in Jerusalem, whose construction arguably damaged the city's architectural beauty.

Impact on Gateway Communities Outside National Parks and Other Host Communities

Tourism affects the natural landscape and character of "gateway communities," which are adjacent to national parks, and other significant tourist destinations. Development related to tourist activity can be detrimental to cultural and aesthetic aspects of these communities if undertaken in an indiscriminate and/or scattered manner. For example, Tusayan, the town near the south rim of the Grand Canyon is "dominated by a gaggle of fast-food restaurants, motels, and trinket shops along the highway, has been likened to a strip mall on the way to the Vatican".

Positive Impacts

Despite its many adverse impacts, tourism can have positive impacts on both natural and artificially constructed environments, as well as on destination communities. In fact, tourism has motivated the preservation of such sensitive ecosystems as the Everglades National Park in Florida. Furthermore, tourism that focuses on cultural and historic sites (sometimes referred to as "heritage" tourism) can be the impetus for the preservation and rehabilitation of existing historic sites, buildings, and monuments. For example, historic lighthouses and piers in Cape Cod, Massachusetts and historic buildings in Williamsburg, Virginia have been transformed and preserved for the purpose of tourism. In addition, the economic benefits of tourism partially balance its negative environmental impacts. For example, gateway communities adjacent to national parks exist primarily because of the economic benefits of tourism. The parks attract more visitors to these communities, resulting in increased employment opportunities and an improved standard of living.

Upstream and Downstream Impacts

In addition to direct environmental impacts, impacts from tourism occur at every point along the supply chain. The "supply chain" with respect to service industries refers to all the actors involved in the provision of a service, including the consumer. The supply chain in the tourism industry consists of those industries that provide accommodations, provide transportation, make arrangements for travellers, and supply equipment. It also includes the tourists themselves. The degree of environmental impact of tourism can be influenced by actors along the supply chain.

For example, a hotel can exert "upstream" influence on its suppliers to provide products that minimize environmental impacts, such as recyclable toiletries. There are several existing initiatives within the private and non-profit sectors to work with the lodging industry to reduce environmental impacts through supplier relations. The extent to which a hotel can leverage its suppliers depends upon several factors, including type of hotel and type of supplies.

Similarly, travel service providers can have "downstream" impacts by influencing tourists through education and provision of options to reduce resource use. For example, hotels can give guests the option not to have their linens washed daily, and cruise lines can limit the number of tourists that go ashore at sensitive destinations. Downstream influence through tourist education is seen most clearly with ecotourism, defined as travel and tourism that attempts to minimize impacts on the environment. Tour operators specializing in ecotourism influence their customers through provision of environmental guidelines before and during trips.

Impact of Technology on Travel Services

The growth of the Internet has begun to influence the interactions among travel agents, suppliers, and consumers. The sophistication of information technology has already begun to allow tourists to bypass traditional methods of making travel arrangements. For example, Southwest Airlines now sells most of its tickets without the use of travel agents, using the Internet instead. The full impact of this technological change has yet to be realized. However, it has the potential to effect significant changes. The interactive nature of the Internet allows for the values of tourists to register directly with providers of tourist services. If there is a strong demand for environmentally sensitive services, it is likely that the demand will be met.

Regulation of Industry Activities

Regulation of the tourism industry reflects its fragmented nature. Different aspects of the industry are regulated by different (primarily federal) agencies, with some overlap. The Environmental Protection Agency (EPA) and the U.S. Coast Guard regulate oil and sewage discharges from recreational marine vessels. The EPA under the Clean Air Act (CAA) amendments now regulates air emissions from selected marine engines. Emissions from land vehicles are regulated under the Clean Air Act.

The EPA also regulates smoke, hydrocarbons, nitrogen oxide, and carbon monoxide from aircraft engines. The Federal Aviation Administration (FAA) in the Department of Transportation (DOT) is responsible for enforcing those emission standards. The FAA is also responsible for regulating noise pollution from aircraft under the 1990 Airport Noise and Capacity Act.

The cruise industry is regulated by both international and federal regulations. The primary international regulatory framework for the cruise industry is the International Convention for the Prevention of Pollution from Ships, commonly referred to as MARPOL 73/78. Three relevant annexes regulate the discharge of sewage, oil, and solid wastes.

The U.S. Coast Guard is responsible for enforcing these regulations in the United States. The International Maritime Organization (IMO) has requirements for solid waste generation and incineration on board cruise vessels, NOx emission limits, and guidelines to minimize transfer of non-native species. Regulation of the development of tourist infrastructure occurs at the state or local level, through planning and zoning laws. The efficacy of these regulations varies depending on location.

Policy Implications

As indicated by the regulatory framework highlighted above, the fragmented nature of the tourism industry is not conducive to integrated, holistic regulation that encompasses all aspects of the industry. The dispersed nature of the tourism industry produces diffuse impacts that fall under the jurisdictions of different federal, state, and local agencies. Moreover, enforcement and compliance problems make it particularly difficult to regulate tourist activities. For these reasons educational efforts seem more promising than regulation to minimize many of the environmental impacts of tourism that are not now regulated. Education can be used to support existing regulations, and to encourage environmentally responsible behaviour where no regulations exist.

Educational efforts to promote environmentally responsible tourism should be framed in accordance with the targeted audience. Tourists may be more receptive to educational efforts that focus on the environmental benefits of altering their behaviour than to regulatory prohibitions per se. For example, a sign that prohibits anchoring in a sensitive marine ecosystem could be more effective if accompanied by an explanation of the potential damage a boat can do to the ecosystem.

However, educational efforts geared towards industry sectors seem most effective when cost savings and the marketing benefits of "being green" are emphasized. A study of 13 corporate executives of hotel chains found that the two most important factors that contributed to their decision to implement a solid waste program were waste disposal fees and the betterment of public image. Some hotels have found that their environmental initiatives have resulted in an increase in business. Although environmental awareness has had an important impact on the tourism industry, economic motives are still primary. Therefore, educational programs aimed at tourism service providers should emphasize the potential economic and marketing benefits of environmental stewardship.

Environmental Implications of the Tourism Industry

Environmental management in the United States over the past several decades has focused on regulating production industries, such as manufacturing and mining. However, there has been increasing interest in the environmental effects of the service industry. Generally speaking, a service is as an activity done for others. A perhaps even broader definition of a service is "anything sold in trade that cannot be dropped on your foot". The service industry therefore comprises a variety of activities, from restaurants to hospitals to financial institutions. It accounts for 75% of the U.S. gross domestic product ($3.8 trillion in 1997) (U.S. Census Bureau, 1998) and 80% of U.S. employment.

The service industry merits attention because of its large size and consequently its potential for environmental impacts (both negative and positive). There is a small but growing body of literature discussing the influence of the service sector on environmental quality. Three categories of influence have evolved from these discussions:

1) direct impacts of the service itself,
2) upstream impacts, arising from the service provider's ability to influence its suppliers, and
3) downstream impacts, where the service provider can influence its customers' behavioral or consumption patterns.

It is necessary to look at all three categories to develop a complete picture of the influence of the service sector on environmental quality.

The tourism industry is one of the largest components of the service sector, and has considerable ability to influence environmental quality. Travel and tourism contributed $91 billion in revenue into the U.S. economy in 1998, supporting 16.2 million jobs directly and indirectly. Over forty-three million tourists visited the United States in 1998. Furthermore, the tourism industry is projected to be the largest U.S. private employer by 2000, and now represents 10% of the national private gross domestic product.

Tourist destinations tend to be places of the highest amenities, whether the amenities are social, cultural, or natural. These destinations, due in part to their high quality, are often in short supply relative to demand. This scarcity leads to the potential for degradation of tourist areas, as they reach and in some cases exceed their carrying capacity.

The tourism industry is complex; being fragmented into several industries that, taken together, constitute what is commonly referred to as the travel and tourism industry. It comprises components of other industries that do not cater exclusively to tourists; therefore a discussion of the environmental impacts of tourism needs to consider what percentage of use is related to tourism in each industry.

Sectors of the tourism industry include transportation (e.g., airlines, buses, automobiles), lodging, restaurants, the cruise industry, amusement parks and resorts, and general retail and merchandise stores. Included in the definition of the tourism industry is the associated development (e.g., tourist infrastructure) of tourist destinations, and tourist activities. We have identified impacts from tourist-related transportation, tourist-related development, tourist activities including some recreational activities such as boating, and direct impacts of the lodging and cruise industries.

Quantitative data help to illustrate impacts where available; otherwise qualitative data supported by relevant examples are used. Although this discussion focuses on environmental impacts in the United States, some international examples are drawn upon when applicable. After presenting these impacts, we analyse the influence that providers of tourism services can have on their suppliers as well as the tourist. While there are many more industries that provide services to tourists, this discussion focuses on the upstream and downstream leveraging potential of four service providers: the lodging industry, the cruise industry, travel agents, and tour operators.

Section 1 presents both beneficial and adverse environmental impacts of tourism, including tourist activities, development, transportation, and direct impacts of the lodging and cruise industries.

Section 2 explores the relationships among travel agents, tour operators, and service providers, and tourists. The structure of selected components of the tourism industry is presented, and opportunities for upstream leverage on suppliers and downstream leverage on tourists are discussed. Finally, this section briefly analyses the impact of technology on travel services. Section 3 discusses steps within the tourism industry as well as government to lessen the adverse environmental impacts of tourism. This section concludes with a brief presentation of the benefits of educational efforts to minimize impacts.

Environmental Impacts of Tourism

Definition of Tourism: Tourism is "the temporary movement of people to destinations outside their normal places of work and residence, the activities undertaken during their stay in those destinations, and the facilities created to cater to their needs". It is often difficult to distinguish between tourism and recreation, as they are interrelated. Tourism involves travelling a distance from home, while recreation is defined as the activities undertaken during leisure time. Outdoor recreation is even more closely related to tourism.

The extent of the overlap depends in part on the length of time of the activity and its location. For example, a boater who uses his or her boat for one day and who stays near his or her home may be considered a recreational boater; while a boater who travels on his or her boat overnight to a destination may be considered a tourist. Therefore while this discussion paper focuses primarily on tourism, selected recreational activities and their impacts are considered as well. The degree of environmental impact varies, depending on the type of tourist and the intensity of site use. There are day tourists, who visit a destination for a day and then leave; summer residents who are in effect tourists for a season; and tourists on bus tours and other trips that may visit a location for a few minutes or a number of days.

Day tourists have an impact on the environment through their transportation to their destination as well as their activities once there. This is true for summer residents, but these tourists also have a cumulative impact, as they are in one place for a longer period of time. For example, nutrients leaching from the septic systems of tourists' waterfront homes can accelerate eutrophication and contribute to depletion of dissolved oxygen supply of the adjacent water body.

On the other hand, summer residents often are an important force in preserving the natural beauty of an area (e.g., the Adirondacks). Tourists who visit an area for longer than a day and choose to stay in hotels contribute to the impacts that the lodging industry has on the environment. In addition to the length of stay, tourist impacts depend on the type of activity undertaken. Passive activities such as birdwatching have different impacts than more active pursuits, such as snowmobiling or boating. There are environmental impacts from the travel to a destination, the tourist activities in and of themselves at that destination, such as hiking or boating, and from the creation, operation, and maintenance of facilities that cater to the tourist, such as hotels. This discussion addresses impacts from tourism-related transportation, development, the lodging and cruise industries, and tourist activities including selected forms of recreation.

Transportation

Airlines: In 1995, twenty percent of U.S. commercial air travel was attributed to leisure, including rest and relaxation, sightseeing, and outdoor recreation. The total and tourism-related contribution of air pollutants from the air transportation industry. Aircraft emit the most carbon monoxide of any of the five listed air pollutants, but it is a small amount relative to other modes of transportation. In total, aircraft are responsible for approximately one percent of the total ground-level emissions from mobile sources; therefore tourism-related air travel is responsible for only.2% of total ground-level emissions. Furthermore, tourism-related air travel contributes less than 1% of total U.S. emissions of each of the listed criteria pollutants.

Although aircraft contribute only a small amount to total air pollution, emissions from this source is increasing. Between 1970 and 1995, hydrocarbon and NOx emissions from aircraft sources have grown 53%. Projections to 2010 indicate that aircraft emissions will continue to increase. Aircraft emissions in nonattainment areas with large airport facilities in particular are projected to represent a growing percentage of regional sources of air pollutants.

The projections indicate an increase in the aircraft component of total regional emissions between 1990 and 2010 in ten metropolitan regions (nine of which are currently not in attainment of the National Ambient Air Quality Standards (NAAQS) for ozone; the tenth city has attained the ozone standard, but is considered an ozone "maintenance" area).

The 2010 percentages are still relatively low, ranging from 0.2% volatile organic compounds (VOC) in Philadelphia to 5.1% VOC in Charlotte; and 1.8% NOx in Philadelphia to 7.6% in Charlotte. The percentages are higher in Charlotte in part because other sources contribute less. The EPA has had regulations for smoke and hydrocarbon emissions from aircraft engines in place since 1984. In 1997, the agency promulgated new emission standards for nitrogen oxides and carbon monoxide. This rule was adopted to codify the existing voluntary emission standards of the United Nations International Civil Aviation Organization (ICAO). The DOT's Federal Aviation Administration (FAA) is responsible for enforcing these aircraft emissions standards.

With increased awareness of the fragile nature of our planet and its beauty, it is not surprising that there has also been an increased demand for travel to unique and remarkable environments around the world, known as environmental tourism. Environmental tourism is the phenomenon of increasing travel to places of environmental interest. It is travel that focuses on the ecological surroundings of the destination, which is generally a place overflowing with natural beauty and wonder.

Environmental tourism can include travel to unique and endangered areas, such as the Galapagos Islands. In addition to visiting places for its uniqueness, many people engage in environmental tourism as a "voluntourism" mission - this is a form of tourism in which people travel to a destination for a short period of time to volunteer in some capacity. In the case of environmental tourism, volutourism means travelling to an ecologically fragile part of the world to offer assistance in repairing it – such as cleaning an oil spill.

The concept of environmental tourism is that people will become more engaged with the ecological and sociocultural concerns of the world through firsthand experience, and thus be more active in conservation and making change. The idea evolved in the late 1980s along with growing consumer awareness of issues surrounding conservation and consumption. Not only is environmental tourism an adventure into the wilderness aimed at helping save the planet, but it also expands the profitable travel industry to developing countries where jobs are scarce and economies are struggling. Although the objectives of environmental tourism are well meaning, there are consequences that arise from the practice.

When people travel to places that have historically been disparately inhabited, the presence of increased and new populations inevitably impacts the environment and the culture of the location. The first impact on the environment comes from getting to the destination. Travel to remote locations where wildlife thrives can be costly to the environment using more fuel than that of an ordinary vacation, at times. Lodging and living are further strains the local environment.

Constructing new lodging often means destroying a natural ecosystem and bringing a Western lifestyle to a developing country often means improper disposal of the increased amounts of waste. In a sociocultural sense, environmental tourism can present a problem with the displacement of people and their resources as well as impede and endanger their daily customs by introducing new difficulties and cultures.

Tourism's Three Main Impact Areas

Negative impacts from tourism occur when the level of visitor use is greater than the environment's ability to cope with this use within the acceptable limits of change. Uncontrolled conventional tourism poses potential threats to many natural areas around the world. It can put enormous pressure on an area and lead to impacts such as soil erosion, increased pollution, discharges into the sea, natural habitat loss, increased pressure on endangered species and heightened vulnerability to forest fires. It often puts a strain on water resources, and it can force local populations to compete for the use of critical resources.

Depletion of Natural Resources

Tourism development can put pressure on natural resources when it increases consumption in areas where resources are already scarce.

Water resources: Water, and especially fresh water, is one of the most critical natural resources. The tourism industry generally overuses water resources for hotels, swimming pools, golf courses and personal use of water by tourists. This can result in water shortages and degradation of water supplies, as well as generating a greater volume of waste water..

In dryer regions like the Mediterranean, the issue of water scarcity is of particular concern. Because of the hot climate and the tendency of tourists to consume more water when on holiday than they do at home, the amount used can run up to 440 litres a day. This is almost double what the inhabitants of an average Spanish city use.

Golf course maintenance can also deplete fresh water resources. In recent years golf tourism has increased in popularity and the number of golf courses has grown rapidly. Golf courses require an enormous amount of water every day and, as with other causes of excessive extraction of water, this can result in water scarcity. If the water comes from wells, over pumping can cause saline intrusion into ground-water. Golf resorts are more and more often situated in or near protected areas or areas where resources are limited, exacerbating their impacts.

Local resources: Tourism can create great pressure on local resources like energy, food, and other raw materials that may already be in short supply. Greater extraction and transport of these resources exacerbates the physical impacts associated with their exploitation. Because of the seasonal character of the industry, many destinations have ten times more inhabitants in the high season as in the low season. A high demand is placed upon these resources to meet the high expectations tourists often have (proper heating, hot water, etc.).

Land degradation: Important land resources include minerals, fossil fuels, fertile soil, forests, wetland and wildlife. Increased construction of tourism and recreational facilities has increased the pressure on these resources and on scenic landscapes. Direct impact on natural resources, both renewable and nonrenewable, in the provision of tourist facilities can be caused by the use of land for accommodation and other infrastructure provision, and the use of building materials. Forests often suffer negative impacts of tourism in the form of deforestation caused by fuel wood collection and land clearing. For example, one trekking tourist in Nepal-and area already suffering the effects of deforestation-can use four to five kilograms of wood a day.

Pollution

Tourism can cause the same forms of pollution as any other industry: air emissions, noise, solid waste and littering, releases of sewage, oil and chemicals, even architectural/visual pollution.

Air pollution and noise: Transport by air, road, and rail is continuously increasing in response to the rising number reported that the number of international air passengers worldwide rose from 88 million in 1972 to 344 million in 1994. One consequence of this increase in air transport is that tourism now accounts for more than 60% of air travel and is therefore responsible for an important share of air emissions. One study estimated that a single transatlantic return flight emits almost half the CO2 emissions produced by all other sources consumed by an average person yearly. (Mayer Hillman, Town & Country Planning magazine, September 1996. Source: MFOE).

Transport emissions and emissions from energy production and use are linked to acid rain, global warming and photochemical pollution. Air pollution from tourist transportation has impacts on the global level, especially from carbon dioxide (CO2) emissions related to transportation energy use. And it can contribute to severe local air pollution. Some of these impacts are quite specific to tourist activities. For example, especially in very hot or cold countries, tour buses often leave their motors running for hours while the tourists go out for an excursion because they want to return to a comfortably air-conditioned bus.

Noise pollution from airplanes, cars, and buses, as well as recreational vehicles such as snowmobiles and jet skis, is an ever-growing problem of modern life. In addition to causing annoyance, stress, and even hearing loss for it humans, it causes distress to wildlife, especially in sensitive areas. For instance, noise generated by snowmobiles can cause animals to alter their natural activity patterns.

Solid waste and littering: In areas with high concentrations of tourist activities and appealing natural attractions, waste disposal is a serious problem and improper disposal can be a major despoiler of the natural environment-rivers, scenic areas, and roadsides. For example, cruise ships in the Caribbean are estimated to produce more than 70,000 tons of waste each year. Today some cruise lines are actively working to reduce waste-related impacts. Solid waste and littering can degrade the physical appearance of the water and shoreline and cause the death of marine animals.

In mountain areas, trekking tourists generate a great deal of waste. Tourists on expedition leave behind their garbage, oxygen cylinders and even camping equipment. Such practices degrade the environment with all the detritus typical of the developed world, in remote areas that have few garbage collection or disposal facilities. Some trails in the Peruvian Andes and in Nepal frequently visited by tourists have been nicknamed "Coca-Cola trail" and "Toilet paper trail".

Sewage: Construction of hotels, recreation and other facilities often leads to increased sewage pollution. Wastewater has polluted seas and lakes surrounding tourist attractions, damaging the flora and fauna. Sewage runoff causes serious damage to coral reefs because it stimulates the growth of algae, which cover the filter-feeding corals, hindering their ability to survive. Changes in salinity and salutation can have wide-ranging impacts on coastal environments. And sewage pollution can threaten the health of humans and animals.

Aesthetic Pollution: Often tourism fails to integrate its structures with the natural features and indigenous architectural of the destination. Large, dominating resorts of disparate design can look out of place in any natural environment and may clash with the indigenous structural design.

A lack of land-use planning and building regulations in many destinations has facilitated sprawling developments along coastlines, valleys and scenic routes. The sprawl includes tourism facilities themselves and supporting infrastructure such as roads, employee housing, parking, service areas, and waste disposal.

Physical Impacts

Attractive landscape sites, such as sandy beaches, lakes, riversides, and mountain tops and slopes, are often transitional zones, characterized by species-rich ecosystems. Typical physical impacts include the degradation of such ecosystems.

An ecosystem is a geographic area including all the living organisms (people, plants, animals, and microorganisms), their physical surroundings (such as soil, water, and air), and the natural cycles that sustain them. The ecosystems most threatened with degradation are ecologically fragile areas such as alpine regions, rain forests, wetlands, mangroves, coral reefs and sea grass beds. The threats to and pressures on these ecosystems are often severe because such places are very attractive to both tourists and developers. Physical impacts are caused not only by tourism-related land clearing and construction, but by continuing tourist activities and long-term changes in local economies and ecologies.

Physical Impacts of Tourism Development

- Construction activities and infrastructure development: The development of tourism facilities such as accommodation, water supplies, restaurants and recreation facilities can involve sand mining, beach and sand dune erosion, soil erosion and extensive paving. In addition, road and airport construction can lead to land degradation and loss of wildlife habitats and deterioration of scenery.

  In Yosemite National Park (US), for instance, the number of roads and facilities have been increased to keep pace with the growing visitor numbers and to supply amenities, infrastructure and parking lots for all these tourists. These actions have caused habitat loss in the park and are accompanied by various forms of pollution including air pollution from automobile emissions; the Sierra Club has reported "smog so thick that Yosemite Valley could not be seen from airplanes". This occasional smog is harmful to all species and vegetation inside the Park.
- Deforestation and intensified or unsustainable use of land: Construction of ski resort accommodation and facilities frequently requires clearing forested land. Coastal wetlands are often drained and filled due to lack of more suitable sites for construction of tourism facilities and infrastructure. These activities can cause severe disturbance and erosion of the local ecosystem, even destruction in the long term.
- Marina development of marinas and breakwaters can cause changes in currents and coastlines. Furthermore, extraction of

building materials such as sand affects coral reefs, mangroves, and hinterland forests, leading to erosion and destruction of habitats. In the Philippines and the Maldives, dynamiting and mining of coral for resort building materials has damaged fragile coral reefs and depleted the fisheries that sustain local people and attract tourists.

Overbuilding and extensive paving of shorelines can result in destruction of habitats and disruption of land-sea connections (such as sea-turtle nesting spots). Coral reefs are especially fragile marine ecosystems and are suffering worldwide from reef-based tourism developments.

Evidence suggests a variety of impacts to coral result from shoreline development, increased sediments in the water, trampling by tourists and divers, ship groundings, pollution from sewage, overfishing, and fishing with poisons and explosives that destroy coral habitat.

Physical Impacts from Tourist Activities

- Trampling Tourists using the same trail over and over again trample the vegetation and soil, eventually causing damage that can lead to loss of biodiversity and other impacts. Such damage can be even more extensive when visitors frequently stray off established trails.

Trampling impacts on vegetation	Trampling impacts on soil
Breakage and bruising of stems	Loss of organic matter
Reduced plant vigour	Reduction in soil macro porosity
Reduced regeneration	Decrease in air and water permeability
Loss of ground cover	Increase in run off
Change in species composition	Accelerated erosion

Source: University of Idaho

- Anchoring and other marine activities In marine areas (around coastal waters, reefs, beach and shoreline, offshore waters, uplands and lagoons) many tourist activities occur in or around fragile ecosystems. Anchoring, snorkelling, sport fishing and scuba diving, yachting, and cruising are some of the activities that can cause direct degradation of marine ecosystems such as coral reefs, and subsequent impacts on coastal protection and fisheries.

- Alteration of ecosystems by tourist activities Habitat can be degraded by tourism leisure activities. For example, wildlife viewing can bring about stress for the animals and alter their natural behaviour when tourists come too close. Safaris and wildlife watching activities have a degrading effect on habitat as they often are accompanied by the noise and commotion created by tourists as they chase wild animals in their trucks and aircraft. This puts high pressure on animal habits and behaviours and tends to bring about behavioural changes. In some cases, as in Kenya, it has led to animals becoming so disturbed that at times they neglect their young or fail to mate.

Loss of Biological Diversity

The effects of loss of biodiversity:

- It threatens our food supplies, opportunities for recreation and tourism, and sources of wood, medicines and energy.
- It interferes with essential ecological functions such as species balance, soil formation, and greenhouse gas absorption.
- It reduces the productivity of ecosystems, thereby shrinking nature's basket of goods and services, from which we constantly draw.
- It destabilizes ecosystems and weakens their ability to deal with natural disasters such as floods, droughts, and hurricanes, and with human-caused stresses, such as pollution and climate change.

Tourism, especially nature tourism, is closely linked to biodiversity and the attractions created by a rich and varied environment. It can also cause loss of biodiversity when land and resources are strained by excessive use, and when impacts on vegetation, wildlife, mountain, marine and coastal environments and water resources exceed the carrying capacity. This loss of biodiversity in fact means loss of tourism potential.

Introduction of exotic species: Tourists and suppliers-often unwittingly-can bring in species (insects, wild and cultivated plants and diseases) that are not native to the local environment and that can cause enormous disruption and even destruction of ecosystems.

Depletion of The Ozone Layer

The ozone layer, which is situated in the upper atmosphere (or stratosphere) at an altitude of 12-50 kilometres, protects life on earth by absorbing the harmful wavelengths of the sun's ultraviolet (UV) radiation, which in high doses is dangerous to humans and animals. For instance, one of the reasons scientists have put forward for the global decrease of amphibian populations is increased exposure to UV radiation.

Ozone depleting substances (ODSs) such as CFCs (chlorofluorocarbon) and halons have contributed to the destruction of this layer. The tourism industry may be part of the problem; direct impacts start with the construction of new developments and continue during daily management and operations. Refrigerators, air conditioners and propellants in aerosol spray cans, amongst others, contain ODSs and are widely used in the hotel and tourism industry. Emissions from jet aircraft are also a significant source of ODSs. According to Tourism Concern, scientists predict that by 2015 half of the annual destruction of the ozone layer will be caused by air travel.

UNEP's OzonAction Programme works with governments and industries, including the tourism industry, to phase out ODSs and find safer alternatives. UNEP has developed extensive information and guidance on how many types of businesses can eliminate ODSs and contribute to preservation of the ozone layer. For further reading see the publication How the Hotel and Tourism Industry can Protect the Ozone Layer.

Climate Change

Climate scientists now generally agree that the Earth's surface temperatures have risen steadily in recent years because of an increase in the so-called greenhouse gases in the atmosphere, which trap heat from the sun. One of the most significant of these gases is carbon dioxide (CO_2), which is generated when fossil fuels, such as coal, oil and natural gas are burned and when there are changes in land use, such as deforestation. In the long run, the accumulation of CO_2 and other greenhouse gases in the atmosphere can cause global climate change-a process that may already be occurring.

Global tourism is closely linked to climate change. Tourism involves the movement of people from their homes to other destinations and accounts for about 50% of traffic movements; rapidly expanding air traffic contributes about 2.5% of the production of CO2. Tourism is thus a significant contributor to the increasing concentrations of greenhouse gases in the atmosphere. Air travel itself is a major contributor to the greenhouse effect. Passenger jets are the fastest growing source of greenhouse gas emissions. The number of international travellers is expected to increase from 594 million in 1996 to 1.6 billion by 2020, adding greatly to the problem unless steps are taken to reduce emissions.

For more information on the relationship between energy and the environment, see UNEP's Energy Programme, which provides information and publications on energy efficiency and alternative energy sources to reduce the environmental impacts of energy use and of transportation.

How Global Environmental Impacts Affect Tourism

Natural disasters: Catastrophes like floods, earthquakes, wildfires, volcanoes, avalanches, drought and diseases can have a serious effect on inbound and domestic tourism and thus on local tourism industries. The outbreak of the foot and mouth disease epidemic in England earlier this year (2001), for instance, has severely affected Great Britain's inbound tourism market. A BHA/Barclays Hospitality Business Trends Survey found that 75% of hotels in England, 81% in Scotland and 85% in Wales continued to be affected by the foot and mouth outbreak, and over 60% forecast a decline in business in the June-September 2001 period.

Climate change: Tourism not only contributes to climate change, but is affected by it as well. Climate change is likely to increase the severity and frequency of storms and severe weather events, which can have disastrous effects on tourism in the affected regions. Some of the other impacts that the world risks as a result of global warming are drought, diseases and heat waves.

These negative impacts can keep tourists away from the holiday destinations. Global warming may cause:

- Less snowfall at ski resorts, meaning a shorter skiing seasons in the Alpine region. In already hot areas like Asia and the Mediterranean, tourists will stay away because of immense heat, and out of fear of diseases and water shortages.
- Harm to vulnerable ecosystems such as rainforests and coral reefs because of rising temperatures and less rainfall. A major risk to coral reefs is bleaching, which occurs when coral is

stressed by temperature increases, high or low levels of salinity, lower water quality, and an increase in suspended sediments. These conditions cause the zooxanthallae (the single-celled algae which forms the colours within the coral) to leave the coral. Without the algae, the coral appears white, or "bleached"- and rapidly dies. The Great Barrier Reef, which supports a US$ 640 million tourism industry, has been experiencing coral bleaching events for the last 20 years.

- Rising sea levels, the result of melting glaciers and polar ice. Higher sea levels will threaten coastal and marine areas with widespread floods in low-lying countries and island states, increasing the loss of coastal land. Beaches and islands that are major tourism attractions may be the first areas to be affected.
- Increased events of extreme weather, such as tornadoes, hurricanes and typhoons. These are already becoming more prevalent in tourist areas in the Caribbean and South East Asia. Hurricane Mitch in 1998, for instance, heavily affected tourism in the Caribbean. Wind damage, storm waves, heavy rains and flooding caused major losses in the local tourism sector.

Effects of Other Industries on Tourism

Impacts from other industries often have a more dramatic effect on the environment and can seriously affect tourism.

- Oil spills, like the oil tanker disaster that occurred off the Galapagos Islands (Ecuador) in January 2001, can cause severe short-term damage to tourist attractions. In that case, a freight ship loaded with 160,000 gallons of diesel fuel and 80,000 gallons of other petroleum products ran aground on the coast of San Cristóbal and spilled nearly all of its load. Unique local marine and land species and the tourism potential of the area were badly affected.
- Agricultural runoff or industrial discharges can cause water pollution and may cause algae blooms like those that occurred in the Adriatic Sea in the early 1990s. In spite of improved control of sewage from tourism developments, the Mediterranean sea floor is increasingly carpeted with these quick-growing invaders, many rising 30 inches or more above

anchoring runners. They appear equally adept at colonizing rock, mud, and sand in a virtually continuous swath that can extend from the beach out to a depth of about 150 feet, smothering coral reefs, fish and other sea flora and fauna in the process.

- Destructive practices such as blast fishing, with poisonous chemicals like cyanide, and muro-ami netting (pounding reefs with weighted bags to scare fish out of crevices) directly destroy corals. They can also destroy a major draw for tourists.

How Tourism Can Contribute to Environmental Conservation

Financial contributions:

- Direct financial contributions: Tourism can contribute directly to the conservation of sensitive areas and habitat. Revenue from park-entrance fees and similar sources can be allocated specifically to pay for the protection and management of environmentally sensitive areas. Special fees for park operations or conservation activities can be collected from tourists or tour operators.
- Contributions to government revenues: Some governments collect money in more far-reaching and indirect ways that are not linked to specific parks or conservation areas. User fees, income taxes, on sales or rental of recreation equipment, and license fees for activities such as hunting and fishing can provide governments with the funds needed to manage natural resources. Such funds can be used for overall conservation programs and activities, such as park ranger salaries and park maintenance.

For Costa Rica, for example, tourism represents 72% of national monetary reserves, generates 140,000 jobs and produces 8.4% of the gross domestic product. The country has 25% of its territory classified under some category of conservation management. In 1999, protected areas welcomed 866,083 national and foreign tourists, who generated about US$ 2.5 million in admission fees and payment of services.

Improved Environmental Management and Planning

Sound environmental management of tourism facilities and especially hotels can increase the benefits to natural areas. But this requires careful planning for controlled development, based on analysis of the environmental resources of the area. Planning helps to make choices between conflicting uses, or to find ways to make them compatible. By planning early for tourism development, damaging and expensive mistakes can be prevented, avoiding the gradual deterioration of environmental assets significant to tourism.

Cleaner production techniques can be important tools for planning and operating tourism facilities in a way that minimizes their environmental impacts. For example, green building (using energy-efficient and non-polluting construction materials, sewage systems and energy sources) is an increasingly important way for the tourism industry to decrease its impact on the environment. And because waste treatment and disposal are often major, long-term environmental problems in the tourism industry, pollution prevention and waste minimization techniques are especially important for the tourism industry. A guide to sources of information on cleaner production (free) is available here.

Environmental Awareness Raising

Tourism has the potential to increase public appreciation of the environment and to spread awareness of environmental problems when it brings people into closer contact with nature and the environment. This confrontation may heighten awareness of the value of nature and lead to environmentally conscious behaviour and activities to preserve the environment. For instance, Honduran schoolchildren from the capital city of Tegucigalpa are routinely taken to visit La Tigra cloud forest visitor centre, funded in part by eco-tourist dollars, to learn about the intricacies of the rainforest.

If it is to be sustainable in the long run, tourism must incorporate the principles and practices of sustainable consumption. Sustainable consumption includes building consumer demand for products that have been made using cleaner production techniques, and for services-including tourism services-that are provided in a way that minimizes environmental impacts.

The tourism industry can play a key role in providing environmental information and raising awareness among tourists of the environmental consequences of their actions. Tourists and tourism-related businesses consume an enormous quantity of goods and services; moving them toward using those that are produced and provided in an environmentally sustainable way, from cradle to grave, could have an enormous positive impact on the planet's environment.

Protection and Preservation

Tourism can significantly contribute to environmental protection, conservation and restoration of biological diversity and sustainable use of natural resources. Because of their attractiveness, pristine sites and natural areas are identified as valuable and the need to keep the attraction alive can lead to creation of national parks and wildlife parks.

In Hawaii, new laws and regulations have been enacted to preserve the Hawaiian rainforest and to protect native species. The coral reefs around the islands and the marine life that depend on them for survival are also protected. Hawaii now has become an international centre for research on ecological systems-and the promotion and preservation of the islands' tourism industry was the main motivation for these actions.

Grupo Punta Cana, a resort in the Dominican Republic, offers an example of how luxury tourism development and conservation can be combined. The high-end resort was established with the goal of catering to luxury-class tourists while respecting the natural habitat of Punta Cana. The developers have set aside 10,000 hectares (24,700 acres) of land as a nature reserve and native fruit tree garden. The Punta Cana Nature Reserve includes 11 fresh water springs surrounded by a subtropical forest where many species of unusual Caribbean flora and fauna live in their natural state.

Guests can explore a "nature path" leading from the beach through mangroves, lagoons of fresh water springs and dozens of species of Caribbean bird and plant life. The Punta Cana Ecological Foundation has begun reforesting some parts of the reserve that had been stripped of their native mahogany and other trees in the past. Other environmentally protective policies have been put into effect at the resort, such as programs to protect the offshore barrier reefs and the recycling of wastewater for use in irrigating the grounds.

The fairways of the resort's new golf course were planted with a hybrid grass that can be irrigated with sea water The grass also requires less than half the usual amounts of fertilizer and pesticides. The resort has also established a biodiversity laboratory run by Cornell University.

Tourism has had a positive effect on wildlife preservation and protection efforts, notably in Africa but also in South America, Asia, Australia, and the South Pacific. Numerous animal and plant species have already become extinct or may become extinct soon. Many countries have therefore established wildlife reserves and enacted strict laws protecting the animals that draw nature-loving tourists. As a result of these measures, several endangered species have begun to thrive again.

Alternative Employment

Tourism can provide an alternative to development scenarios that may have greater environmental impacts. The Eco-escuela de Espanol, a Spanish language school created in 1996 as part of a Conservation International project in the Guatemalan village of San Andres, is an example.

The community-owned school, located in the Maya Biosphere Reserve, combines individual language courses with home stay opportunities and community-led ecotours. It receives around 1,800 tourists yearly, mostly from the US and Europe, and employs almost 100 residents, of whom around 60% were previously engaged in mostly illegal timber extraction, hunting and *milpas*, or slash-and-burn agriculture. Careful monitoring in 2000 has shown that, among the families benefiting from the business, the majority has significantly reduced hunting practices, and the number and extension of "slash-and-burn" agricultural plots. Furthermore, as most families in the village benefit directly or indirectly from the school, community-managed private reserves have been established, and social pressure against hunting has increased.

Regulatory Measures

Regulatory measures help offset negative impacts; for instance, controls on the number of tourist activities and movement of visitors within protected areas can limit impacts on the ecosystem and help maintain the integrity and vitality of the site. Such limits can also reduce the negative impacts on resources.

Limits should be established after an in-depth analysis of the maximum sustainable visitor capacity. This strategy is being used in the Galapagos Islands, where the number of ships allowed to cruise this remote archipelago is limited, and only designated islands can be visited, ensuring visitors have little impact on the sensitive environment and animal habitats.

Tourism and the Environment

Tourism plays an important role in the economies of. both Goa and the Maldives. For the Maldives, it provides 17 percent of the gross domestic product, over 25 percent of government revenue and around 60 percent of the foreign exchange earnings; and for Goa, it generates 13.7 percent of the state's net domestic product, 7 percent of employment, and 7 percent of state tax revenues.

Although both states capitalize on their comparative environmental advantages, that is beach and sunshine, Goa also capitalizes on its unique historical and cultural heritage while the Maldives on its unique archipelagic and coral reef marine environment. Their products and approaches to tourism development are very different: Goa promotes heterogeneous tourism development with upscale and inexpensive charter tourism to international and domestic audiences while the Maldives concentrates on upscale, international tourism.

The experiences in tourism of Goa and the Maldives vary in terms of their environmental impacts, social issues and conflicts and institutional responses. There is much that Goa and the Maldives can learn from each other. Other states could also learn from the experiences of these two tourist spots in South Asia.

Tourism and the Environment

The two papers included in this set, presented at an EDI/SAARC Regional Seminar on. Economic Globalization and Environmental Sustainability in Goa in June 1997, review the impacts of tourism on the environment in the State of Goa, India and in the Republic of the Maldives. Compared with their giant neighbouring states, Goa (population 1.2 million) and the Maldives (population 244,000) are small, but blessed among others with local attractions, good beaches and sunshine that draw tourists from near and far.

Tourism plays an important role in the economies of both Goa and the Maldives. For the Maldives, it provides 17 percent of the gross domestic product, over 25 percent of government revenue and around 60 percent of the foreign exchange earnings. For Goa, tourism generates 13.7 percent of the state's net domestic product, 7 percent of employment and 7 percent of tax revenues. Both states capitalize on their comparative environmental advantages: beach and sunshine. Goa also capitalizes on its unique historical and cultural heritage while the Maldives on its unique archipelagic and coral reef marine environment. Their products and approaches to tourism development are very different: Goa promotes heterogeneous tourism development with upscale and inexpensive charter tourism to international and domestic audiences. The Maldives concentrates on upscale, international tourism. The experiences in tourism of Goa and the Maldives vary in terms of their environmental impacts, social conflicts and institutional responses. After reviewing both experiences, there is much that Goa and the Maldives can learn from each other. Other states could also learn from the experiences of these two tourist spots in South Asia.

The preservation of the natural environment, the prudent use of natural resources, disposal of solid waste and sewage, and the depletion and deterioration of ground-water attributable to tourist inflows are, among others, issues which both governments face. In Goa, the growth of coastal tourism has been rapid and uncontrolled, notes the paper by Sawkar *et al.* Tourism development has resulted in, the loss of biodiversity, erosion of sand dunes, declining fish catches, accretion and salutation and depletion of ground-water.

Although the environmental diversity and sensitivity of Goa has been widely known, a complex mixture of customary rights, land ownership, a variety of stakeholders with very differing interests, and ineffective institutional and political structures seem to have made it difficult for Goa to define a tourism strategy and to enforce its implementation. In the Maldives, the rapid increase, *albeit* government controlled, in the number of resorts over the last two decades has also taken its toll on the environment. The paper on the Maldives by Saeed, acknowledges environmental damage from beach erosion, an alteration of ocean currents, loss of biodiversity, water, soil and nutrient pollution and damage to its coral reefs most notably from mining for construction, anchoring of boats and diving. The Government has played a key role in promoting tourism on unoccupied islands (or abandoned islands where customary usufruct rights were compensated) through certain traditionally powerful families and with certain funding arrangements to encourage foreign investments; the government has been closely monitored the development of tourism.

Tourism development has many social impacts. The Maldives has avoided much social conflict due to its relatively isolated geographical location and small, somewhat homogenous population and culture. The

Maldives strategy of separating foreign tourists from the local residents by developing tourist resorts on uninhabited islands is critical to minimizing social impacts.

This strategy has managed thus far to avoid social conflicts, but with the leakage of information from tourist areas, and the separation of resort employees from their families, the sustainability of this strategy under existing institutional and political structures remains to be seen. In contrast, as Goa does not have land which is untitled or unowned or which is not of some historical significance, the needs of tourists and the local population in Goa come into frequent conflict over the use of local resources. The Goan social scene is further complicated by the states porous borders with the rest of India. While Goas geographical location improves domestic demand for tourism, it has also lead to a large influx of labour from adjoining states, further exasperating social impacts.

Conflicts over resource use and institutional responses to them is another area in which the experiences of Goa and the Maldives differ. The situation in Goa is rather complex due largely to the number of stakeholders involved in tourism: luxury hotels, family-run guest houses, the needs of tourists, local residents, and other sectors of the economy. Mechanism for resolving conflicts among the various resource users do exist, such as the panchayats (.communidades.) and the courts, but the long backlog of cases has delayed justice.

The high number of conflicts among users suggests that an improved institutional response is necessary. Comparatively, the situation seems less complex in the Maldives. At this point, legislating and enforcing environmental quality controls for tourism appears to create fewer conflicts among residents because of the geographical separation of resorts, the small number of facilities and the limited number of stakeholders involved in tourism. As tourism expands in the Maldives, additional review of potential conflicts over resource use must be considered. Environmental legislation and regulatory mechanisms are in place in both states. The Maldives has developed its institutional capacity to address these problems and to facilitate unique solutions. Having carried out a proper evaluation of tourism in 1983 and a survey in 1995 to identify the major existing environmental problems facing the resorts, the Maldives seems further down the road in its development of tourism. But, while the Maldives has increased its regulation of tourism, it tends to focus on future environmental damage, viewing current damage as more aesthetic rather than a serious threat.

The sustainability of such policy is questionable. In Goa, while a Master Tourism Plan is in place, the implementation of the laws and regulations appears to be somewhat tardy. Although the paper alludes to several government department charged with varies aspects of tourism planning in Goa, institutional strengthening is a clear issue. Similarly, a systematic study of the environmental impacts of tourism and the implementation of a monitoring and management system would also aid Goa. Fortunately, some of these issues will be covered by the. India Environmental Management Capacity Building Technical Assistance Project, supported by the World Bank, in which Goa is included.

In sum, these two cases provide a brief introduction to the complexity of pursing tourism as an avenue to development. Much can be highlighted from the two. The Maldives has excelled in moving forward with strengthening its environmental regulatory and enforcement framework. Not only has it increasingly developed its institutional capacity to address environmental problems related to tourism, but it has also concentrated its efforts on the polluter pays principle. In Goa, although institutional responses and the development of a tourism strategy which integrates the needs of all stakeholders has lagged, the active lobby of its citizenry at all levels, which has intensively documented its environmental impacts and brought environmental concerns to the public agenda, should be highlighted. The active participation of all stakeholders in the planning process lends itself to greater sustainability of tourism in the long-run.

Clearly the complexity of both cases requires that Goa and the Maldives carefully review the sustainability of their approaches and how to strike a balance between tourism development and protecting the natural and social environments. As in any other sector of an economy, tourism requires a sound, well-defined and executed approach in which the government, the various stakeholders and the public cooperate. We wish to acknowledge the contributions of the two papers and the comments of Mr. Gert van Santen.

Issues of Concern in the Coastal Zone of Goa

When Goa joined the Indian Union in December 1961, its only large industry was the export of its rich ores of iron and manganese.

Goans depended on indigenous fish and coconuts for their vital nutritional requirements. The popularity of milk and vegetables amongst local inhabitants was low, and most of their dietary and other consumer items were imported. Before 1961, Goa had very little development in the modern sense of the term. With rich coastal biodiversity and abundant natural resources, the quality of life and the social fabric was good.

Its main assets were its genial and peace loving people, a tranquil and unspoiled environment, and an absence of population pressure. Tourism was adopted as a key sector for Goa development, not only for the well-established reasons of increasing income and employment but also for its potential to generate non-manual employment in a state with an increasingly educated work force and limited industrial growth. Fearing industrial pollution, the planners and decision-makers opted for tourism as an avenue to earn the states income over increased industrial development in addition to mining.

Except at academic levels, very little awareness and understanding existed back then among planners about the processes of the life support systems of the coastal environment and the interactive roles played by each component. This paper highlights the issues and the implications of tourism on the coastal marine and the socioeconomic environment of Goa.

Nature and Growth of Tourism in Goa

Most of the tourism in Goa is concentrated in the coastal stretches of Bardez, Salcete, Tiswadi and Marmagao. Over 90 percent of domestic tourists and over 99 percent of the international tourists frequent these areas. Consequently, beach tourism is the only type that is avidly encouraged by policy makers and other concerned parties alike.

Goa is visited by two types of tourists with distinct needs which this state satisfies. The first is the domestic tourists, who comprise 80 percent of all tourists. These people come in search of the culture that is different from the rest of India, as the Goan image holds a degree of mysticism, a sense of freedom and unconventional dress style. The second is the international tourists who visit Goa purely for the natural environment sun and beaches. Within the category of international tourists are there are two sub-categories: backpackers and charter tourists. Although both visit Goa for the beaches, they stay away from each other. The backpackers are not found in areas of charter tourists; they prefer to mingle and live with the local communities. Whereas, the charter tourists tend to stay in the luxury starred hotels. Domestic and international tourists also differ in terms of the areas they frequent. For the domestic tourist, the beaches hold limited appeal, so domestic tourists remain away from the places frequented by the international tourists.

The timings of visits are clearly different for the domestic and the international tourists. In previous decades, a clear off season for all tourists could be identified, today this is not so for domestic tourists, who come throughout the year albeit in larger numbers in the non-monsoon months. Conversely, international tourists avoid the monsoon months, as for them the use of the beach is the prime attraction to come to Goa.

In the earlier years, the international tourist was one in search of alternative lifestyles and mingling with local communities; however, in more recent years, a considerable homogenization of the traveller has occurred in terms of package tourism. In the 1980s, the domestic tourist came from the middle class and from the adjoining states; however, now domestic tourists that come to Goa are diversifying, as the place attracting a number of the rich young elites from more distant states.

In response to these changes, the tourism industry in Goa has evolved into a curious mix of low-budget tourism and up-market hotel development, a mix that is marked with tensions and potential conflicts over the appropriation of resources.

Impacts of Tourism in Goa

Tourism development among policy-makers tends to be discussed in terms of the factors that are of concern to the national and the state governments. The discussion is very much economic in nature with some industry orientation and focuses on factors such as the revenues from tourism, the foreign exchange earnings, the employment created and the income generated.

The focus has always been on the implications of tourism development on the economy of Goa and on the relations among the various components of its tourism industry. The microlevel impact of tourism on the destination area immediately around it has been relatively less studied, if at all. The impacts of such a large-scale, diversely interactive activity as tourism should be more inclusive of all components. Tourists travel to and from their destinations, are accommodated, fed and entertained. All these activities require extensive infrastructural networks and support services that may not remain limited to the geographical positions of a tourists movements. Moreover, the effects result very much from the interactions among the tourists and the agents in the destination area.

Economic Aspects

The foreign exchange earning potential of the tourism industry is one of the main attractions for its support by national governments, while state governments are more concerned with its contribution to local income, taxes and employment. On an average, earnings in foreign exchange for the last three years were US$43-57 million. It is estimated that tourism contributes to around 13.7 percent of Net State Domestic Product; 7 percent of employment and 7 percent to state tax revenues. The money spent by domestic and international tourists is received by different segments of the industry which provide the supporting goods and services.

Tourist receipts can be classified into five categories: accommodation and food, shopping, internal travel, entertainment and miscellaneous items. An overview of the distribution of expenditures among the five categories for international and domestic tourists. Moreover, in 1992, about 90 percent of the domestic tourists who came to Goa spent less than US$35 per capita per day. Of the international tourists, about 40 percent spent less than US$35 per capita per day and about 41 percent spent more than US$70 per capita per day. As mentioned earlier, however, this trend is changing today. In the last few years indications are that the domestic tourist coming to Goa is increasingly from the more affluent segments of society, and the international tourist have increasingly been more of the inexpensive charter packages.

As previously mentioned, most of the tourism development in Goa is concentrated in the four coastal stretches of Bardez, Salcete, Tiswadi and Marmagao. These areas are, similarly, the most developed regions of Goa, accounting for approximately 66 percent of Goa's Gross State Domestic Product (GSDP). They have dense settlements and are more developed in terms of infrastructural support services.

About 70 percent of small-scale units, 78.5 percent of the capital investment in small industry and over 68 percent of the employment in this sector are found here. Historically, the region developed relatively faster than the rest of the state due to its coastal location, which provided easy access for sea trade and was attractive for settlement.

There are a number of interesting locations with tourism potential exist in the hinterland; however, very little has been done to develop them. Hence, there is a considerable imbalance between the coastal and the hinterland regions in infrastructural and other indicators of economic development. Investment in the Tourist Industry Since tourisms acceptance as the primary avenue through which to develop, it has grown in scope to be comparable with mining, the only other industry in Goa. State expenditures on the tourism industry has doubled over a period of 10 years. Expenditures amounted to approximately Rs.15 million in 1986-87, and they grew to approximately Rs.30 million by 1996-97.

Private investment also increased. If the investment per room by hotel category, which was estimated by Kirloskar Consultants 1994, investment in the hotel industry has risen from Rs.2.08 billion to Rs.3.25 billion in 1996, an increase of Rs.1.19 billion in just 2 years. If the type of hotels that have been built over the last two years is analysed, investment in starred hotels increased by 39.5 percent during this period while that in other hotels has gone up by 47.5 percent. Tourism studies suggest that the financial performance of the hotel industry is poor compared to several other industries in the state although no evidence has been presented to back this claim.

From the statistics available and through observation, local participation in the tourism industry is high in terms of the number of small hotels and paying guest accommodations, yet the bulk of economic investment is concentrated in just a few hotels. Thus, using just the accommodation sector as a proxy for the tourism industry as a whole in 1996, almost half of all investment in the sector was in the hands of just four large hotels; the largest hotels together controlled 69 percent of all investment, and the balance was made up by smaller hotels. Seasonality of Income and Employment The industry peaks and troughs: October-February being the good months and June-August being the lean months due to the monsoon. This seasonality requires the tourism industry to respond by adjusting the output in terms of the services it provides which affects hotels, restaurants and their employees. Because of the search and initial training costs that the employer faces, and because of the need to cater to sudden spurts of demand, a hiring and firing policy is not cost-effective to an employer. The first reaction of employers is to keep labour, but reduce the work hours, a situation akin to holding inventories of labour in excess of demand. This strategy is supported by employing unskilled labour during the peak season, who are then laid off during the off season as the costs of hiring and firing unskilled labour are not high. A sample survey indicates that the highest seasonality of income (in terms of lower off season earnings) and the highest seasonality of employment (in terms of hours worked per week) are experienced by the smaller hotels. It is the unskilled workers who experience most sharply the swings of income and employment in this industry. This is a social cost of the industry to which hitherto scant attention has been paid.

Shifts in Population and Traditional Occupations

In the tourist belts of Calangute-Candolim in Bardez, a shift in the composition of the resident population has occurred to include a large number of migrants from the states of Karnataka, Rajasthan and Kashmir due to potential employment in the tourism industry. Most of these people are engaged in selling artisanal pieces, handicrafts and garments. It cannot be denied that tourism has also given a boost to local art and handicrafts; however, the commercialisation of such arts and crafts has resulted in a certain deterioration in their quality as they are being manufactured for bulk sale. At another level, Goan cultural practices are being used as tourist attractions, such as Carnival and Shigmo, which have been given a certain orientation to suit the demand of tourists. Much of the spontaneity of these practices has been lost.

Moreover, some of the villages along the coasts have become very tourist-oriented and thus, shifted away from their traditional occupations. A couple of decades ago, these villages were predominantly fishing-or agricultural-oriented. Tourism has increased land prices and encouraged locals to sell their land, thereby sharply increasing the competition for land in the tourist belt. It can be argued that tourism has accelerated the decline of agriculture in Goa, by providing a viable alternative for the lateral transfer of investment capital, land, and labour by the locals. In the tourist belt, land conversion from agriculture to non-agriculture uses has occurred. In the fishery sector, while fishermen do not always compete with tourists for shore space, there are instances on the Goan coasts where traditional fishing operations have been constrained by lack of shore space. In some areas, fishing ports and the houses of fishermen have been displaced by resort development. Economic forces are driving social forces here. On the one hand, expectations of higher returns, from the sale of land to builders and/or from hiring out houses to tourists rather than from actively engaging in agriculture or fishing are creating incentives for shifting occupations.

On the other hand, social forces are at work in the sense that tourism provides locals with an opportunity to keep their women at home rather than have them till the soil or sell fish in the market. This is perceived as a movement upwards for the locals, and a factor that cannot be ignored in the dynamics of the intersectoral movement of land and labour. Often large tourism development projects require the displacement of some of the original inhabitants of the area. Some of those displaced by present projects, chose to invest their compensations in capital assets, e.g., taxis, and have become to a degree upwardly mobile in an economic sense. However, there are others who due to their initial circumstances are unable to move along the same path, and instead become marginalized, having to replace self-employment for menial jobs in the very resorts that have displaced them. The issue of income distribution needs to be examined.

Impacts on the Goans. Sense of Community

One of the impacts of tourism on the Goan community is the creeping expropriation felt by the locals. This feeling of being pushed out arises from the fact that starred hotels have effectively gained control over beach resources, which locals have used for generations, and are selling access to them at a price. The area that is available to them as commons is increasingly reduced and overpopulated, causing the locals to avoid the beaches as a whole. Consequently, the growth of tourism in Goa has been accompanied by strong anti-tourism activism. Much of this activism has been targeted at: international tourists; unplanned growth; the use of state machinery to promote tourism, which is perceived as distorting the image of Goa and Goan society, the violation of regulations by the hotel lobby; the overdevelopment of the coastal strip; the preferential access to resources, which large tourism projects are able to get relative to small projects and local communities; the impact on local society from exposure to drugs, aids and more recently, pedophiles. The bottom-line is that there has been little involvement of the public in the policy decision-making process resulting in a strong sense of alienation about decisions that are affecting the lives of the local community.

Environmental Aspects

Coastal zone environment is particularly fragile and can be divided into two areas: the marine part and the land part. For the purpose of this discussion, coastal waters, bays, backwaters, creeks, tidal inlets, and estuaries are considered as components of the marine part of the coastal zone. The sandy beaches along with two dunes (one which runs along the seashore, and another that runs parallel but about 100 to 500 meters away from the seashore) and their vegetation are considered components of the land part. In between these dunes there lies a sandy plain, which acts as a buffer zone between the main land and the sea.

Impacts to the Marine Part of the Coastal Zone

The marine part of the coastal zone provides many functions and in the present context are:

- To support marine flora including subtidal varieties, such as mangroves. The mangrove ecosystem itself serves as a habitat for diverse types of species of birds and marine biota, in addition as the protection of the coastline from erosion, tides and storms.
- To support a wide variety of marine organisms including mammals. The marine organisms among themselves form a very intricate, well-established food chain starting with the chemical constituents of sea water called nutrients.
- To function as a natural thermostat which balances the climate on the subregional, regional and global scales.
- To disperse riverine load effectively in near-shore regions.

Most of the above functions are interactive in nature. In the coastal current movement, the most important force is the tidal cycle, which drives the sea water along the shoreline, bays, creeks and upstream through the mouths of rivers and estuaries. Other important forces are the near shore and riverine, or estuarine currents. All these currents carry natural sediment load and any other marine discharge, resulting from man-made activities, and deposits them at a site defined by an equation containing parameters, such as current velocity, counter currents, topography of the seabed or riverbed and other oceanographic factors. The transportation capacity of the currents has to be understood in terms of its effect on marine biota. For example, a rise of a few degrees in temperature of a sea water body would adversely effect species occurrence and predominance among biota, which in turn could influence other life forms. Also, a sudden appearance or disappearance of a species due to anthropogenic factors may cause stress in other species. Given the interactiveness and complexities of the coastal environment, any developmental activity should to be preceded by the Environmental Impact Assessment studies to forestall environmental degradation.

The following impacts on the marine part of the coastal zone have been observed while surveying the ecosensitive coastal areas of Goa. They have been represented in a flowchart in the Annex. The work was carried out by National Institute of Oceanography on request from the Ministry of Environment and Forests, Government of India, in August/September, 1996.

- Loss of mangroves. Thick mangroves on the outskirts of Panaji, at Sao Pedro near Old Goa, around Talpona backwaters and at innumerable other locations are being reclaimed. In addition to the biological impacts of the loss of mangroves, the tidal waters could flood the surrounding coastal areas causing erosion and thus opening the estuarine banks to storm surges.
- Reduced fish catch and species: A steady decrease in the total annual fish catch has been observed in Goa. The catch has declined from 105.44 thousand tones in 1993-94 to 101.90 in 1994-95 and in 1995-96, to 87.82 thousand tones. More specifically, at Sancoale-Chicalim Bay, the decrease in production of certain varieties of shellfish and crabs, both local delicacies, is believed to be due to the land reclamation of mangrove swamps and to the construction of roads to the Sao Jacinto Island and at Talpona. More generally, one or more of the following factors may be responsible for the reduction in fish catch:

a) Unscientific fishing practices: These can include the use of nets with a mesh size smaller than permissible during spawning periods and the fishing beyond sustainable yields. These practices are pursued due to high demand for fresh seafood in the market.

b) Loss of spawning grounds: Reasons for this could be mangrove deforestation, land reclamations and salutation. Short-term economic gains from the development of these areas is obviously preferred over the long-term benefits of the conservation of ecology.

c) Introduction of anthropogenic material: Any disturbance at any step in the marine food web may inadvertently affect other species. The introduction of untreated sewage and waste to the environment would give rise to toxic algal blooms wiping out many species. Increased turbidity and sedimentation can also affect the benthic communities.

- Erosion: Dispersion of sediment load at any given point depends upon a number of parameters related to marine currents. Any activity which causes disturbances in these parameters, could alter the sites of deposition and result in erosion, accretion or salutation and changes in the ecology of that area, such as land reclamations, the extraction of sand or the construction of jetties. Consequently, there are a large number of cases where coastal stretches have been subjected to the forces of erosion. Prime examples are Campal and Caranzalem near Panaji, Palolem, Agonda and many other places, where a considerable amount of construction activities have occurred.
- Accretion/salutation: Accretion and salutation is occurring. An island is in the process of formation upstream of the mouth of River Talpona. Due to sand bar formation at the mouth itself, which has been more pronounced in the last few years, the river is navigable only during high tides. In addition, local fishermen have noted salutation in the river bed. All these observations suggest disturbances in the natural sediment load dispersion patterns in the River Talpona. Impacts to the Land Part of the Coastal Zone

The land part of the coastal zone mainly comprises sandy areas along with the dunes and its vegetation cover. This part provides the following functions:

- To protect the coast from the forces of the oceans,
- To replenish the sand on the beach that is carried away by the sea,
- To gather the sand that is blown landward by the wind with the help of dunes and its vegetation, and
- To serve as habitats for numerous organisms, including turtles. Sandy areas are also used for tourism development:
- To mix the sand with cement for construction purposes, and
- To develop the land.

All along the coastline of Goa, for example, between Chapora and Sinquerim in Bardez, Caranzalem and Miramar in Panaji, Salcete Coast in Central Goa and in Galgibaga, Talpona, Palolem in South Goa, there has been a boom in construction activities, most of which are for tourism or for associated purposes. To make space for and to use them as a component of cement for construction, sand is being extracted in substantial amounts.

When the environmental functions are weighed against the economic services that sand performs, the fact that the former are not priced, tilts the demand in favour of the economic user-groups. There is need to quantify and monitor such sand losses and their ecological impacts.

The following impacts have been observed on the coastal stretches of Goa due to development activities:

- Loss of sand dunes: Sand dunes have borne the brunt of construction activities along the coastal stretches of Goa. Anjuna and Baga-Calangute-Candolim stretches in North Goa, and Salcete beaches comprising Betalbatim, Colva, Varca, Cavelossim and Mobor in central Goa, were the first beaches to lose their dunes. Our survey showed South Goa to be the next in line as in Galgibaga, two dunes, 10 meters high, have already been flattened into plateaus at half the heights to make way for construction.
- Endangered species: Four species of turtles have been reported to frequent the beaches at Morjim, Miramar, Bogmalo and

Palolem, covering almost the entire stretch of the Goan Coast. The Save The Turtles. campaign of the Goa Foundation, a local Non-Governmental Organization, carried jointly with the Forest Department of the Government of Goa, reported that the number of seaturtles visiting their nesting sites on different beaches in Goa particularly in Morjim, is steadily decreasing.

- Tidal ingress: The ceaseless mining of sand and sand-dunes have effectively razed gentle slopes of sand which stop the tides from rushing further on the shore. The consequent tidal ingress has reduced the area of beach at different places, such as Miramar in Panaji, Baga-Calangute-Candolim-Sinquerim stretch and Anjuna in Bardez, and in Salcete and Mormugao on the north and central coasts of Goa.

Impacts of Recreational Activities

Recreational facilities affecting the coastal environment are generally, but not limited to, those related to upscale tourist activities. These are:

- *Swimming pools:* The water for this is invariably drawn from subsurface aquifers. The withdrawal of large amounts of ground water in a limited area can be detrimental to the water table of the region, particularly since it is a source of drinking water. Additionally, some parties owning wells with a good underground stream of fresh water sell their water at Rs.100 (US$2.5) per 500 litre tank to fill these swimming pools. Consequently, the ground-water levels in some coastal areas is decreasing and is frequently accompanied with salt water intrusions. The manifestation of sea water intrusions in the form of salt water in wells along the coastal belt from Chapora to Aguada has been observed in coastal aquifer studies.
- *Water sports:* Motor boats used in shallow coastal waters continuously disturb the habitats of endangered species and other marine life. Moreover, they tend to degrade water quality by the discharge of oil and grease.
- *Beach driving:* Tourists regularly drive on the beaches during low tide. Concrete ramps have even been constructed to take the vehicles on the beaches such as at Palolem.
- *Beach accommodations:* In the initial states of tourism in Goa, beach shacks became popular due to their small numbers,

economical rates and simple decor; however, after several decades, these structures crowd the shorelines without any comfortable space among them, and they lack ecofriendly toilet facilities and proper refuse collection, all of which often result in waste invariably find its place in the coastal waters.

- *Sanitation:* Goa lacks modern treatment and disposal systems for both sewage and garbage. Even the internationally famous beach stretch of Baga-Calangute-Sinquerim, does not have rudimentary toilet facilities. Tourists, locals, shop owners and the hordes of migrant labourers, who are employed by construction companies along the beaches, have no other option than to use the beaches to answer the call of the nature.
- Beach litter: Plastics are among the very serious problems in a number of Goas beaches, and an action plan is urgently needed to mitigate the problem. Both the last mentioned problems could be solved through improved enforcement of regulations and infrastructual improvements.

Impacts of Expanded Transport

Even though tourists in Goa are almost exclusively accommodated in coastal areas, they arrive and depart Goa by some kind of transportation operating in other areas of the state. While the air and sea travel would cause negligible damage to the environment in broad terms, motor vehicles cause air pollution by their uncontrolled exhaust fumes. Also, the alignment of the Konkan Railway has broad reaching environmental impacts. The laying of the tracks for the railway in Goa, especially through wetlands and tidal marshes at Maxem and between Bali and Mayem along with numerous bridges on the Mandovi-Zuari estuarine fronts, has been done without proper hydrodynamic and geomorphological studies. The gigantic embankments, several kilometres long, supporting the rail lines along the lowlands of Goa have lead to substantial alterations in physical, chemical, biological and geomorphological setups. Blocking, diminuting or increasing the tidal flow has resulted in a major redistribution of sediments giving rise to erosion/deposition or deposition/erosion with conspicuous changes in shorelines or near-shore realms.

Mangrove swamps have been destroyed; tidal regimes disrupted; paddy fields flooded, and the embankments are sinking due to soft underlying strata 32. A comprehensive analysis of the environmental impacts of the Konkan Railway alignment is needed to study such questions as the following. Is the salutation taking place in the backwaters and estuarine regions of Canacona in South Goa due to river runoffs carrying haphazardly dumped material from the digging out of the railroad? To what extent has the Konkan Railway Alignment through ecosensitive areas contributed to the environmental degradation of estuarine/coastal areas of Goa? In board terms, factors other than tourism could be responsible for the observations made above, but the contributions of the tourism industry in all these situation should be identified given the criticality of the coastal environment demands.

Tourism Policy

In the wake of the report, Our Common Future, by United Nations Commission on Environment and Development in 1983, India passed its own Environment Protection Act in 1986. This was followed by a Notification in February 1991, inviting the governments of Indias coastal states and union territories to prepare Coastal Zone Management Plans for their respective territories. The much publicized Rio Summit in June 1992, along with Indian environmental norms, started a land race for coastal development regardless of the laws, regulations and conventions in vogue. The land race got started probably because the coastal resource users experienced inertia in the implementation of various legislation on the part of the authorities.

It seems increasingly clear that (i) despite several important pronouncements and regulatory mechanisms in place, local planning does not always adhere to guidelines and regulations and (ii) where it does adhere, planning and development regulations have been observed in the breach. Thus, the Government of Goa, in October 1988, published its Regional Development Plan, anticipating, among other activities, the growth of tourism by 2001 A.D. In this plan, a strategy is outlined:

Location of new beach resorts should be considered not only from point of view of land availability but also from the consideration of beach resource ecology, based on the Environmental Assessment Studies. Further, spreading thinly on all available sandy beach stretches from Tlerekhol/Arambol in the north to Betul/Agonda in the south is not advisable from the standpoint of conservation of resources both natural and man-made. Instead, it is suggested that beach-head developments at certain selected centres should be encouraged. Despite these admirable commitments toward conservation and the protection of the coastal environment and ecology, the Regional Development Plan for Goa 2001 A.D. does not contain any reference to the no development zone. of 200/500 meters from the high-tide line along the seashores, which had been much debated around the country in the early 1980s; nor does it mention the Environment Protection Act of 1986 of the Government of India. Moreover, the Coastal Zone Management Plans, prepared by the Department of Town and Country Planning of Goa in 1995 and 1996 for approval by the Central Government, actually recommend tourism-related development for almost the entire length of the Goan coastline, barring only a few places, which contradicts the Departments own guidelines.

The current policies and relaxed enforcement thereof have led to the haphazard and uncontrolled growth of townships. Places like Calangute and Candolim in Bardez and Colva in Salcete have become over commercialized and haphazard in their development pattern. These areas have a number of unauthorized constructions, which have paid little heed to local planning rules, infrastructural supports or aesthetics. During the 1980s and the early 1990s, the lure of catering to tourists especially, international tourists and the hope of making rapid profits have led to considerable investment in resorts and apartments. Today there are signs of over investment, this is spreading a price war. When a certain location is to be developed as a prominent tourist area requiring extensive infrastructural and other support services, it gets developed as a small township.

This increases its real estate value manifold, inducing other sectors of the society to set up business and residences in these areas as well. A quick look at the developments along the coasts of Goa and the future plans for it, reveals that:

(i) these follow the ideas submitted in the CZM plan of Goa (which is yet to be formally approved) rather than its Regional Development plan; and,

(ii) the tourists are almost exclusively accommodated along the 105 km stretch of the coastline while little effort has been made to adhere to the regional plans of creating other types of tourism besides beach tourism.

One successful example of regulated tourism development is Seychelles, an island nation in the Indian Ocean. It spared its beaches from concretization and allowed resorts to come almost entirely amongst the coconut groves just behind the sandy stretches, taking care of the coastal marine environment. This policy, unfortunately, is not in place in Goa where constructions are allowed as close to the waterline as possible.

Conclusions

Although tourism is concentrated along the coastal zone in Goa, it has had a number of positive benefits in terms of increased incomes, increased employment, added avenues for upward mobility for locals, increased revenue and increased foreign exchange earnings. However, there are also some socioeconomic and environmental impacts associated with these benefits that need to be highlighted. These impacts have arisen as a result of the trajectory that tourism has followed in Goa and can be summed up as follows:

1. The growth of coastal tourism has been rapid and uncontrolled.
2. The seasonal nature of tourism has led to swings in employment and income most markedly in the small sector and to the unskilled worker.
3. There has been no clear nor firm policy relating to tourism; most decisions have been on a purely ad hoc basis, except for a marked predisposition to upmarket tourism. The policy initiatives that have been introduced are not attentive to local concerns. This has led to some disaffection among locals toward tourists that needs to be studied.
4. There has been a marked spatial concentration of tourism development along the coast, which is leading to heavy demand for resources in these places. Cumulatively, this results in concentration and congestion of population, enormous increase in the density of construction, and related infrastructure and facilities. Consequently, there has been an overall decline in the agricultural sector in the state.
5. It poses major changes in land use, shortages of resources, such as land and water, and damage to coastal aquifers, the sand dune system, and mangrove vegetation.
6. Spawning and breeding grounds have been lost due to anthropogenic activities related to tourism; consequently, fish

populations are decreasing and traditional fishing activities are on the decline.

7. The principles of sustainability and the norms related to the conservation of the environment and ecology are generally ignored; the coastal environment is becoming irreversibly degraded as evidenced by the concretization of beaches.

It is clear that there is much to be learned about the impacts of tourism in Goa, and that further planning and development requires information gaps to be filled. More specifically, the following actions are needed:

1. A careful study on the type of tourism that best suits Goa: up-scale, low budget or a combination of the two.
2. Recognition that tourism is a vulnerable industry, subject to the fads of the trade; hence, tourism cannot be allowed to permanently change the face of the coast in the long run.
3. A systematic study of the environmental impacts of tourism, through perhaps, a life cycle analysis, and the valuation of the environment to enable its integration into decision-making.
4. An understanding of the processes that make the Goan coast a preferred tourist destination rather than the hills or the hinterland areas.
5. A monitoring and management system to ensure the effectiveness of coastal and environmental regulations. The development of sustainability markers would be a way to ensure this. Such markers will enable both the industry and government to identify the emerging issues and to facilitate mitigation before problems becomes unmanageable. They can also serve as the basis for monitoring changes in the ecosystem, social and economic spheres.
6. The integration of the principles of coastal environment and ecology into the planning stage of any coastal activity, as preventative rather than remedial measures.
7. An environmental impact assessment and studies of Goas coastal stretches including estuaries and backwaters.
8. Policies which recognize the type of interconnections among tourism, local communities and the environment, to ensure that tourism contributes to a sustainable development agenda.

Impacts of Construction Activities in close Proximity to the Marine Environment

The aim of this paper is to assess the impact of tourism on the environment of Maldives and explore the environmental management practices in the tourism industry of Maldives. First, the emergence, growth and present status of tourism development in the Maldives is outlined. Then the environmental impacts of tourism are discussed. Next, the environmental management practices are outlined. The relevant legislation, institutional structure, tourism planning, standards and controls are also presented.

Tourism Development in the Maldives

The Republic of Maldives is a small island, developing state consisting of 26 coral atolls dominated by the sea and is situated in the Indian Ocean, southwest of India. In total, these atolls contain about 1,190 very small islands of which only 200 are inhabited. The capital of the Maldives is Male., an island by itself, and the Male. International Airport also has an island (Hulhule) to itself. Tourism development in the Maldives is based on the principle of isolation of tourists from the bulk of the indigenous population and the physical configuration of tourism development is an unusual one. In the Maldives, the tourism industry is synonymous with resort islands and each resort occupies a separate island and is totally self-contained. This isolation is practical because of the availability of a large number of uninhabited islands that can be developed into tourist resort islands.

According to a tourist opinion survey in 1991 conducted by the Ministry of Tourism, the main attractions in order of priority are white sandy beaches, opportunities for snorkelling and scuba diving among coral reefs and spectacular marine life, sunny weather, clear lagoons and scenic peaceful environments. The expectation is one of a Robinson Crusoe existence without any problems where the Art of Doing Nothing is practiced in a relaxing atmosphere.

Tourism History

Maldivian tourism entered the international scene only in the early 1970s. Tourism commenced with the opening of two resorts in 1972 and about 1,000 tourists visited the islands. Until then the Maldives was virtually unknown to the tourist travel trade. By the late 1970, tour operators, notably from West Germany and Italy, started to feature the islands within their programs and international tourism had become an important source of income for the Maldives. The first decade (1972-1982) in the development of the Maldives tourism industry evolved essentially in an unplanned laissez faire manner. Hulhule Airport was the basic and only gateway entry to the Maldives and the natural hub for tourism development. Thus the first two resorts to be developed were Kurumba and Bandos both on islands in close proximity to Hulhule Airport and Male. In 1973, along with three other resorts, Club Med established itself on Farukolhufushi island, also only 20 minutes by boat from Hulhule Airport.

Tourism in Maldives originated from excursions from Sri Lanka and because of the reputation of Maldives as a diving destination. Tour operators identified the ideal combination of packaging the culturally-orientated product of Sri Lanka with the unique island paradise holiday of the Maldives. During the 1972-1980 period the market changed from the more limited and specialized divers.

Market to the much bigger mainstream market for beach holidays. With the growing importance of the mainstream market for sand, sea and sun holidays, the tour operators found that the market base was sufficient for introducing the Maldives as a separate destination.

With the completion of the runway at Hulhules International Airport in 1981, direct charters from Europe, using wide bodied planes, flew in tourists. The expansion of air travel assisted by various promotional and other concessional fares on scheduled services, together with the rapid growth of charters, has helped the growth and development of the Maldives as a tourist destination. In the beginning the facilities provided for tourists were basic.

The room was furnished with just a bed and the essential cooling fan. Food with no exotic flavours was served by local people with no formal training, and scuba diving and island hopping were the only recreation facilities besides sun bathing and swimming. At present, a diverse range of facilities are offered at different resorts. At the luxurious end of the spectrum, public spaces have expensively tiled finished floors, vast varnished and carved timber frame roofs, elaborate light fittings and plush furniture, impressive reception areas, international cuisine, swimming pools, fountains, piped music and a lush landscape incorporating many ornamental imported species.

Tourism Indicators

Two resorts with a bed capacity of 280 opened in North Male atoll in 1972. By the end of the first decade (1972-1982), 44 resorts became operational and bed capacity rose to just under 4,000. With the spatial policy shift towards opening of Ari Atoll, together with consolidation and upgrading of existing resorts, the next decade (1982-1992) saw the addition of 36 new resorts with over a doubling of bed spaces to reach a total of almost 8,500. By 1995, there were 74 resorts in operation in the Maldives.

During the year of inception of tourism in the Maldives, 1972, only 1097 tourists visited the Maldives. The number of annual tourist arrivals (reaching over 300,000 in 1995) now exceeds the total indigenous population of about 244,000. Europe is the leading generating market followed by the Asian market. Germany and Italy are the two main suppliers of tourists and in 1994, shared 40 percent of the total tourist arrivals to the Maldives.

In the late 1970s, international tourism became an important source of income for the Maldives. The readiness of the Maldives to develop its tourist sector can only be understood in terms of its very limited economic possibilities, especially the absence of local raw materials to diversify into exports of manufactures. At 17 percent of gross domestic product, which provides over 25 percent of the government revenue and contributes around 60 percent of the country foreign exchange earnings, tourism is the second largest contributor to the economy and it is increasing in importance yearly.

Tourism and the Environment

Tourism depends on environmental quality more than any other activity and a central precept that has been preached in tourism is not to kill the goose that lays the golden eggs. Yet, in general, it is characterized by rapid, short-term development which more often than not damages the very environment the tourists come to enjoy and simply moves off elsewhere.

Without careful attention to the balance between the volume and type of tourist activity, and the sensitivity and carrying capacities of the resources being developed, tourism projects can be not only environmentally harmful but also economically self-defeating. Tourism in the Maldives exists solely due to the physical and geographic features of the coral islands. The beauty of the underwater world at the reefs, clean water in the lagoons, white and pristine sandy beaches, a rich island vegetation and ideal tropical climate which form a virtual paradise that attracts tourists from Europe and Australasia.

Environmental Impacts of Tourism

The first proper evaluation of tourism in the Maldives was carried out in 1983 after 10 years of tourism development. It was revealed that the pollution of the sea with garbage, piles of waste found in the resorts often close to the tourist cottages, the picking of corals, the use of spearguns were features present that did not fit into the tourists image of the Maldives. In 1991, after almost two decades of tourism development in the Maldives, the perception of impacts has changed. According to the present perceptions, the islands offer uncommon visual beauty unspoiled by human settlement, virtually unsurpassed marine environment and the strongest of all, unspoiled, under populated tiny tropical islands replete with natural beauty and abundant sea life.

The Environmental Protocol prepared in 1992 by the Ministry of Planning and Environment to determine the carrying capacity constraints in the tourism sector concluded that the natural resources of the Maldives are in a sufficiently pristine state, and of such high aesthetic quality, that a period exists in which environmental deterioration can occur without an adverse effect on tourism. However, concern was expressed that the duration of this period cannot be predicted and with increasing environmental pressures, rising environmental sensitivity, and without compensatory environmental management, adverse effects may be felt sooner than later.

According to a survey carried-out in August 1995 involving the management of 47 resorts, beach erosion was identified to be the major existing environmental problem facing the resorts. The highly dynamic Maldivian beaches erode and build in response to wave action associated with storms, the tidal cycle, and the monsoons. The results of a survey carried out in 1992 showed that 12.8 percent of the total shoreline of 32 resorts surveyed consists of seawalls and groynes and is not sandy. The same survey also showed that 12 of the 32 resorts surveyed (38 percent) had offshore breakwaters to protect the beach. The maintenance of natural beach is of paramount importance to attract clients to the resorts and the construction of artificial structures designed to control and limit beach erosion are not only unsightly but also expensive. Rubbish on beach is the next environmental problem identified by the resort management.

Rubbish on beach mainly results from waste dumped at sea irresponsibly by neighbouring resorts and inhabited islands that get washed ashore onto islands with the current and to some extent from the messy habits of certain tourists. The resort management is quite emotive on this issue as this is one issue that will reflect very badly on the image of the resort environment.

Solid Waste

Solid waste disposal is one of the most obvious impacts of tourist resort operation and one of the easiest environmental management problems to deal with and thus has been addressed in a number of reports on tourism development in the Maldives. The pollution of the sea with garbage and piles of waste found in the resorts often close to the tourist cottages were identified in 1983 among features that was not aesthetically pleasing. In 1985 the Department of Tourism reported that the disposal of non-biodegradable waste was then a serious problem and that there was need for education to increase environmental awareness, and for the use of recycling technology. In the new Tourism Master Plan solid waste is identified as a major issue for resort islands and it is stated that at current tourism levels, problems are probably more aesthetic than environmental.

The plan also points out that while solid waste itself may not currently pose a serious environmental threat, its impact in conjunction (e.g., synergistically) with the effects of other human activities should be considered.

Sewage Disposal

In 1980 only two resorts were reported as discharging saltwater flushed toilets to the open sea. In a survey of methods of sewage disposal reported from 34 resorts in 1992, 23 resorts disposed sewage into the ground while 11 discharged sewage to the sea.

A survey in 1993 revealed that at 67 percent of tourist resorts sewage effluent is piped into septic tanks, and the untreated sludge is dealt with by natural processes and soil absorption. At 33 percent of the resorts analysed, septic tanks and sea outfalls were the reported practices. Measures to protect the environment in cases of direct sewage discharge include the siting of outfall pipes 100m from the island and 30m below mean sea level.

Sewage disposal has both health implications and environmental consequences. Aquifer contamination by faecal coliform bacteria or the contamination of bathing waters could give rise to health problems. Since a very small percentage of resorts pump sewage into the sea and even so, these resorts have a very small population it might be concluded that the current levels of sewage emission into the coastal waters of the resorts do not pose very serious problems to human health.

The capacity constraints survey carried out in 1992 showed that the sewage discharges from resorts are relatively small and the observed effects were limited. Even though the volume of waste matter disposed is quite small, nutrients from sewage could build up over time, especially if the process of discharge is not managed well. However, volumes of water and rates of water exchange are large and in view of the productive fisheries, the atolls are probably already subject to relatively high nutrient input from upwellings as oceanic currents hit them.

Ground-water

There is an increasing move away from using ground-water as a resource in tourist resorts. Drinking water in tourist resort comes from rainwater which is collected on roofs and stored in large tanks and is now supplemented by desalinated water and imported bottled mineral water. There has also been a move away from the system in which ground-water was used for showering and flushing toilets to one in which saltwater is used for flushing with the wastewater pumped out to sea and desalinated water used for showering.

Ground-water quality deterioration could be caused through increasing abstraction of ground-water which depletes the already thin freshwater lends; salt water intrusion into the freshwater aquifer; and contamination of ground-water from sewage discharges. In addition to sewage, ground-water can also be contaminated through the use of contaminated soils; the excessive use of fertilizers; the use of pesticides; and inappropriate solid and liquid waste disposal.

An analysis of ground-water quality and pollution in tourist resorts, based on the results of Maldives Water and Sanitation Authority Surveys and consultants opinions showed that ground-water quality in the resorts is deteriorating. However, the capacity constraints study in 1992 concluded that whilst there is some evidence that ground-water quality has deteriorated on some resorts through tourism, the deterioration is not significant and is unlikely to be irreversible. The study also suggested a number of factors mitigating any possible deterioration and they are:

1. The sources of pollution are relatively benign though more and more pesticides are being used and rubbish buried on islands.
2. High rainfall backed up by evidence that salinity vary widely on many of the islands between the wet and dry season indicates that flushing rates, and oxidation, of contaminants are likely to be rapid.
3. Before upgrading, resorts traditionally used ground-water flushing for toilets and for showering, this minimizes the historic loss of ground-water.
4. The contaminant adsorption properties of coralline soils are generally extremely limited.

One advantage of this is that any contaminants should be flushed out eventually. This is good for the state of the ground-water but not so good for adjacent lagoon waters..

Coral Reefs

On tourist resort islands reef damage has been caused by scuba divers, and by snorkelers and bathers walking out across the reef flat. The greatest threat at present almost certainly arises from snorkelers and bathers, from both inadvertent breakage and deliberate removal of coral and coral fauna for souvenirs. A study at Kurumba Village has assessed the effects of snorkelers on the reef flat/crest at depths up to about 1.5 m. Results indicate breakage of 18 percent of all Arcopora corals/month. Hence most or all coral colonies of this genus stand to get broken each year, suggesting a significant effect from snorkelers.

The present evidence on reef degradation from sewage in the Maldives is inconclusive. The Environment Protocol reported that none of the 32 resorts surveyed in 1992, and none of the 70 dive base operators on 41 resorts, identified sewage as a problem causing reef deterioration. Direct and indirect damage to reefs is also caused by divers and tourists. demands. However, the greatest impact to reefs in the Maldives has originated from coral mining for construction purposes.

Island Vegetation

The image of a palm fringed sandy beach and lush tropical vegetation is integral to the perception of, and satisfaction, with Maldives as a tourist designation. At present there is no requirement to survey and consider the vegetation of an island as part of the planning approval process prior to resort development. In the construction process trees and shrubs are cut down and coastal vegetation is removed. Exotic ornamental and fast growing species are imported to replace the vegetation removed and for new resort gardens. The introduction of exotic species not only reduces the ability of the island to recover to its natural state but also the exotic species may overcome local ones directly or through the introduction of pests.

There is also the matter of maintaining the natural perception of the island for marketing purposes. Whilst the palm is the most important vegetation feature on an island, there are local plants that have historic and cultural importance and so have marketing value which imported exotics do not have.

Soil and fertilizer have largely been imported to improve the growth prospects of exotic imports. These imports are very much on trial and error basis and there is little doubt that many soils and a variety of fertilizers have been tried. This process detracts from efforts to use local vegetation which is already adapted to local conditions, and so should not have to be sustained artificially. Imports may also introduce soil associated pests and diseases for which local plants have limited resistance.

Environmental Management

National Legislation: The Department of Tourism and Foreign Investment was organized in 1978 and made responsible for supervision, coordination and maintaining standards of tourist services in the country. To develop and regulate tourism, and simultaneously to strengthen the institutional framework for administering and monitoring the industry, this department was renamed the Department of Tourism in November 1982 and made solely responsible for tourism management. In 1984, the Tourism Advisory Board was established as a consultative body affiliated to the tourism authority.

The tourism sector was given elevated status in 1988 with the establishment of the Ministry of Tourism, according to the designating law 3/68 J under 1/69 J as at 1993, to provide ways to develop the tourism industry in the Maldives, to plan methods of income generation through tourism, to provide guidelines, and to administer the industry. The Ministry of Planning and Environment was established in 1988. This Ministry is responsible for the formulation of policies on environment, environmental guidance to other development sectors, the implementation of environmental impact assessment and the designation of protected areas.

Policy and Planning

During the first decade of tourism development, there was no specifically planned development; rather, tourism took place according to individual private sector initiatives in locations that offered market advantages principally related to the access opportunities offered by Hulhule Airport. This essentially informal development managed to generate almost 3,500 bed spaces of international quality and the industry was achieving enviable occupancy rates of up to 80 percent in the high season. The first formal initiative to plan, in an integrated way, the future development of the tourism industry in the Maldives, came when the Department of Tourism and Foreign Investment commissioned Dangroup International in November 1980 to carry out a Maldives Tourism Development Plan. This long-range (10 years), tourism development plan was prepared for the Maldives in May 1983 and some, but not all, of its recommendations were considered feasible for implementation.

The tourism plan provided some ideas for development. However, to date, most of the tourism planning and management has resulted from government initiatives, based on its evaluation of the best forms and standards of development. Many of the governments present approaches and standards have evolved through the monitoring of the earlier phases of development to determine what is most suitable. Approaches and standards have been refined and some abandoned based on the experience gained from previous types of development.

By government policy, the resorts are located on uninhabited islands, in order to reduce any possible sociocultural impacts. Also most islands are too small to contain both resorts and traditional villages. These islands are owned by the government and it can allocate them for resort use as needed. The resort developer receives a long-term lease and pays an annual rent that is calculated individually for each island. The resorts must supply their own infrastructure of electric power, water supply, sewage and solid waste disposal, boat dock and recreation facilities. They must also provide housing and related facilities for the resort employees. The families of the resort employees remain on their home islands, often some distance away.

The government policy has been to expand tourism for its economic benefits, but in a systematic manner of staged development. In the late 1980s, Kaafu Atoll was considered saturated with resort development. This decision was made within the framework of maintaining high environmental standards for the existing resorts, and retaining sufficient land for village and urban expansion and recreation parks.

All new resort development was then programmed to take place in Alif Atoll, which is accessible by sea and air from the international airport. In parallel the government policy turned to encourage expansion and upgrading of existing resorts to higher standards, including meeting present environmental quality standards. This upgrading was considered necessary to maintain the viability and competitiveness of these resorts and to maintain all tourism development at a reasonably high level, catering to quality tourist markets.

As an inducement to achieve these objectives, resort leases were extended from 10 to 21 years and much of this upgrading has been accomplished. The Third National Development Plan (1991-1993) recommended the development of a ten-year zoning plan (1991-2000).

Under strategies and policies to achieve the main objectives of tourism development, the NDP (1991-1993) included a proposal to assess environmental impacts of resort developments and operations, and further strengthen measures taken to protect and conserve the environment and natural setting for tourism, and to adopt remedial measures on environmental degradation. The issues that are examined in the new Tourism Master Plan draft include new markets, priority markets, air travel and other transportation issues, tourism infrastructure development, legal aspects, human resource development, gender situation, sociocultural aspects and environmental impacts.

Environmental Impact Assessment

The Environmental Protection and Preservation Act of Maldives (4/93) provided the basic framework for the Environmental Impact Assessment (EIA) process in the Maldives and under Article 5 (1) of the Act, an impact assessment study shall be submitted to the Ministry of Planning, Human Resources and Environment (MPHRE) before implementing any activity that may have an impact on the environment. According to the EIA guidelines issued by MPHRE all new resort developments require an EIA study before approval for development can be made.

Carrying Capacity Limits

As an important basis for deciding the number of rooms and extent of resort facility development allowed on each resort island, the government has established carrying capacity standards. These are based on several factors. The cutting of trees is controlled so that the natural appearance and facade of the island are maintained and no buildings are allowed to appear above the tree tops. The maximum area of the island to be occupied by buildings is 20 percent, with two story buildings allowed to conserve land area if there is sufficient vegetation to conceal these buildings from the ocean view. To preserve the tourists perceptions and image of beach orientation, all guest rooms should be facing the beach, with a minimum of 5 meters of linear beach available in front of each room. Only 68 percent of the beach length can be allocated to guest rooms as 20 percent has to be allocated to public use and 12 percent left as open space. Construction on reef flat and lagoon are discouraged; however, as over water bungalows are very popular among tourists, they are permitted provided that equal open space is left on the land for each building developed on the lagoon.

Architectural and Design Controls

The design of resort buildings is controlled so that they are well integrated into the island environment, take advantage of the tropical climate and use local building materials to the extent possible, such as thatch roofs. Previously many buildings were constructed from coral mined from the reefs. However, the use of coral is now restricted and use of imported materials is now encouraged, although these are expensive by local standards. Coral and sand mining from resorts and their house reefs is strictly prohibited. Hard engineering solutions for dynamic coastlines are discouraged and construction of solid jetties and groynes are controlled. Design of boat piers and jetties should be in such a way that they do not obstruct the original flow of currents or disrupt the wave climate within the lagoon.

Biodiversity Conservation

To protect and preserve marine biodiversity a number of measures have been prescribed. Spear, poison and dynamite fishing are strictly prohibited. Net and trap fishing are controlled and confined to certain areas. Removal of shells, juvenile lobsters and lobsters ready to lay eggs are strictly prohibited.

The catching of turtles is strictly prohibited and trade in all turtle products is banned. The commercial exploitation and export of a number of other species is also banned. Resort operators also voluntarily prohibit the catching of reef fish from the house reef or tourist resorts. Fifteen important dive sites have been declared as protected areas in 1994, where fishing, anchoring, removal of coral and other destructive activities are prohibited.

The Ministry of Tourism recognizes the importance of vegetation in maintaining the natural beauty of the islands and there are a number of regulations which aim to secure this resource. These include a limit of 20 percent of the islands for building, the requirement that no buildings be put up that disrupt the natural facade of the island, that there be a minimum setback limit of 5 meters from the vegetation line of the island, and that no buildings should appear above the tree tops.

Waste Disposal

According to the regulations issued by the Ministry of Tourism, garbage from tourist resorts should be disposed off in a manner that would not cause any damage to the environment. All garbage disposed into the sea should be done as far away into the sea as necessary in order to ensure that it does not get washed onto any islands with the current.

Tourist resorts are required to have incinerators and compactors adequate in size to burn all flammable materials and crush all the cans respectively. Those who lack these facilities are not allowed to operate. Plastic or polythene bags should not be thrown into the sea and such material should be burnt. Those who contravene these regulations are subject to fines and penalties.

Two airlines have joined in the effort to keep Maldives clean by arranging for waste to be carried back to Europe. Under this program all tourists who fly in to the Maldives in these airlines are given a bag and asked to bring to the airport, all the waste they produce during their stay in the Maldives when they depart. The airlines carry the waste to the original destination for recycling free of charge.

Under sewage and excreta disposal the tourism book of regulation specifies that the sewage system should be prepared such that pollution of water supplies, beaches and other areas are prevented; nuisance, ugly sights, and unpleasant odors do not occur, human wastes do not come into contact with people, animal and food; and breeding of flies and mosquitoes will be prevented.

Conclusion

Tourism in the Maldives began in 1972 and it then evoke the image of a lost paradise. The tourism industry of the Maldives is dependent entirely on environmental quality and since it established itself in the tourism market it has maintained its strong position in a rapidly growing market. A few critics in the 1980s proclaimed that environmental pollution had begun to rear its ugly head in the Maldives. However, the natural resources of the Maldives are still in a sufficiently pristine state and of very high aesthetic quality and environmental concerns are few.

Environmentally unsound practices in solid waste and sewage disposal pose the most serious threat from tourism to the delicately balanced coral reef ecosystem of the Maldives. Though solid waste is a cause of environmental concern, at current level it is more of an aesthetic problem. In the past the portion of waste and garbage which could not be burned was dumped into the sea. This practice is now prohibited by law and waste incinerators and crushers have to be used in all resorts. Sewage effluent is discharged into the sea by the resorts. However, their discharges from resorts are very small and the evidence on reef degradation from sewage discharges is inconclusive. Some of the resorts are turning to the latest technology in sewage treatment using UV radiation to produce virtually pure water.

The Maldives has developed a very suitable form of tourism, appropriate for the small island environment. The present form of tourism development has not generated any serious environmental impacts. This has been accomplished through careful management. The government has developed appropriate policies, legislation and plans and instituted mechanisms to apply strict standards and regulations.

Bibliography

Andrew, N; Flanagan, S & Ruddy, J: *Tourism Destination Planning*, Dublin, Dublin Institute of Technology, 2002.

Apostolopous, Y and Leivadi, S: *Sociology of Tourism, The: Theoretical And Empirical Investigations*, London, Retailed, 1996.

Ashworth, G J and Dietvorst, A G J: *Tourism and Spatial Transformations: Implications For Policy and Plan*, Wallingford, CAB International, 1995.

Ashworth, Greg and Larkham, P J: *Building a New Heritage: Tourism, Culture & Identity in the New Europe*, London, Routledge,1994.

Baum, Tom: *We're all Going on a Summer Holiday: Images of Tourism Past and Person*, Buckingham, University of Buckingham, 1995.

Beeho, A & Prentice, R: *Conceptualising The Experiences of Heritage Tourists*, 1997.

Beeton, Sue:: *Film-Induced Tourism*, Clevedon, Channel View, 2005.

Belie et al.: *Tourism and the Inner City: An Evaluation of / Impact of Grant Assist*, London, HMSO, 1990.

Benefice, Brian G, and Cooper, Chris: *Geography of Travel and Tourism*, The, London, Heinemann, 1987.

Bolshevism, Germy: *Coping with Tourists: European Reactions to Mass Tourism*, Oxford, Berghahn Books, 1995.

Boniface, Priscilla and Fowler, Peter: *Heritage and Tourism: In the Global Village*, London, Retailed, 1993.

Bosselman, Fred P: *In The Wake of the Tourist: Managing Special Places in Eight Countries*, Washington, DC, Conservation Foundation, The, 1978.

Briguglio, L and Vella, Leslie: *Competitiveness of the Maltese Islands in Mediterranean in Tourism*, Chichester, John Wiley, 1995.

Brown, Dona: *Inventing New England: Regional Tourism in the Nineteenth Century*, Washington DC, Smithsonian Institution, 1995.

Brunt, Paul: *Market Research in Travel and Tourism*, Oxford, Butterworth Heinemann, 1997.

Burkart, A and Medlik, S: *Management of Tourism*, The, London, Heinemann, 1975.

Chambers, Erve: *Native Tours: The Anthropology of Travel and Tourism*, Prospect Heights, Waveland Press, 2000.

Chandler, Harry and Carter, John: *Chandler's Travels: A Tour of the Life of Harry Chandler*, London, Quiller Press, 1985.

Clark, Colin: *Tourist Services and Guidance: Heritage and Information*, Strasbourg, Council of Europe Press, 1989.

Coccosis, Harry and Nijkamp, Peter: *Sustainable Tourism Development*, Aldershot, Avebury, 1995.

Cohen, Erik: *Towards a Sociology of International Tourism*, 1972.

Dann, Graham M S: *Language of Tourism*, The, Wallingford, CAB International, 1996.

Davidson, R and Maitland, R: *Tourism Destinations, London*, Hodder and Stoughton, 1997.

Davidson, Rob: *Travel and Tourism in Europe*, Harlow, Addison Wesley Longman, 1998.

Ecotec: *Calderdale: Tourism Impact Study*, Calderdale, ECOTEC/Calderdale Council, 1990.

Edensor, Tim: *Tourists at the Taj*, London, Retailed, 1998.

Edgell, David L: *International Tourism Policy, New York*, Van Nostrand and Reinhold, 1990.

Elliott, James: *Tourism: Politics and Public Sector Management*, London, Retailed, 1997.

Fairgrieve, James: *Geography in School*, London, University of London Press, 1926.

Foster, Douglas: *Travel and Tourism Management*, London, Macmillan Educational, 1985.

Frechtling, Douglas C: *Practical Tourism Forecasting*, Oxford, Butterworth Heinemann, 1996.

Gamble, P. R: *The Educational challenge for Hospitality and Tourism Studies*, Tourism Management, 13, 1992.

Ghimire, Krishna: *The Native Tourist*: Mass Tourism within Developing Regions, London, Earthscan, 2001.

Goeldner, C. R: *The Evaluation of Tourism as an Industry and a Discipline, Paper Presented to*, International Conference for Tourism Educators, Guildford, University of Surrey, 1988.

Gunn, Clare and Var, Turgut: *Tourism Planning*, London, Retailed, 2002.

Hall, C Michael *Tourism Planning: Policies, Processes and relationships*, Harlow, Prentice Hall, 2000.

Hall, Colin and Jenkins, John: *Tourism and Public Policy*, London, Retailed, 1995.

Hall, Colin Michael: *Tourism and Politics*: Policy, Power, & Place, Chichester, Wiley, 1994.

Harrison, Lyndon: *Tourism Means Jobs*, Chester, Lyndon Harrison, 1996.

Harron, S and Weiler, B: *Ethnic Tourism*, Belhaven/Wiley, 1992.

Inkpen, G: *Information Technology for Travel and Tourism*, Harlow, Addison Wesley Longman, 1998.

Inskeep, Edward *National and Regal Tourism Planing*: Methodologies & Case Studies, London, Routledge/WTO, 1994.

Irwin, William *The New Niagara*: *Tourism, Technology, And the Landscape of Niagara Fal*, University Park, PA, University of Pennsylvania, 1996.

Jack, G and Phipps, A: *Tourism and Intercultural Exchange*: *Why Tourism Matters*, Clevedon, Channel View, 2005.

Jakle, John: *Tourist, The: Travel in Twentieth Century North America*, University of North Nebraska, 1985.

Jennings, Gayle: *Tourism Research*, Chichester, Wiley, 2001.

Judd, D R: *Promoting Tourism* in US Cities, 1995.

Karski, A: *Urban Tourism* - A Key to Urban Regeneration?, 1990.

Kotler, Philip et al: *Marketing Places*: *Attracting Investment, Industry & Tourism etc*, New York, free press, 1993.

Labarge, Margaret Wade: *Medieval Travellers*: *The Rich and Restless*, London, Hamish Hamilton, 1982.

Laws, Eric: *Tourist Destination Management: Issues, Analysis & Policies*, London, Routledge, 1995.

Leed, Eric J: *Mind of the Traveller, The: From Gilgamesh to Global Tourism*, New York, 1991.

MacCannell, Dean: *Tourist, The: A New Theory of the Leisure Class*, London, Macmillan, 1976.

Machin, Alan: *Retracing the Steps: Tourism as Education, Janus*, Fin, ATLAS / FUNTS, 2001.

Opperman, Martin and Chon, Kye-Sung: *Tourism in Developing Countries, London*, International Thomson Business Press, 1997.

Patullo, Polly: *Last Resorts*: *The Cost of Tourism in the Caribbean*, London, Cassell, 1996.

Pearce, Douglas: *Tourism Today*: *A Geographical Analysis*, Harlow, Longman, 1995.

Pearce, P L: *Social Psychology Of Tourist Behaviour*, The, Oxford, Pergamon, 1982.

Peters, M: *International Tourism*, London, Hutchinson, 1969.

Ringer, Greg: *Destinations: Cultural Landscapes of Tourism*, London, Routledge, 1998.

Ritchie, Brent: *Managing Educational Tourism*, Clevedon, Channel View, 2003.

Robinson, H: *Geography of Tourism*, A, London, Macdonald and Evans, 1976.

Robinson, M, Evans, E & Chalazion, P: *Tourism and Cultural Change, Sunderland*, Business Education Publishers Ltd, 1996.

Rogers, H Anthea and Slinn, Judy A: *Tourism: Management of Facilities*, London, Pitman: M & E, 1993.

Schwaninger, M: *Trends in Leisure and Tourism for 2000 - 2010*, Prentice Hall, 1989.

Scottish Tourist Board: *Visitor Attractions: A Development Guide*, Edinburgh, Scottish Tourist Board, 1991.

Seaton, A V et al: *Tourism: The state of the Art*, Chichester, John Wiley, 1994.

Shaw, G and Williams, A: *Tourism and Tourism Spaces*, London, Sage, 2004.

Stevens, Terry: *Island Tourism*: Malta, , WTO, 1993.

Trench, R: *Travellers in Britain*, London, Aurum, 1990.

Tribe, John *Corporate Strategy for Tourism, London*, International Thomson Business Press, 1997.

Urry, John: *Tourist Gaze*, The, London, Sage, 1990.

Van den Berg et al: *Urban Tourism: Performance and Strategies in Eight European Cities*, Aldershot, Avebury, 1995.

Van Harssel, Jan: *Tourism: An Exploration*, New York, Prentice Hall, 1994.

Veal, A: *Leisure and Tourism*: Policy and Planning, Wallingford, CABI, 2001.

Wahab, S A: *Tourism Management*, Tourism International Press, 1975.

Walle, Alfred H: *Cultural Tourism*: A Strategic Focus, Boulder, Co, Westview Press, 1998.

Wilkinson, Paul: *Tourism Policy and Planning: As Studies from the Caribbean*, Elmsford New York, Cognizant Communications Corporation, 1997.

Yale, Pat: *From Tourist Attractions to Heritage Tourism*, Huntingdon, Elm, 1991.

Zarkia, Cornelia: *Philoxenia: Receiving Tourists*-but *not Guests-on a Greek Island*, Oxford, Berghahn Books, 1996.

Index

F

G

H

I

J

L

M

N

□□□